NOT OUTSIDERS

• • •

Asian Americans' political activism
from the 19th century to today

I0089698

ALSO BY HELEN RALEIGH

Confucius Never Said

Invest Like a Zen Master and Live Happily Ever After

Backlash: How China's Aggression Has Backfired

The Broken Welcome Mat: America's unAmerican immigration
policy, and how we should fix it

NOT OUTSIDERS: ASIAN AMERICANS' THREE HISTORICAL WAVES OF
POLITICAL ACTIVISM FROM THE 19TH CENTURY TO PRESENT DAY
Copyright © 2025 by Helen Raleigh.

Cover design by Ebooklaunch.com

LCCN: 2024925083
ISBN: 978-173600855-3

All rights reserved. In accordance with the U.S. Copyright Act of 1976, the scanning,
uploading, and electronic sharing of any part of this book without the permission of the
publisher constitute unlawful piracy and theft of the author's intellectual property.

For Lucas, Allie, and Mike

CONTENTS

NOT OUTSIDERS

• • •

*Asian Americans' political activism
from the 19th century to today*

PROLOGUE

The seed of this book was planted when some progressives started to describe Asian Americans as being "white adjacent." I was so stunned by this derogatory term that I decided to embark on a journey to understand the progressive thinking behind it.

According to Layla Saad, author of *Me and White Supremacy: Combat Racism, Change the World, and Become a Good Ancestor,* "white adjacent" refers to a person of color "who holds white privilege" but is not white, including "persons who may be biracial, multiracial, or white-passing people of color who benefit under systems of white supremacy from having lighter skin color than visibly Brown, Black or Indigenous people." Self-identified anti-racist blogger Nimisha Barton claims, "Asian Americans – even dark-skinned South and Southeast Asian Americans like myself – most clearly fall into the category of white-adjacent people of color" because Asian Americans' "model minority myth furnished us with a fragile adjacency to whiteness."[1]

The "model minority" phrase refers to Asian Americans' reputation of achieving stellar academic and economic success. It is not a myth that the educational attainment and economic well-being of

1

Asian Americans as a group have been above the average for decades. For example, in 2019, Pew Research found that more than half of Asians ages 25 and older (54%) have a bachelor's degree or more education, compared with 33% of the U.S. population in the same age range. The median annual household income of households headed by Asian Americans was $85,800, compared with $61,800 among all U.S. households.[2] Asian Americans credit their strong work ethic and a shared culture of valuing education as the root causes for their success.

However, the progressives have denounced Asian Americans' "model minority" label as a myth that "minimize[s] the role racism plays in the struggles of other minority groups, such as Black Americans."[3] They would rather attribute Asian Americans' success to acting white and adopting white culture, as if only whites work hard and value education. Hence, the progressives started calling Asian Americans "white adjacent." In recent years, especially in the aftermath of a nationwide racial reckoning since George Floyd's tragic death in 2020, the progressives, including influential figures such as the *New York Times'* Nikole Hannah-Jones (co-author of the highly controversial and inaccurate 1619 Project), have publicly declared Asian Americans should not be part of the "People of Color" coalition.

Of all the racial slurs against Asian Americans, the term "white adjacent" stands out as particularly offensive, carrying with it a weight of discrimination and marginalization. It robs all Asian Americans of agency and dignity. It discounts the long history of discrimination and segregation Asian Americans have endured in the United States. It erases Asian Americans' significant and often overlooked contributions to the Civil Rights movement. It ignores courageous political movements that Asian Americans have led and participated in since the mid-19th century, all of which have helped make this nation closer to its founding ideal of "All men are created equal." Accusing Asian Americans of benefiting from so-called "white" traits such as hard work and pursuing educational attainment is an insult to Americans, regardless of their ethnicity and race, because having a good work ethic and doing well in school are valued by all cultures.

Categorizing Asian Americans as "white adjacent" is not only demeaning but also has led to policies, such as race-based college admissions, that specifically discriminate against Asian Americans and threaten our constitutional right to equal protection.

I decided to write this book to refute the "white adjacent" label of Asian Americans. However, I soon realized the challenges I faced. First, I had to answer the question: who are Asian Americans? According to Pew Research, the term "Asian American" is a political construct that emerged out of Berkeley, California, in the 1960s as a reaction to the long history of discrimination and exclusions Asians faced in the country. This discrimination includes the Chinese Exclusion Act of 1882 and the internment of Japanese Americans during World War II. Today, more than 22 million Asian Americans trace their roots to more than 20 countries in East and Southeast Asia and the Indian subcontinent.[4] Many within the Asian American community feel the label has failed to fully capture the rich diversity in each subgroup's unique histories, cultures, languages, religious beliefs, and other characteristics. If I covered all the subgroups within the Asian American community, this book would be longer than Tolstoy's *War and Peace*. Since 85 percent of Asian Americans in the U.S. are represented by six subgroups: Chinese, Indian, Filipinos, Vietnamese, Koreans, and Japanese (see Appendix 1), I chose to center on the experiences of a few large subgroups in this book.

My second challenge was that writing about every aspect of every large subgroup's experience in America would still be a massive undertaking. To keep this writing project manageable, I focused on only a few of the most significant subgroups' political activism from the 19th century to the present. These subgroups were selected based on their population size and historical significance: Chinese, Japanese, Koreans, and Indians. Since these four subgroups arrived in the United States at different times and sometimes faced various challenges, their political activism didn't happen all at the same time or in the same forms; readers will notice that some groups' activities and experiences are emphasized more than others, depending on the historical period.

Lastly, I emphasized the importance of recognizing and sharing Chinese Americans' experiences and political activism for these reasons: Chinese Americans, with their long history in the U.S., are the largest subgroup, comprising 5.4 million people, which is 24% of the total Asian American population. They are also one of the most politically active subgroups within the Asian American community. This unique historical significance provides a wealth of material to explore. It's crucial to understand that sharing more about Chinese Americans does not diminish the experiences, efforts, and contributions of other subgroups within the Asian American community. As history has shown, the political activism of every Asian American subgroup has played a crucial role in advancing equality for all races and ethnicities in this country.

As the fastest-growing ethnic group in the U.S., Asian Americans are projected to reach a population of 46 million by 2060.[5] This growth trajectory not only underscores the increasing diversity of the U.S. but also suggests a promising future with a surge in political activism from a diverse range of Asian American subgroups. This anticipation of increased activism is a cause for optimism, and I am confident that future writers will do justice to these subgroups by sharing their experiences with the world.

PART I

· · ·

Asian Americans' First Wave
of Policial Activism:
From the 1850s to the 1920s

INTRODUCTION

One common misperception about Asian Americans is that most Asian Americans are newly arrived immigrants. This misperception is often reinforced by viral videos like the one titled "Where are you from?" The video depicts a conversation between two joggers, one of whom is an Asian woman. When she stood by one side of the road to stretch, a man passed by and decided to initiate a conversation. He talked about the weather and asked her, "Where are you from? Your English is perfect." The woman – who speaks perfect American English – responded with a touch of sarcasm: "San Diego. We speak English there." He kept rephrasing the same question, including, "Where are *your people from*?" He was only satisfied after she disclosed, "My great-grandma was from Seoul."[1] This video is an effective illustration of the impact of such questions on Asian Americans, highlighting the underlying assumptions and stereotypes that often accompany them.

I can relate to this young woman's experience because I have to answer the "where are you from" question often. Since I speak English with a Chinese accent, I get why people are curious about my country of origin. On a standalone basis, the question itself is innocent, and often, those who ask are driven by curiosity rather than malicious intent. It's important to understand that for Asian Americans, this question can be offensive, and the constant need to justify our American identity can be exhausting. In my case, after living in the United States for more than two decades and having been a naturalized U.S. citizen for more than ten years, I see myself as an American inside and out. It's frustrating that my answer to the "Where are you from?" question with "I'm from Colorado" is never enough until I say "China." But it doesn't change who I am.

Many of my Asian American friends share my frustration because the diversity of the Asian American community means when and how different subgroups arrived in the U.S. varies, and some subgroups have lived in America for generations. A few Asian friends can trace their family tree in America back to the American Civil War. Yet, Asian Americans, more than any other ethnic group, have to fight back against the perception of being "perpetual outsiders." Both the far right and the far left have told Asian Americans to "go back to where you come from." Especially noticeable is that in recent years, influential people on the left, such as the *New York Times'* Nikole Hannah-Jones, have been using their massive public platforms to spread misinformation such as "Asian Americans are not people of color" and "most Asian Americans arrived after legal segregation and discrimination, thanks to the Black resistance struggles,"[2] implying the majority of Asian Americans neither suffered racial discrimination nor had done much to contribute to the Civil Rights movement. Neither of these claims is true. Unfortunately, such misinformation has been widely accepted. No wonder Asian Americans have experienced the lowest sense of belonging compared to other racial/ethnic groups in the U.S. A survey by the liberal Brookings Institute found only 29% of Asian Americans feel they belong entirely and are accepted in the U.S., compared to Black Americans (33%), Hispanic Americans (42%), and white Americans (61%).[3]

Asian Americans' political activism is deeply intertwined with their American experiences, making it valuable to explore the history of some of the major subgroups in the U.S. This section specifically focuses on the experiences of Chinese and Japanese immigrants, who both arrived in the U.S. around the mid-19th century, driven by similar reasons: their native countries were undergoing profound changes, and these early immigrants sought a better life for themselves and their families in America. Both subgroups faced discrimination and had to learn to defend their rights in this new land. One significant difference between the two immigrant subgroups was that early Japanese immigrants congregated mainly in Hawaii, while Chinese immigrants congregated in mainland America. Therefore, the early Chinese immigrants' political activism was more visible and better documented than that of Japanese immigrants. This section delves into how early Chinese immigrants defended their rights through labor strikes and lawsuits, highlighting their resilience and determination. The section culminates in the 1920s, a pivotal moment in Asian American history, as the passing of the 1924 Immigration Act severely reduced migration from Asia, casting a long shadow on all Asian Americans' experiences in this country.

CHAPTER 1

• • •

Why Did Some Asians Choose to Migrate to America?

Asian immigrants began arriving in the United States and its controlled territories as early as the 1850s. These early Asian immigrants, like many migrants today, were disheartened by their home country's internal turmoil and economic challenges. They were willing to travel thousands of miles to seek a better life for themselves and their families. This chapter focuses on the experiences of two groups of Asian Americans—Japanese and Chinese immigrants—between the mid-19th century and the early 20th century, answering two questions: what motivated them, and what were the lives of these early immigrants like?

1.1. The Early Japanese American Experience

After nearly 200 years of self-imposed isolation beginning in the mid-17th century, Japan was forced to open its ports for international trade after U.S. vessels led by Commodore Perry sailed into Tokyo Bay in 1853. The event became a turning point for Japan and had far-reaching implications on the global stage. The Japanese government quickly realized they had to reform and learn from the West. Led by Emperor Meiji, Japan launched decades of reforms between 1868 and 1912 (Emperor Meiji died in 1912), and this period is referred to as the "Meiji Restoration." These reforms brought drastic political, social, and economic changes in Japan, including establishing a Western-style cabinet and parliament system, expanding international trade, and modernizing the military. The Meiji Restoration propelled Japan into becoming a world power in mere decades, a testament to the nation's resilience and adaptability. This rapid transformation from a secluded nation to a global powerhouse is a remarkable feat that continues to inspire awe.

However, not every Japanese citizen benefited equally from the Meiji Restoration. The country's swift industrialization and modernization caused social and economic disruptions for Japanese people at the bottom of the economic ladder. Japanese farmers and owners of mom-and-pop shops struggled to survive against cheap imports and competition from the West. Many farmers lost their land, and some business owners lost their shops. With nothing more to lose, these destitute Japanese decided to look for a better life somewhere else.

During the entire span of the Meiji Restoration, Hawaii was an independent kingdom. American businessmen and missionaries arrived at the Hawaiian Kingdom in the early 1800s. It didn't take long for them to realize that Hawaii's tropical weather was perfect for sugar production, a commodity that was nicknamed "white gold" due to the high demand globally. The opening of the first sugar plantation on Kaua'i in 1835 was a pivotal moment, as it propelled agriculture to become a dominant sector of the Hawaiian Islands' economy. At the time, sugar production was highly labor-intensive. It created a vast demand for farming and plantation laborers. Recruiters, working on behalf of plantations, began to travel to places including China, Japan, and the Philippines to entice migrant workers to work on sugar plantations under labor contracts.

The first group of Japanese workers, 149 people, arrived in Honolulu in 1868 as contract laborers. They were known as *gannenmono*, or "first-year men," because 1868 was the first year of Emperor Meiji's reign.[1] Although most returned to Japan after three years, some stayed. In Japan, the success of the Meiji Restoration unfortunately also bred nationalism and the radical racial belief that the Yamato race, which most Japanese people belong to, was superior to all other racial and ethnic groups in Asia. Thus, the Japanese government banned its citizens from emigrating to Hawaii to do manual work, fearing such work would undermine the superior image of the Japanese race. Still, those early Japanese migrant workers had left such a good impression that Hawaii's King Kalakaua let the Japanese government know that he would like to welcome more Japanese to his kingdom.[2]

In 1885, Japan established its first consular facility in Hawaii. Tarō Andō, one of the Japanese migrants who came to Hawaii in 1868, became Japan's first consul general to the Kingdom of Hawaii. By then, the Japanese government had lifted the migration ban, recognizing the potential of emigration to the West as a pathway to wealth and respectability. The government's significant interest was evident as it often handpicked emigrants, favoring ambitious young men with good connections. This strategic planning and support from the government was crucial, as many prospective emigrants sought the backing of influential citizens to finance their journey to the U.S.

The Kingdom of Hawaii experienced political turmoil in the late 19th century. The United States annexed it through the Newlands Resolution in 1898, and Hawaii officially became a U.S. territory in 1900. It was not until 1959 that Hawaii was admitted as a U.S. state, the 50th state in the union. However, many Japanese Americans still consider the arrival of the first Japanese migrants in Hawaii the starting point of Japanese American history.

Many Japanese people came to Hawaii – between 1885 and 1924, an estimated 180,000. The majority returned to Japan eventually, but about 39,000 stayed.[3] Most of them worked at sugar plantations. Historical documents show they usually worked for twelve-hour days, making less than six cents an hour.[4] Furthermore, "Even the process of dressing for work was arduous. Plantations workers had to get up before dawn to clad themselves in an armor of button-up leggings, long underwear, arm protectors, and other specific articles of clothing meant to protect their skin and prevent centipedes from crawling inside clothing."[5] A folk song Japanese migrant workers used to sing while working in the fields suggested how they felt about the hardship of the work:

Hawai', Hawai'i
I saw as in a dream
Now my tears are flowing
In the canefields.[6]

These Japanese migrant workers not only demonstrated a willingness to endure the hardship of doing backbreaking work at the plantations, but also to stand up for their rights. In May 1909, several thousand Japanese plantation workers staged the first industry-wide strike in Hawaiian labor history, demanding equal pay between Japanese and white workers. Trying to shut down the strike quickly, local police arrested many strikers and landlords issued 24-hour eviction orders to kick striking workers and their families out of plantation-provided housing units. In Honolulu, about 5,000 Japanese migrants suddenly were displaced and in desperate need of housing. Still, the strike lasted about four months before most strikers returned to work. The strikers were not discouraged that they couldn't claim any immediate victory. Later that year, planters quietly raised Japanese workers' minimum wage to $22 a month, the amount the strikers originally demanded.[7] Thus, this first strike was a success story after all.

Over the years, Japanese migrants gradually branched out from working on plantations to other fields, such as fishing and gardening. Some brought their wives to Hawaii and started families. The Japanese community began flourishing, establishing language schools, Buddhist temples, and Japanese-owned stores. Known as Issei, these Japanese immigrants became integral to Hawaii's diverse community, contributing to and enriching the local culture and economy. By 1930, 51% of the babies born in Hawaii were of Japanese ancestry, and Japanese became the largest ethnic group on the island.

Japanese immigrants settled first in Hawaii. Later they made their way to the mainland of the United States. Between 1886 and 1911, more than 400,000 Japanese migrated to the U.S. and U.S.-controlled territories. Japanese immigrants formed communities, often called "Japan towns," within small and big cities.

The early Japanese immigrants played a significant role in the farming industry and laid the groundwork for future generations. Those who arrived first created Japanese cooperative organizations across the United States, demonstrating remarkable community support and unity. These organizations were more than just social groups; they were essential lifelines, providing crucial financing and services to newly arrived immigrants. With their guidance, many Japanese newcomers ventured into entrepreneurship by starting their own farms and restaurants. This underscores the vital importance of community support in overcoming the challenges of a new land. By 1920, Japanese immigrant farmers were managing more than 450,000 acres of California land, contributing more than 10% of the state's crop revenue. Notably, at least one Japanese immigrant farmer became a self-made millionaire.[8]

1.2. The Early Chinese American Experiences

Turkish and Arab merchants brought opium to China in the late 6th or early 7th century as a medicine to relieve tension and pain. In the 17th century, opium smoking became popular throughout the country. By the 18th century, the Yongzheng emperor who ruled from 1722 to 1735 recognized opium as a highly addictive narcotic drug and banned opium sales and smoking inside China. However, his ban failed to eliminate the demand for opium and only forced the opium trade to go underground.

The Portuguese soon discovered that they could illegally export opium from India to China and make a significant profit. The British learned about the opium trade in 1773 and gradually became the leading supplier of illegal opium to China through its East India Company. Later, other Western powers, including the United States, also joined the opium trade. Around this time, China embarked on a path of steady decline due to corruption, internal conflicts, and self-imposed isolation from the rest of the world. The internal governance was so weak that many local officials ignored the central government's opium ban. Therefore, despite repeated government bans, the amount of opium imported into China increased from about 200 chests (each chest weighed about 140 pounds) annually in 1729 to roughly 40,000 chests in 1838. Before the illegal opium trade, China managed to maintain a trade surplus with its foreign trade partners because the West developed an insatiable appetite for China's tea and silk. At the same time, China imported little from the West. However, the illegal opium trade and the widespread use of opium led to a decline in productivity, increased crime rates, and became a significant drain on the economy, leading to a shift in the balance of trade and a loss of wealth for China.

The Chinese government tried to enforce its opium bans through a variety of means. In 1839, a high-level official burned about 20,000 chests of opium he confiscated from British merchants' warehouses in Guangdong, the only port city in Southern China where foreign traders were allowed to operate. The British Navy later responded by attacking a Chinese port. The first "Opium War" (1839–1842) erupted between China and Britain. China lost the war and was forced to sign the Treaty of Nanjing. Under that Treaty, China agreed to pay the British government the indemnity of 21 million silver coins over three years and ceded the control of Hong Kong to the British. The Treaty only brought China temporary peace. The second Opium War erupted between China, Britain, and France between 1856 and 1860 and only ended with China's defeat and the signing of another treaty with crushing terms, including forcing the opening of more ports for Western traders.

Yet, these humiliating defeats failed to compel the ruling Qing court to adopt radical reform to transform and modernize China. Instead, the Chinese government intensified its oppression of the Chinese people. The Qing court imposed heavy taxes on the Chinese people to pay millions in indemnities to England and other foreign nations. Some Chinese responded to the government's oppression with armed uprisings. The Taiping Rebellion (1850–1864) is the most well-known. It's worth mentioning that the rebellion's leader, Hong Xiuquan, led a religious cult influenced by his misunderstanding of Christianity. He claimed that he was also a son of God and the brother of Jesus. He attracted millions of followers and engaged in military conflict with the Qing army. Ironically, the Western nations that defeated the same Qing army during the Opium War chose to support the Qing court and its army against the rebels who claimed to be Christians. The foreign force and the Qing army defeated Hong and his rebels in 1864. Between 20 million and 70 million people were killed during the Taiping Rebellion – one of the deadliest conflicts in Chinese – and world – history.

The social and economic upheavals caused by wars, rebellions, and increasing financial strain compelled some Chinese individuals to seek a better life elsewhere. Starting in the 1840s, a few Chinese laborers from Southern China, who had interacted with foreign traders and Christian missionaries, departed their homeland in search of manual work in Southeast Asia and later South America. The discovery of gold in California in 1848 triggered a gold rush to the state. Stories of mountains made of gold in California eventually reached southern China. The Chinese translation of the United States' name is "beautiful country," a name that held a powerful allure for these destitute laborers and landless farmers. They embarked on the journey to the "beautiful country," driven by the hope of striking it rich to afford marriage, family, debt repayment, and ancestral honor.

The first Chinese arrived in San Francisco in 1848. By 1851, California had about 25,000 Chinese immigrants, most young men from poor families who spoke little English and had received no formal education. Most came as indentured laborers because they couldn't otherwise afford the long and expensive journey from China to the United States. It was the wealthy locals, acting almost like today's venture capitalists, who financed these young men's trips, and expected to be paid back and then profit from their ventures. This economic dynamic played a significant role in the early Chinese immigration to the United States.

These early Chinese immigrants quickly learned there was no mountain of gold waiting for them. Mining was hard, and the outcome was often uncertain. Hostile locals ridiculed Chinese workers' language, clothing, and living habits.

Life in cities for Chinese migrants was just as challenging as they were forced to live in the least desirable part of the cities, thus giving birth to so-called Chinatowns.

> In Marysville, Yreka, and elsewhere, Chinese Americans could live only along the river, which was subject to flooding. In Mendocino, they could live only on the swampy headlands next to the ocean... While some White businesses were allowed to locate in the Chinese section, no Chinese American homes or businesses were permitted in the White section of Fiddletown.[9]

Such racial segregation meant that Chinese communities didn't have access to local fire departments, and Chinese immigrants' children were not allowed to attend public schools with white children. Therefore, Chinese immigrants had to find their own solutions, including establishing schools to educate their kids and creating organizations to govern the community and provide social welfare services.

One form of such organizations was called *huiguans*, a community organization that gave Chinese immigrants the social welfare support they needed but couldn't get elsewhere. The first *huiguan* was founded in 1850 by the Kong Chow Company. The company spun into six companies, and the *huiguans* they operated were eventually combined into the Chinese Consolidated Benevolent Association (CCBA). Still, many Chinese immigrants referred to the CCBA as "the Six Companies." The services CCBA provided included arranging transportation, and room and board for new arrivals; offering translation services for immigrants who didn't speak English; negotiating labor contracts on behalf of Chinese workers; looking after the sick, the poor, and the elders in the community; arranging to send the remains of the deceased immigrants back to China for traditional burials; and providing legal consultation and filing lawsuits on behalf of Chinese immigrants. The last function became more and more critical as the discrimination against Chinese immigrants, sanctioned by the state, became increasingly severe. The CCBA played a crucial role in addressing this discrimination and advocating for the rights of Chinese immigrants.

The majority of these early Chinese immigrants had debts to pay and families to support back home, which drove them to take any jobs, including those that Americans considered "dirty," such as mining, railroad construction, and laundry work. These Chinese immigrants' wages were low by American standards but relatively high by Chinese standards. They lived a very frugal life in America, often in cramped and unsanitary living conditions, and sent most of their earnings home without saying much about all the challenges they faced in America. Their remittances not only helped pay off the cost of their trip but also enabled their families in China to build big houses and their siblings to get married. As these immigrants' families showed off their new-found wealth, more young Chinese men from poor families were inspired, and they took off for America as well.

As the influx of Chinese immigrants into California continued and the state's gold mines were mined out, employment in other fields became a necessity. A handful of these brave individuals even made their way to the East Coast during America's Civil War and participated in the conflict. Historian Ruthanne Lum McCunn estimates that approximately 50 Chinese immigrants fought for the Union Army. Among them was John Tomney, who courageously joined the New York Infantry in 1861 and tragically lost his life at the Battle of Gettysburg in 1863. In the same year, William Ah Hang made history by becoming the first Asian American to enlist in the U.S. Navy. The highest-ranking Chinese American in the Union Army was Joseph Pierce, a corporal in the Army of the Potomac.[10]

While most Chinese immigrants remained on the West Coast and continued to make a living by doing manual jobs, some started businesses, including brothels, gambling dens, laundromats, restaurants, and shops. Others joined Tongs – a form of gangs typically made up of people from the same hometowns or regions back in China. Early Chinese immigrants initially formed these Tongs out of necessity because mainstream American institutions, charitable organizations, and even many government agencies didn't extend their services to Chinese immigrants or inside Chinatowns. Thus, Chinese immigrants formed Tongs to look after newly arrived Chinese immigrants and provide community services for existing Chinese residents. However, due to the challenging living conditions and the lack of legal protection, some Tongs evolved into criminal organizations that also ran illicit drug trades and human trafficking, collected "protection fees" from local Chinese businesses, and fought each other in turf wars. It is fair to say that these criminal Tongs did more to terrorize fellow residents in Chinatown than to help them.

There weren't many Chinese women in California in the 1850s. Most men would return to China to get married and have children and then leave their new families in China while returning to America to find work so they could send money home. Therefore, most of the Chinese women in California were trafficked to the U.S. by smugglers and sold either to brothels as prostitutes or wealthy Chinese businessmen as concubines, sometimes for as little as $300.

One of the most remarkable Chinese women in America during this period was Ah Toy, who, in 1848, was only the second Chinese woman to arrive in San Francisco. Ah Toy set out for America with her husband, but he died of illness on the boat. At age 19 and newly widowed, Ah Toy was alone in a strange land. Without language or other skills, her survival depended on selling the most valuable possession she had — herself. She became the first recorded Chinese prostitute and later the highest-paid one. Rumor had it that Ah Toy charged an ounce of gold (sixteen dollars) for her "peek show."[11] After saving enough money, Ah Toy opened her own brothel in San Francisco's Chinatown and became a madam. By 1852, Ah Toy was running the most prominent brothel in Chinatown, counting police officers and well-known political figures of the city of San Franciso as her clients.

The Tongs in Chinatown were annoyed that a woman ran the most successful brothel in their territory, and they started seeking ways to teach her a lesson. Yee Ah Tye, head of one of the most notorious Tongs in Chinatown, demanded Ah Toy pay him a "protection fee." Had the incident taken place in China, Ah Toy would have paid the extortion without uttering any objection. After all, prostitutes were regarded as one of the lowest of the low social classes in China, only slightly better than beggars and criminals. But after living in America for a few years, Ah Toy understood that she had rights that weren't recognized in China, and she had the means in America to defend herself that weren't available to people in China. Rather than sucking up and paying the extortion to Yee Ah Tye, Toy did something very daring and American — refusing to pay up and threatening to take Yee Ah Tye, the gang leader, to court. *The Alta California,* a local newspaper, applauded Ah Toy for standing up to the head of a Tong:

Miss Ah Toy knows a thing or two, having lived under the folds of the Star-spangled Banner for three years and breathed the air of Republicanism, and she cannot be easily humbugged into any such measures. Besides she lives near the Police Office and knows where to seek protection, having been before the Recorder as a defendant at least fifty times herself. A-Thai had better be particular as to the powers he assumes, or he may find his dignity wiped away, he being dumped in the lock-up.[12]

Although Ah Toy didn't press any charges in the end, Yee Ah Tye ended up in prison a year later, anyway, for assault and burglary.

Unlike Ah Toy, who was willing to defend her rights in the American justice system, most Chinese immigrants chose to remain inconspicuous, focusing on laboring in various physically demanding jobs. Their exceptional work ethic and almost superhuman ability to endure hardship became so well-known that American employers actively sought out Chinese workers for the most physically taxing and often perilous jobs.

After California passed the Swamp and Overflow Act to encourage levee building in 1861, American developers hired several thousand Chinese immigrants to build the levee. These developers knew that only the Chinese would be willing to endure the hard work, which entailed standing in waist-deep water for long hours in an area where malaria was endemic. The Chinese workers' dedication and hard work led to the construction of hundreds of miles of levees in the Sacramento–San Joaquin Delta region, which helped California reclaim a total of 88,000 acres of fertile farmland from the swamps between 1860 and 1880.[13] The value of these reclaimed lands quickly increased from $1 to $3 per acre up to $100 per acre, demonstrating the significant economic benefits of the Chinese workers' efforts. A former surveyor general of the state estimated that by the mid-1870s, "the increase in the value of the property in the state due to Chinese labor building the railroads and reclaiming tule lands was $289,700,000."[14]

It is important to note that not all Chinese immigrants around this time were poor and uneducated laborers. Some early Chinese immigrants came to the U.S. to go to school. Yung Wing (1828–1912) was often believed to be the first-known Chinese student to graduate from Yale College in 1854. According to Yale's website:

> A native of Guangdong Province, Yung excelled in his studies and impressed Samuel Robbins Brown, a Yale-educated missionary, who brought him to the United States for preparatory school at Monson Academy and then sent him to Yale in 1850. At Yale, Yung Wing was a member of the choir, played football, was a member of the Boat Club, and won academic prizes for English competition.[15]

Yung's influence extended far beyond his own achievements. He enjoyed his American experience so much that he succeeded in lobbying the Manchu court in China to send a Chinese Educational Mission to the U.S. Between 1872 and 1881, Yung led about 120 young Chinese students to study science and engineering in the U.S. These students, upon their return to China, became leaders in education, engineering, and science, and played a pivotal role in modernizing China. They built factories and railroads, started newspapers, and established new schools to teach Chinese youths science and Western ideas, thereby extending Yung's influence to a wider audience. Yung's impact was profound, and his students' contributions to China's modernization were significant. In 1876, Yung was awarded an honorary Doctor of Law degree by Yale University; the same year, he married Mary Kellogg, an American. In appreciation of his Yale education, two years later, Yung donated many of the 1,237 volumes of his Chinese book collection to his alma mater. This generous gift formed the basis of Yale University's East Asia Library.

Yung's educational mission was soon met by perilous challenges. According to the Museum of Chinese in America's official website:

American sponsors rejected the mission's applications to Military and Naval Academies on the basis of race, and his Chinese overseers, who were already suspicious of Americanization, pulled the plug on the program after Wing's promise of military education failed. Yung strongly supported reform in China, which put him in great political peril – after fleeing to Hong Kong, he attempted to return to the U.S. but in 1902 was told his U.S. citizenship had been revoked under the Naturalization Act of 1870. Yung was able to sneak into the U.S. in time to see his youngest son graduate from Yale.[16]

Yung spent the rest of his life improving Sino-U.S. relations. He died in 1912 and was buried at Cedar Hill Cemetery in Hartford, Connecticut.

1.3 The Chinese Railroad Workers' Strikes

In 1862, President Abraham Lincoln signed the Pacific Railway Act, which chartered the Central Pacific and the Union Pacific Railroad Companies to build a transcontinental railroad linking the United States from east to west. The two companies would race toward each other. The western portion, starting from Sacramento, California, was the most challenging because it had to go through the Sierra Nevada: workers had to cut through thick rocks, build tunnels, and lay tracks across deep canyons. In addition to the unforgiving environment, workers were often attacked by hostile Native tribes who didn't want the white men's "iron horse" passing through their land.[17]

The transcontinental railroad construction started in 1863 with workers of European descent. Soon, those workers began to quit in droves over the physically demanding and hazardous working conditions. The labor shortage forced the Central Pacific Railroad (CPRR) to recruit Chinese workers, an idea that sparked intense opposition from some CPRR executives, including construction superintendent James Strobridge. Strobridge thought Chinese workers lacked the physical strength and intellect to build railroads. Additionally, he was concerned that white workers wouldn't want to work alongside Chinese workers.

While having his own anti-Asian bias, Leland Stanford, president of the CPRR, wouldn't let his racial prejudice stand in his way of making money. Under Stanford's leadership, CPRR hired 50 Chinese workers from nearby mining towns as a trial. The supervisors were impressed by these Chinese workers' dedication, work ethic, dependability, and intelligence. This led to the company hiring more Chinese laborers for the transcontinental railroad construction. By late 1865, 80 to 90% of the CPRR workforce was Chinese. At the peak of the railroad construction, there were between 10,000 and 15,000 Chinese railroad workers, showcasing their dedication to handling everything from low-skilled assignments, such as removing dirt and trees, to highly-skilled ones, including carpentry and handling explosives. Some Chinese workers even found new applications of skills they had obtained in China. For example, "the techniques of masonry they brought from China were used to construct many retaining walls along the railroad routes."[18]

Samuel S. Montague, the railroad's acting chief engineer, was initially skeptical about whether Chinese workers could perform challenging assignments. However, as he witnessed their hard work, skills, and dedication, he was quickly won over. In his 1865 annual report, Montague praised Chinese workers for being "faithful and diligent, and under proper supervision, soon become skillful in performing their duties. Many of them are becoming very expert in drilling, blasting, and other departments of rock work."[19] Montague's transformation in his perspective is a testament to the significant contribution of Chinese workers to the construction of the transcontinental railroad.

It is worth emphasizing that Chinese workers were usually assigned the toughest and most hazardous jobs during the railroad construction. In a stretch called Cape Horn, Chinese workers had to "negotiate a precipitous, rocky bluff about 1,200 feet high above the American River east of Colfax, California." Some reports describe "Chinese workers hanging over sheer precipices in woven baskets to drill holes in the rock for explosives. Once a worker lit the fuse, he signaled to be drawn up to avoid the blast, knowing that he would lose his life if the basket was not drawn up quickly enough."[20]

As challenging as Cape Horn was, it paled in comparison to the task of building 15 tunnels at high elevations through the Sierra Nevada. One of the most difficult tunnels was the Summit Tunnel, which "cut through solid granite, 1,695 feet long and 124 feet below the mountain's surface." [21] The construction didn't stop during winter. "Snow from raging blizzards blocked tunnel entrances, and avalanches swept away camps of Chinese workers, carrying many to their deaths." Poor living conditions also meant "a good many [Chinese workers] was [sic] frozen to death."[22] Sadly, there was no accurate estimate of how many Chinese workers died during the construction. Researchers estimate there were hundreds, possibly more than a thousand.[23]

During the transcontinental railroad's construction, for doing the most challenging work six days a week and 10–12 hours a day, Chinese workers, on average, earned only $26 per month, significantly less than white workers' monthly wage of $40. The CPRR management later raised monthly wages for new hires from $26 to $35 monthly, hoping to attract more Chinese laborers. Even after the increase, Chinese workers' wages still fell short of those of white workers. In addition, while the CPRR paid for white workers' meals, lodging, and tools, Chinese workers had to pay for everything out of their own pockets. This disparity in treatment and pay was a clear injustice. When summer arrived in 1867, overworked and underpaid Chinese workers had had enough. They learned from their white counterparts that a strike was their only way to send a message to CPRR management that it must treat Chinese workers equally and fairly.

On June 25, 1867, the CPRR management woke up to shocking news: about 5,000 Chinese railroad workers who toiled at the railroad construction sites between Cisco, California, and Truckee, Nevada, staged a strike. While white workers frequently launched strikes during this time to demand better wages and working conditions, Chinese workers rarely took part, mainly because they weren't invited by the white workers, who regarded Chinese workers as adversaries rather than part of the labor movement. Therefore, the 1867 strike, a bold and unprecedented move by the Chinese workers, was one of the earliest recorded labor actions by Chinese Americans in the United States, and a significant event in the history of the labor movement.

The striking Chinese workers' primary demand was wage parity with white workers. Executives at CPRR, however, were not bothered by the wage disparity between Chinese and white workers. In fact, they actively perpetuated it. The more the company could save labor costs by squeezing Chinese workers, the higher profit the company would generate, and the richer the CPRR's executives, such as Leland Stanford, would become. Therefore, CPRR had every intention of exploiting those "quiet" and "obedient" Chinese workers, most of whom didn't even speak English, for as long as they could. However, they underestimated the determination of the Chinese workers. These workers, quick learners, soon realized that they must stand up for themselves.

Besides seeking wage parity, the striking Chinese workers also asked for better working conditions and shorter work days. Their demands were modest, reflecting their simple desire for fair treatment: reducing the daily working hours from 11 to 10 hours and shorter shifts in some of the most hazardous assignments, e.g., digging tunnels. The striking Chinese workers maintained a remarkable level of discipline and order, reassuring all with their peaceful protest. Their protest was devoid of any violence or riots. Instead, they chose to sit quietly in their camps. According to Gordon Chang, a professor at Stanford University who has done extensive research about Chinese railroad workers, "The strikers exhibited remarkable organization and discipline. The workers were spread out over several miles of the line in numerous camps, but they communicated closely with one another and coordinated the work stoppage."[24]

Charles Crocker, the CPRR superintendent, found the striking Chinese workers' discipline and peaceful manner astonishing. He later remarked, "If there had been that number of white laborers on strike, it would've been impossible to control them." Still, Crocker played hardball because he was concerned that any compromise would give the impression that the Chinese bossed him around. He and other CPRR executives considered recruiting African Americans from the East Coast as replacements for Chinese workers. When that plan failed to come through, rather than negotiating with the striking Chinese workers, Crocker cut off their access to food and supplies. After starving Chinese workers for a week, Crocker issued the request to the Chinese workers, "If the hungry Chinese workers returned to work immediately, they would only be fined, but if they continued on strike, they would not get paid for the whole month of June."[25] The Chinese workers displayed remarkable resilience despite the widespread hunger and the fear of losing a month's pay. They eventually gave up their strike and returned to work, but their determination in the face of such adversity is truly inspiring.

Although the Chinese workers returned to work without getting what they requested, the 1867 strike was a monumental historical event. It was the largest labor strike of its era and marked the beginning, not the end, of the first wave of Asian American political activism. [26] The CPRR and other employers learned they couldn't take Chinese workers for granted.

The 1867 strike didn't diminish demand for Chinese railroad workers. On the contrary, CPRR wanted to bring more Chinese laborers to help with the railroad construction. In 1868, the United States and the Manchu emperor in China signed a new treaty to bring more Chinese laborers to the U.S., promising them "the right to free immigration and travel within the United States and allowed for the protection of Chinese citizens in the United States by the most-favored-nation principle."[27] The 1868 treaty, often known as

the Burlingame-Seward Treaty, was named after two key negoti-
ators: U.S. Secretary of State William Seward and Anson Burlingame. Burlingame, an American diplomat, made a significant sacrifice by giving up his post to negotiate on behalf of the Chinese
government, a unique and commendable act that underscores the
treaty's historical significance.

Privately, executives at CPRR were in awe of Chinese workers'
bravery, intelligence, and work ethic. Leland Stanford wrote to
President Andrew Johnson, "Without them [the Chinese labor], it
would be impossible to complete the western portion of this great
national enterprise within the time required by the Acts of
Congress." [28] Yet, CPRR's management, including Stanford,
wouldn't recognize Chinese workers' immense contribution publicly due to deep-rooted anti-Asian racism. When the railroad was
completed on May 10, 1869, a Chinese crew was selected and
joined an Irish crew to place the last 10 miles of rail as a symbol to
honor their hard work. However, images of Chinese railroad workers are nowhere to be found in Andrew Russell's famous photo
commemorating this historic achievement, *East and West Shaking
Hands at Laying Last Rail.* This lack of recognition for Chinese railroad workers' significant contributions is a stark injustice.

Still, some local and national newspapers recognized the essential
role of Chinese workers. One newspaper compared Chinese workers to "artists with shovels or drills, wheelbarrows and carts." A
commentary reprinted in many newspapers, such as *American Railroad Journal* and *Scientific American,* between May and September
1869, stated that without the "skill and industry" of the Chinese
worker, "the Central Pacific Railroad might not now have been
carried eastward of the Sierras." The author concluded, "The bands
of Chinamen now organized by the Central Company are as fine
railroad builders as can be found anywhere."[29] With this kind of
endorsement, Chinese rail workers were in high demand. In the
two decades after the completion of the transcontinental railway,
other U.S. companies hired Chinese workers to construct railroads
nationwide, from West to East, North to South, and from cross-

country to local lines. Chinese workers even built some railways in Canada. These workers took lessons learned from the 1867 strike and continued to stand up for their rights. They refused to be exploited.

For instance, on July 19, 1887, about 300 Chinese workers employed by Sisson & Crocker went on strike after the company deducted $4 from each person's pay to cover the cost of transporting workers to the site. The striking Chinese workers insisted that their contracts promised free transportation. Although the company cut off these workers' access to food and water and the local law enforcement threatened them with violence, the striking Chinese workers remained resilient in their fight for justice. A few days later, *San Bernadino Daily Courtier* reported that the Chinese workers resumed working after the company paid their wages in full.[30]

It is important to note that none of the striking Chinese workers received any support from unions made up of white Americans. Instead, the mainstream American labor movement was consistently the loudest voice in America's anti-Chinese sentiment. White unions didn't allow Chinese workers to become members and had no interest in supporting pay parity between white and Chinese workers.

In the summer of 1877, white workers in San Francisco formed a Workingman's Union, with Denis Kearney, an Irish immigrant from the East Coast, as its secretary. Kearney's story is particularly poignant, as he had arrived in California riding trains on tracks laid down by Chinese railroad workers. However, he quickly became one of the most vocal anti-Chinese labor leaders in California, punctuating every speech with the infamous cry, "The Chinese must go!" On July 23, 1877, a Workingman's Union meeting, initially intended to support labor strikes, took a dark turn and descended into one of the most violent racial riots in the nation, mainly due to Kearney's influence:

[Mobs] went on a rampage that lasted three nights, killing several Chinese, destroying Chinese laundries, and raiding the wharves of the Pacific Mail Steamship Company, which transported Chinese immigrants to America. The rioters burned adjacent lumberyards and hay barns, but were unable to burn the company's steamships.[31]

After the 1877 San Franciso riots, the Workingman's Union formed the Workingman's Party and became a powerful political force in California.[32] The party supported legislators who drafted many discriminatory bills against Chinese immigrants:[33]

- The Sidewalk Ordinance of 1870 banned the Chinese method of carrying vegetables and carrying laundry on a pole, while in San Francisco,
- The Queue Ordinance of 1873 outlawed the wearing of long braids by men, a Chinese custom.
- Laundry ordinances mandated Chinese American laundries to pay higher taxes than other laundries, and regulated the types of buildings in which laundry businesses could be housed.
- In 1879, California revised its constitution to limit the ownership of land to aliens who are of "the white race or of African descent." Later in 1913, the state passed the Alien Land Law that prohibited aliens ineligible for citizenship from owning property or entering into leases longer than three years.
- Chinese immigrants were prohibited from working for federal, state, and local governments, and from educating their children in public schools.
- Chinese immigrants were prevented from testifying in court against Americans of European descent— effectively placing thousands of immigrants outside the protection of the law.

In 1881, during the first meeting of the Federation of Organized Trades and Labor Unions of the US and Canada, C.F. Burgman, Chief of the San Francisco Cigar Makers Union (a precursor to the American Federation of Labor), called on members to "use...our best efforts to get rid of this monstrous immigration."[34] Consequently, American labor unions became the driving force behind many discriminatory laws against Chinese. Hostile union workers were often the instigators of violent acts against Chinese immigrants. Through their deliberate efforts, American labor unions have largely erased the history of Chinese workers from the history of the American labor movement.

CHAPTER 2

• • •

"See You in Court!"

No matter what they did for a living, the early Asian immigrants faced a formidable challenge in the form of persistent racism, and often such racism was sanctioned by government laws and regulations. These early immigrants quickly recognized that they must become adept at defending their rights and dignity with all the tools available within America's justice system, including filing lawsuits. This section explores a few well-known cases where Asian Americans fought unjust laws ranging from immigration to local ordinances. These lawsuits were not just legal battles. They were also significant milestones in the history of civil rights, carrying the weight of challenging the status quo and paving the way for future generations.

Chy Lung v. Freeman (1875)

In 1875, California enacted a law that granted state immigration officials the power to scrutinize new immigrants and bar those deemed 'lewd and debauched' from entering the U.S. This law was created in a specific historical context, where unfounded assumptions and racial prejudices often led to discriminatory immigration policies. The law assumed that all Chinese women in the U.S. were prostitutes and they carried sexually transmitted diseases. The fear was that if Chinese women were allowed into the U.S., they would corrupt white men and spread disease.

Shortly after the law's enactment, about 22 Chinese women, including Chy Lung, arrived on a Japanese steamer in San Francisco. As no men were in their company, California's immigration officials, operating under the assumption that these women were prostitutes, denied them entry and held them captive, demanding a $500 gold bond from the ship's captain. The CCBA in San Francisco filed a writ of habeas corpus, initiating a legal battle that eventually reached the U.S. Supreme Court. That court ruled in favor of the women, ordering their release. The opinion of the majority read:

> It is hardly possible to conceive a statute more skillfully framed, to place in the hands of a single man the power to prevent entirely vessels engaged in a foreign trade, say with China, from carrying passengers, or to compel them to submit to systematic extortion of the grossest kind…if citizens of our own government were treated by any foreign nation as subjects of the Emperor of China have been actually treated under this law, no administration could withstand the call for a demand on such government for redress…. **The passage of laws which concern the admission of citizens and subjects of foreign nations to our shores belongs to Congress, and not to the states**[1] [emphasis added].

In reaction to the Supreme Court's ruling, the U.S. Congress passed the Page Act of 1875. This act, which prohibited the importation of labor from "China, Japan, or any Oriental country" that was not "free and voluntary" or who was brought for "lewd and immoral purposes," had a significant impact on Asian immigrants, especially the Chinese since it was the largest immigrant group from Asia at the time. The law explicitly forbids "the importation of women for the purposes of prostitution."[2] In practice, the Page Act subjected Chinese women to rigorous screening by U.S. immigration officials at port cities, resulting in the unjust prevention of most Chinese wives and women who were not prostitutes from coming to the U.S. Fewer Chinese women emigrated to the U.S. after the Page Act went into effect. "Between 1880 and 1882, over 50,000 men immigrated from China yet only 550 women arrived in the country."[3] The Act exacerbated the problem of life without families among Chinese male immigrants, making it difficult for them to start families and set roots in the U.S., and thus, effectively made Chinese immigrants a declining population.

Yick Wo v. Hopkins (1886)

In San Francisco, Chinese Americans were able to overturn several of the city's discriminatory ordinances through lawsuits. One of the most well-known cases was *Yick Wo v. Hopkins*. The city of San Francisco issued a laundry ordinance in 1880, requiring all laundries in wooden buildings to have a permit issued by the city's Board of Supervisors. The real purpose of the ordinance was to drive the Chinese out of the laundry business because most of the laundries run by Chinese Americans were housed in wooden buildings in Chinatown. After the laundry ordinance went into effect, the Board of Supervisors didn't grant any Chinese owners of laundry operations a permit, even though the Chinese dominated the city's laundry business. Two Chinese laundry business owners, Yick Wo and Wo Lee, continued to run their businesses without a permit. When confronted by the local authorities, they refused to pay a $10 fine. The city's sheriff, Peter Hopkins, arrested Wo and Lee and imprisoned them.

Wo and Lee sued Hopkins for a writ of habeas corpus, arguing that the ordinance and Hopkins' enforcement violated their rights under the Equal Protection Clause of the Fourteenth Amendment. Their case went to the U.S. Supreme Court, which sided with Wo and Lee unanimously. Writing the opinion on behalf of the court, Justice T. Stanley Matthews found:

> Both petitioners have complied with every requisite deemed by the law or by the public officers charged with its admin-istration necessary for the protection of neighboring property from fire or as a precaution against injury to the public health. No reason whatever, except the will of the supervisors, is assigned why they should not be permitted to carry on, in the accustomed manner, their harmless and useful occupation, on which they depend for a livelihood. And while this consent of the supervisors is withheld from them and from two hundred others who have also peti-tioned, all of whom happen to be Chinese subjects, eighty others, not Chinese subjects, are permitted to carry on the same business under similar conditions. **The fact of this discrimination is admitted. No reason for it is shown, and the conclusion cannot be resisted that no reason for it exists except hostility to the race and nationality to which the petitioners belong, and which, in the eye of the law, is not justified** [emphasis added]. The discrim-ination is, therefore, illegal, and the public administration which enforces it is a denial of the equal protection of the laws and a violation of the Fourteenth Amendment of the Constitution. The imprisonment of the petitioners is, there-fore, illegal, and they must be discharged.[4]

According to legal scholars, the legacy of Wo and Lee's lawsuit was monumental. Not only did they overturn the city's bigoted laundry regulations, but their lawsuit also "established the principle that a law is discriminatory, even if its wording is not discriminatory but if it is applied in a discriminatory manner."[5]

Interestingly, some of the lawsuits challenging San Francisco's discriminatory ordinances were filed by white Americans who were reliant on Chinese American workers. For example, the California legislature passed a law in 1879 prohibiting American businesses holding state charters from employing "any Chinese or Mongolian." With its hefty penalties and potential imprisonment, this law immediately presented a problem for Sulphur Bank Mine, a quicksilver mine in Lake County. The mining company had a difficult time recruiting white American workers because the working conditions at the mine were highly challenging:

> The entire area abounded in hot springs, and it was found impossible to work at any distance below the surface... The men had to wear rain suits, hats, and shoes with wooden soles. The heat was so intense that the men worked in 20-minute shifts, then went to a cooling room where the air was pumped from the outside.[6]

Unsurprisingly, nearly two-thirds of Sulphur Bank Mine's employees were Chinese Americans. Without them, the mining company would have gone out of business because white workers refused to work underground in certain areas they regarded as unsafe; only Chinese Americans would, despite knowing the danger. One of the worst incidents involved six Chinese workers. They were in the cooling room "when a landslide crushed the pipe bringing in cool air. The men were killed by heat and steam."[7]

Sulphur Bank Mine's president, Tiburcio Parrott, defied the state law and continued to hire Chinese American workers. He was soon arrested and tried. Some speculated that Parrott's actions were a deliberate ploy to expose the absurdity of the state law that excluded Chinese Americans from employment. On March 22, 1880, the Ninth Circuit Court made a historic decision, ruling in favor of Parrott and striking down the unjust state law. This decision reverberated in history as it was found to be "in contravention of both the Burlingame Treaty and the Fourteenth Amendment to the Constitution."[8]

Given that the majority of Asian Americans were immigrants, federal immigration laws, such as the Chinese Exclusion Act and the 1924 Immigration Act, were a cause for concern for Asian Americans. These laws, which prevented Asian immigrants from obtaining U.S. citizenship, had severe economic and political implications. U.S. citizenship was a legal status and a key to a better life. Without it, they could not own land in California. They faced restrictions on reentering the U.S. if they left. In addition, any children who had been born in the U.S. risked losing their citizenship, thereby facing a future of uncertainty and severely limited opportunities in this country. On top of the unjust federal immigration laws, Asian Americans faced additional discriminatory laws at the state level. For example, the California legislature passed the Alien Land Law (a.k.a. the Webb-Haney Act) in 1913, which prohibited "aliens ineligible for citizenship" from owning agricultural land or possessing long-term leases over it but permitted leases lasting up to three years. This unfair law had a devastating impact on the economic survival of immigrants from China, Japan, India, and Korea, making it a struggle for them to make a living and provide for their families. Naturally, Asian Americans brought several cases to the Supreme Court to challenge what they regarded as unfair immigration laws that either denied their citizenship or sought to prevent them from becoming Americans.

United States v. Wong Kim Ark (1895)

In 1882, the U.S. Congress passed the Chinese Exclusion Act, the first immigration law that prevented immigration and naturalization based on race and nationality. The act suspended immigration for ten years for Chinese laborers (skilled or unskilled). The law didn't expel Chinese immigrants who were already in the U.S., but it did prevent them from receiving U.S. citizenship. The Exclusion Act also required every Chinese person traveling in or out of the country to carry a certificate identifying their status as a laborer, scholar, diplomat, or merchant.[9] This act was extended for another decade in 1892, made permanent in 1902, and not repealed until 1943. The Exclusion Act severely impacted the Chinese American community. Rather than passively accept this unjust law, they challenged the constitutionality of the act through the lawsuit that became known as *United States v. Wong Kim Ark.*

Wong Kim Ark's personal story adds a human touch to this landmark case. Wong was born in 1873 in San Francisco to Chinese immigrants Wee Lee and Wong Si Ping, who ran a butcher shop and general store in San Francisco for many years. After the passage of the Chinese Exclusion Act, Lee and Ping returned to China, leaving Wong behind. In December 1894, Wong left the U.S. to visit his parents in China and returned in August 1895. When he went through U.S. customs, he presented a departure statement with his photograph and an affidavit signed by prominent white Americans to attest his U.S. citizenship and residency in San Francisco. The statement included this sentence, "WHEREAS, Wong Kim Ark, whose photograph is hereto attached is about to depart for China, intending to return to the United States, and is entitled to return thereto."[10]

However, John H. Wise, collector of customs, decided that based on the 1882 Chinese Exclusion Act, Wong was ineligible for birthright citizenship due to his parents being Chinese immigrants. Wise kept Wong locked on a ship in San Francisco Bay for several months, intending to deport Wong back to China. However, Wong, with the support of the CCBA, chose to fight for his birthright citizenship. The CCBA's attorneys filed a writ of habeas corpus, arguing that Wong was being unlawfully restrained on the ship, violating his rights as a U.S. citizen. They pointed out that Wong was a natural-born U.S. citizen, per the Fourteenth Amendment to the Constitution. This amendment declares that "all persons born or naturalized in the United States, and subject to the jurisdiction thereof, are citizens of the United States." Wise was defended by U.S. District Attorney Henry S. Foote and legal scholar George Collins, arguing birthright citizenship was not applicable to Chinese children born to noncitizens. After U.S. District Judge William Morrow sided with Wong, declaring him an

American citizen, Wise had to release Wong under the court order. Yet, the Department of Justice (DOJ) appealed the case to the U.S. Supreme Court on behalf of Wise, attempting to use this case to exclude Chinese born in the U.S. from the Fourteenth Amendment.

While the U.S. Supreme Court was reviewing Wong's case, a small group of Chinese Americans who were born and raised in the U.S. realized that they must respond to discrimination against Chinese Americans and especially their rights as citizens in a more organized way. Chun Dick led the group to found the first Chinese American civil rights organization, called "Native Sons of the Golden State," in San Francisco in 1895. The organization's goal was to help Chinese Americans "quicken the spirit of American patriotism…and to make secure their citizen's rights." [11] As the organization's name implied, its initial membership was limited to Chinese males born within the state of California.

In 1898, the U.S. Supreme Court made a landmark ruling in Wong's favor. The justices concluded that Wong's parents satisfied the "subject to the jurisdiction" requirement of the Fourteenth Amendment because Wong's parents "have a permanent domicile and residence in the United States, and are there carrying on business, and are not employed in any diplomatic or official capacity under the Emperor of China, [Wong] becomes at the time of his birth a citizen of the United States." Furthermore, the court interpreted the citizenship clause through the principle of "jus soli," establishing that birthright citizenship applies to children born in the U.S. to foreign parents, with limited exceptions, like children of foreign diplomats. Importantly, the justices did not consider the parents' immigration status, as the legal concept of illegal immigration did not exist at that time.

The case of The United States vs. Wong Kim Ark stands as a pivotal moment in Asian American history, marking the first time a Chinese American served as a plaintiff in the Supreme Court. Wong's victory transcended the courtroom; it became a powerful beacon of hope for the entire Chinese American community. His success demonstrated that it was possible to uphold constitutional rights and receive equitable treatment in the face of rampant racial discrimination. In the early 20th century, following the permanent establishment of the Chinese Exclusion Act and the extension of its restrictions to other Asian immigrants, Wong inspired many others to stand up for their rights.

Ozawa v. United States and United States v. Bhagat Singh Thind

The first naturalization law in our nation's history – the Uniform Rule of Naturalization of 1790 – stated that "any Alien being a free white person" can become a U.S. citizen if the person had resided "within the limits and under the jurisdiction of the United States for the term of two years," could prove that they were "a person of good character," and took a court-administered oath. The passing of the Fourteenth Amendment in 1868 was a monumental step forward, extending U.S. citizenship and equal civil and legal rights to African Americans and formerly enslaved people who had been emancipated after the Civil War. However, U.S. immigration law at the time still excluded Asian Americans who weren't born in the U.S. from becoming naturalized U.S. citizens.

While not being able to become naturalized U.S. citizens, Asians except the Chinese could emigrate to the U.S. to live and work, and were not affected by the immigration restrictions set by the 1882 Chinese Exclusion. But in 1900, the Democratic Party platform demanded the 1882 Chinese Exclusion Act be applied to all Asian races, including the Japanese. California's anti-Chinese labor union groups formed the Japanese and Korean Exclusion League in 1906. On October 11, 1906, the San Francisco Board of Education passed a resolution, calling for segregating all Japanese, Korean, and Chinese students from white students. After the Japanese government protested such a resolution, the U.S. President Theodore Roosevelt and the Japanese government reached a "Gentleman's Agreement" in 1908. Consequently, President Roosevelt pressured the San Francisco Board of Education to repeal its Japanese American school segregation order. In exchange, the Japanese government agreed to "deny emigration passports to Japanese laborers, while still allowing wives, children and parents of current immigrants to enter the United States."[12]

The rising hostility against Asian immigrants in the U.S. hadn't dampened some Asian Americans' desire to become a U.S. citizen. Takao Ozawa was born in Japan but had lived in the United States for 20 years. On paper, he couldn't be more American:

> He was a graduate of the Berkeley, California, high school, had been nearly three years a student in the University of California, had educated his children in American schools, his family had attended American churches, and he had maintained the use of the English language in his home. [13]

Ozawa applied for United States citizenship in 1914 in Hawaii. However, his application was denied due to the Naturalization Act of 1906, which allowed only "free white persons" and "persons of African nativity or persons of African descent" to become naturalized citizens. Ozawa filed a lawsuit, arguing: "My honesty and industriousness are well known among my Japanese and American friends. In name, Benedict Arnold was an American, but at heart, he was a traitor. In name, I am not an American, but at heart I am a true American."[14]

Ozawa's case reached the Supreme Court, and in 1922, the majority of the Court ruled against Ozawa. Justice George Sutherland delivered the majority's opinion. While conceding that Ozawa "was well qualified by character and education for citizenship," Justice Sutherland deemed Ozawa racially "ineligible" for citizenship:

> The term 'white person,' as used in Rev. Stats. § 2169 and in all the earlier naturalization laws, beginning in 1790, applies to such persons as were known in this country as "white," in the racial sense, when it was first adopted, and is confined to persons of the Caucasian Race... A Japanese,

born in Japan, being clearly not a Caucasian, cannot be made a citizen of the United States under Rev. Stats. § 2169 and the Naturalization Act. P. 260 U. S. 198.[15]

Merely a year later, however, Justice Sutherland's interpretation of the term "white person" took a significant turn when he ruled in another case, *United States v. Bhagat Singh Thind*. Thind, an immigrant from India and a U.S. Army veteran from World War I, applied for and was granted citizenship in Oregon. Yet, a federal immigration official denied Thind's application because he was not white. Thind, in a bold move, filed a lawsuit, arguing he was of "high-caste Hindu stock, born in Punjab, one of the extreme north-western districts of India, and classified by certain scientific authorities as of the Caucasian or Aryan race." Despite the anthropological evidence supporting Thind's claim, Justice Sutherland still deemed him ineligible for naturalization. Writing on behalf of the majority, Justice Sutherland stated in his opinion that the phrase "white person" in the Naturalization Act was "synonymous with the word 'Caucasian' only as that word is popularly understood." This ruling effectively meant that a "white person" was defined as someone who not only belonged to the Caucasian race but also had a white complexion. This decision profoundly and personally impacted Thind's life, essentially limiting his future opportunities in this country. Justice Sutherland concluded:

Congress, by the Act of February 5, 1917, 39 Stat. 874, c. 29, § 3, has now excluded from admission into this country all natives of Asia within designated limits of latitude and longitude, including the whole of India. This not only constitutes conclusive evidence of the congressional attitude of opposition to Asiatic immigration generally, but is persuasive of a similar attitude toward Asiatic naturalization as well, since it is not likely that Congress would be willing to accept as citizens a class of persons whom it rejects as immigrants.[16]

Although Ozawa and Thind's pursuit of U.S. citizenship was unsuccessful, their lawsuits compelled the court to defend the unjust law that excluded Asian immigrants from U.S. citizenship. The legal opinions revealed contradictions and the need for the U.S. Congress to take action to right historical wrongs. Asian Americans understood that they must take actions to foster a nationwide political change.

In the early 1900s, the Chinese American civil rights organization, The Native Sons of the Golden State, expanded its footprint beyond California. Given the organization's growing membership nationwide, it changed its name to the Chinese American Citizens Alliance (CACA) in 1915. Its New York chapter, CACAGNY, was founded a year later in 1916. In addition to lobbying the U.S. Congress to repeal the 1882 Chinese Exclusion Act, CACA provided other services the Chinese community needed. For instance, due to prevalent discrimination, Chinese Americans had a hard time obtaining life insurance to provide their families with a financial safety net. Thus, CACA created a "death benefit fund" for its members. When a member passed away, CACA would collect a thousand dollars from the rest of the members and pay the sum to the deceased member's surviving family members.[17]

Unfortunately, Asian Americans' efforts to seek political change faced a grave setback in the 1920s as the public sentiment in the nation was dominated by isolationism. The U.S. Congress raised tariffs to keep imports out and started to draft a restrictive immigration act. When lawmakers were discussing the 1924 Immigration Act, their initial focus was to limit immigrants from Southern and Eastern Europe. However, V.S. McClatchy, the influential publisher of *The Sacramento Bee* and an advocate for labor unions, convinced Congress to include a Japanese exclusion clause in the 1924 Immigration law. This clause aroused more opposition within the U.S. than did the 1924 Immigration Act as a whole. More than forty major newspapers condemned the Japanese exclusion. American religious groups and members of the academic community testified against the law's inherent racism. At its annual meeting in 1924, the National Association of Manufacturers criticized Congress's methods of passing the exclusion clause. Despite these oppositions, President Calvin Coolidge signed the 1924 Immigration Act into law.

The 1924 Immigration Act severely cut the total number of immigrants allowed into the U.S. each year and effectively stopped all immigration from Asia. It introduced strict national origin quotas: "two percent of the total number of people of each nationality in the United States as of the 1890 national census." The objective of the quota system was to favor immigrants from Northern and Western Europe. Furthermore, the Act stipulated that only white people or people of African nativity or descent were eligible for naturalization, effectively eliminating the path to citizenship for Asian Americans who were already in the U.S., leading to a significant decline in immigration from Asia to the United States. This trend only reversed after World War II.

One positive aspect of the 1924 Immigration Act was its provision that allowed Asian students to pursue education in the United States. This provision led to the increase of students and intellectuals from China, Korea, and Japan at several prestigious universities on the East Coast, including Columbia, New York University, Harvard, and Yale. Their presence undoubtedly enriched the academic landscape of these institutions.

After the passing of the 1924 Immigration Act, Chinese Americans united with other Asian communities in a series of concerted efforts to overturn this restrictive immigration law, as well as to repeal the 1882 Chinese Exclusion Act. Their collective actions, spanning nearly two decades, and the influence of World War II, finally led to the political change they had been striving for.

PART II

• • •

Asian Americans' Second Wave of
Political Activism:
From WWII to the 1990s

INTRODUCTION

By the 1930s, due to immigration restrictions, many Asians in the U.S. were native-born U.S. citizens. Yet, the American public still perceived Asian Americans as being "outsiders." Such a perception was also often influenced by international affairs that Asian Americans had little to do with nor had control over. The internment of Japanese Americans during World War II is a stark example of the injustices faced by Asian Americans. In response to such injustices, Japanese Americans demonstrated their patriotism by defending America on the battlefields, protecting their constitutional rights in the courtroom, and setting examples for other Asian Americans, invoking empathy from their fellow citizens.

This segment covers three significant examples of Asian Americans' political activism in the 20th century: the internment of Japanese Americans in WWII, the murder of Vincent Chin and the Pan-Asian Civil Rights movement it sparked in the 1980s, and the political awakening of Korean Americans after the Los Angeles (LA) riots in the 1990s.

CHAPTER 3

• • •

"Are You Loyal to America?" – How the
Internment Reshaped the Japanese American
Experience

In the 1930s, Japan's military aggression in Asia, especially its full invasion of China in 1937, alarmed the United States. Since Japan's military actions hurt U.S. commercial and geopolitical interests in the Asia Pacific, the U.S. supported China's Nationalist government against Japan. Before the U.S. officially entered World War II, Washington not only strengthened its diplomatic relations with China and provided economic aid (and stealth military aid) but also made concerted efforts to promote goodwill toward China and the Chinese people in America.

The United States government extended its first loan to China in 1938. A year later, in 1939, Washington terminated the 1911 Treaty of Commerce and Navigation with Japan and began restricting war matériel exports to Japan. After Japan signed the Tripartite Pact with the Axis powers (Germany and Italy), the United States government took further steps, cutting off all commercial and financial relations with Japan, freezing the Japanese government's assets in the U.S., and declaring an embargo on shipments to Japan – petroleum and other essential war materials. Most Americans were unaware of the blockade. Thus, they didn't know how much the Japanese people resented this blockade because they saw themselves being unfairly victimized. This embargo severely impacted Japan's economy, as the island nation is significantly dependent on foreign imports, especially energy imports. However, the economic blow from the U.S. failed to tame Japan's military aggression in Asia. In fact, Japan reacted by accelerating its conquest of China and Southeast Asian nations, including the Philippines, for resources its economy needed and secretly planning revenge against America that would shock the world.

While the relations between the U.S. and Japan were deteriorating, Americans' previous anti-Chinese sentiment started to recede, thanks to a pro-China propaganda campaign in the U.S., coming in various forms, including articles, films, and news reports. Pearl Buck's novel *The Good Earth*, which depicts Chinese farmers' strong work ethic and devotion to their land, was adapted into a film and won two Oscars, including the Best Actress award for Louise Rainer, a white actress who played a Chinese woman with heavy yellow makeup. For many Americans who had never known much about China or its people before, this book and movie cast the Chinese people positively. It helped Americans see that the Chinese people shared many of the same values as Americans, such as love for their families and an appreciation for farming. Henry Luce, founder of *Time* magazine, grew up in China, and his parents were missionaries who spent many years there. Luce's personal connection to China and his influential role in the media industry allowed him to shape the American perception of China. He put Generalissimo Chiang Kai-shek, head of the Nationalist government in China, on the cover of *Time* magazine twice: 1938 and 1942. The magazine also wrote numerous articles to inform readers about Chinese people's courageous resistance and their suffering at the hands of the Japanese invaders.

The American public's friendly sentiment toward China reached its height when China's First Lady Mayling Soong, wife of General-issimo Chiang Kai-shek, visited the United States in 1943. Madam Soong's connection with the U.S. was deep-rooted. She first came to the U.S. in 1908, when she was only 11. She was educated in the U.S., attending Wesleyan College (in Georgia), and graduating from Wellesley College. When she returned to China in 1917, Soong was thoroughly Americanized, a devout Christian who spoke fluent English with a Southern accent. This Americanization was not just linguistic but also cultural assimilation that further strengthened her bond with the U.S. Madam Soong was often credited with helping Chiang convert to Christianity.

Madam Soong's American education and experiences paid dividends when she visited the U.S. in 1943 as China's first lady. She became the first Chinese and only the second woman to deliver a speech to a joint session of the U.S. Congress. She skillfully reminded American lawmakers that China had "bled and borne unflinchingly the burden of war for more than five and a half years." China and the U.S. embarked on a "united effort to free mankind from brutality and violence."[1] Her speech received a standing ovation. She successfully aroused much sympathy toward China and the Chinese people among the American public. Many Americans donated to United China Relief, a U.S.-based charity dedicated to raising funds for China's war effort.

Thanks to the changing public perceptions toward China and the lobbying effort by organizations including the Chinese American Citizens Alliance (CACA), the U.S. government not only provided China with financial aid and military assistance to fight the war against Japan but also reversed the discriminatory immigration law against the Chinese by repealing the 1882 Chinese Exclusion Act through the 1943 Magnuson Act. In a letter to Congress to express his support for the Magnuson Act, President Franklin D. Roosevelt wrote that repealing the Chinese Exclusion Act was vital to correcting a "historic mistake" and was "important in the cause of

winning the war and of establishing a secure peace." [2] The
Magnuson Act, a milestone in U.S.-China relations, established an
annual quota of 105 immigration visas for Chinese immigrants,
marking a new era in Chinese immigration to the United States.
The Act was not only a triumph for Chinese Americans, but also
had a ripple effect, becoming the model to overturn immigration
exclusion of several other Asian countries that were allies of the
United States in WWII, such as the Philippines and India. This
broader impact further underlines the significance of the repeal.[3]

On January 18, 1944, a significant day in U.S. history, Edward
Bing Kan, the son of a Chinese vegetable peddler and an inter-
preter who worked for the Immigration and Naturalization
Service's (INS) Chicago office for 35 years, became the first
Chinese American to take the oath and become a U.S. citizen after
the repeal of the Chinese Exclusion Act, a testament to the changing tide of immigration policies in the U.S.

Unfortunately, while the anti-Chinese sentiment in America was
receding due to the allyship in WWII, the anti-Japanese sentiment
in the nation was on the rise. The Japanese American community in
the U.S. consisted of two groups:

- The Issei – Japanese immigrants who were not born in the
  U.S. and were not allowed to become naturalized U.S.
  citizens due to the 1924 Immigration Act, which excluded
  all Asian immigrants from the legal path to citizenship.
- The Nisei – Japanese Americans born in the U.S. with
  birthright citizenship. They grew up like any other American kids, speaking English, playing sports, pledging
  allegiance to the American flag, and celebrating America's
  founding on July Fourth each year. Japan was a remote
  concept the Nisei rarely thought about.

By 1930, Nisei made up about half of Japanese Americans. One
of the Nisei organizations, The Japanese American Citizens League
(JACL), declared in its creed in 1940:

I am proud that I am an American citizen of Japanese ancestry, for my very background makes me appreciate more fully the wonderful advantages of this nation... I pledge myself...to defend her against all enemies, foreign and domestic.[4]

The patriotism of the Nisei and their faith in America would soon be tested. Japan's military conquest of China threatened America's economic and geopolitical interests and also sparked Washington's paranoia about Japanese Americans. As early as 1932, the U.S. government and the U.S. Navy began to express concerns about Japanese Americans' loyalty to the U.S., based on the assumption that "the homogeneity and ethnic loyalty of the Japanese would lead to acts of sabotage against the United States."[5] By 1941, as the likelihood of a war between the U.S. and Japan rose, the U.S. government took the secret initiative to classify more than 2,000 Japanese in the U.S. into three groups, profoundly impacting the Japanese American community:

> Group A suspects were known to be dangerous and were considered to be at the front line of sabotage... 'Those deemed sinister enough to warrant top surveillance included fishermen, produce distributors, Shinto and Buddhist priests, farmers, influential businessmen, and members of the Japanese Consulate.' Group B suspects had not been fully investigated but were considered to be 'potentially dangerous.' Suspects in Group C were believed to be on the edge of sabotage but were closely watched due to their pro-Japanese beliefs...Japanese language teachers, kibeis, martial art instructors, community servants, travel agents, social directors, and newspaper editors were among the suspects with B or C categories."[6]

President Roosevelt also sent a State Department official, Curtis B. Munson, to the West Coast and Hawaii to determine "the degree of loyalty" among Japanese Americans. Munson found:

> There is no Japanese 'problem' on the Coast. There will be
> no armed uprising of Japanese. There will undoubtedly be
> some sabotage financed by Japan and executed largely by
> imported agents…for the most part, the local Japanese are
> loyal to the U.S. or, at worst, hope that by remaining quiet
> they can avoid concentration camps or irresponsible mobs.
> We do not believe that they would be at least any more
> loyal than any other racial group in the United States with
> whom we went to war.[7]

Munson put his observations in a 25-page report and sent it to
Roosevelt in November 1941. Yet, Munson's favorable assessment
of Japanese Americans' loyalty had failed to ease President Roosevelt's and some of his cabinet officials' fear that Japanese Americans were "enemies from within." The Roosevelt administration
suppressed the findings of the Munson report about Japanese
Americans' loyalty.[8]

Then, on December 7, 1941, the Japanese Navy attacked the
U.S. Naval base at Pearl Harbor, Hawaii. A Japanese proverb says:
"A cornered mouse will bite a cat!" Since the embargo America
imposed on Japan had devastated Japan's economy, most leaders in
the Japanese government and even some ordinary Japanese citizens
regarded the Japanese Navy's action as a righteous response to the
severe economic pains caused by the U.S. embargo. However,
Americans saw the Pearl Harbor attack quite differently. It was the
first and only attack on the U.S. homeland during WWII. All
corners of American society were shocked by the loss of lives,
battleships, and the pain the Japanese Navy inflicted:

> The *Arizona* and the *Oklahoma* were destroyed with great
> loss of life, and six other battleships suffered varying
> degrees of damage. Three cruisers, three destroyers, and
> other vessels were also damaged. U.S. military casualties
> totaled more than 3,400, including more than 2,300 killed.

Heavy damage was inflicted on both army and navy aircraft on the ground.[9]

Contrary to popular belief, the internment of Japanese Americans didn't begin with President Roosevelt's Executive Order 9066, which was issued in February 1942. Right after the Pearl Harbor attack on December 7, 1941, President Roosevelt personally directed the U.S. Immigration and Naturalization Service (USINS) to detain all Japanese previously classified as A, B, and C groups. The next day, before President Roosevelt delivered his declaration of war against Japan in a joint session of the U.S. Congress, the number of detained Japanese Americans had surged from 736 to 1,291. After spending two weeks in local detention centers, these Japanese Americans were transferred to sixteen imprisonment camps operated by the Immigration and Naturalization Service.[10]

When President Roosevelt declared war on Japan on December 8th, he framed Japan's action at Pearl Harbor as "suddenly and deliberately." He gave the impression that his administration didn't expect it at all. Some historians have argued that President Roosevelt had plenty of warning about Japan's imminent attack on America's soil, but that he chose to deliberately leave the U.S. Navy unprepared, his "secret" plan. Then he could frame the heavy losses the U.S. Navy suffered as a "sneaky" and "unprovoked" attack by Japan to convince the American public, who were indifferent to wars going on in Asia and Europe before the Pearl Harbor attack, that the U.S. must join WWII.[11]

What was indisputable was that the Pearl Harbor attack did become a turning point in American public opinion about WWII. Americans were angry about the "unprovoked" attack by Japan and the heavy loss the U.S. Navy suffered. They were eager to seek revenge, and they looked at their fellow citizens of Japanese descent with suspicion and contempt. Cartoons and war posters employed racial stereotypes to ridicule Japanese Americans. Influential publications called for the removal of Japanese Americans from American society. For example, on January 29, 1942, the *San*

Francisco Examiner demanded the U.S. government take tough actions against Japanese Americans:

> Herd 'em up, pack 'em off and give 'em the inside room in the badlands. Let 'em be pinched, hurt, hungry, and dead up against it... Let us have no patience with the enemy or with anyone whose vein carry his blood... Let's quit worrying about hurting the enemy's feelings and start doing it.[12]

The *Seattle Post-Intelligencer* printed a similar opinion on February 19, 1942:

> You can't tell a man's loyalty by looking at him and there isn't time now that we are at war to check on every individual. So why take a chance? The Japanese and the Japanese Americans should be taken into protective custody not only for the good of the United States but for their own welfare as well.[13]

The anti-Japanese sentiment and the call for their removal, which intensified after the Pearl Harbor attack, was a stark contrast to the loyalty of the majority of Japanese Americans. President Roosevelt's decision not to make the Munson report, which affirmed this loyalty, public, was a significant missed opportunity to correct this injustice. His failure to redirect the public's revenge tendencies after the Pearl Harbor attack toward the Japanese government and military instead of their fellow citizens was a grave mistake. Instead, Roosevelt issued his notorious Executive Order 9066 on February 19, 1942, authorizing the Secretary of War, Henry L. Stimson, and assigned military commanders to remove persons of Japanese ancestry, both American citizens and legal residents, from the West Coast.

It is worth noting that some historians believe Roosevelt's EO was heavily influenced by Lieutenant General John L. DeWitt's recommendation. As the commanding general of the Western

Defense Command, General DeWitt held significant sway over West Coast security, particularly in the wake of the Pearl Harbor attack. His influence, combined with the prevailing anti-Japanese sentiment, likely played a crucial role in shaping Roosevelt's decision. DeWitt justified his rationale for the removal of persons of Japanese ancestry from the West Coast this way:

> In the war in which we are now engaged racial affinities are not severed by migration. The Japanese race is an enemy race and while many second and third generation Japanese born on United State soil, possessed of United States citizenship, have become "Americanized," the racial strains are undiluted… That Japan is allied with Germany and Italy in this struggle is not ground for assuming that any Japanese, barred from assimilation by convention as he is, though born and raised in the United States, will not turn against this nation when the final test of loyalty comes. It, therefore, follows that along the vital Pacific Coast over 112,000 potential enemies, of Japanese extraction, are at large today. There are indications that these were organized and ready for concerted action at a favorable opportunity. *The very fact that no sabotage has taken place to date is a disturbing and confirming indication that such action will be taken* [emphasis added].[14]

I always find the last sentence full of irony: the fact that Japanese Americans committed no sabotage before or after the Pearl Harbor attack should have convinced people like General DeWitt not to treat Japanese Americans as an enemy race. Instead, General DeWitt was disturbed by the peace and was even more convinced that Japanese Americans must be removed. Still, ultimately, the buck stopped at President Roosevelt. He was the one who signed the EO to forcefully remove Japanese Americans from their homes, even though he had reviewed the Munson report several months prior.

More than 100,000 people of Japanese ancestry were ordered to leave their businesses, employment, schools, and homes. Lives, schools, and work were interrupted. Identities were reduced to name tags. Since most had only a few days' notice, Japanese families and businesses were forced to sell their assets quickly for a fraction of their actual value. Adding insult to injury, some white Americans took advantage of the situation and offered to buy assets Japanese Americans owned for 5 or 10 cents on the dollar. For example, Yoshimi Matsuura's family had to sell their vineyards for $23/acre instead of their value of $200/acre.[15]

According to historian Sandra Taylor, "Initial [economic] losses were compounded by vandalism and the local officials' indifference to protecting Japanese property." It has been challenging to assess the economic losses Japanese Americans suffered during WWII accurately. Some have estimated it was between $1 and $3 billion (not adjusted for inflation).

Since few states wanted to endanger their security by accepting Japanese Americans, the U.S. government sent them to temporarily built concentration camps in remote areas in Mountain West states including Arizona, Colorado, Montana, and Wyoming. For example, more than 7,500 Japanese Americans were interned at Camp Amache in Colorado. The influx of Japanese Americans instantly turned Heart Mountain, Wyoming, into the third-largest city in Wyoming. Overall, about 127,000 Japanese Americans were impacted; some 70,000 were U.S. citizens and some were veterans of World War I.[16] They were forced to live in concentration camps solely because of their ancestry.

Colorado's Republican Governor Ralph Carr was the only influential public official who publicly denounced Roosevelt's EO that imprisoned Japanese Americans. He called on all Americans to "understand the Japanese Americans instead of fearing them."[17] Carr's opposition to Roosevelt's EO and his public support of Japanese Americans came at a significant political cost, as seen in the loss of his bid for a second term of the governorship in 1943, a stark contrast to his wide margin of victory in 1938. This professional sacrifice underscores the significance of his actions.

A few courageous Japanese Americans, U.S. citizens through birthright citizenship, challenged the constitutionality of President Roosevelt's EO soon after it went into effect. Four of their cases reached the U.S. Supreme Court, carrying immense significance.

Hirabayashi v. United States

Gordon Hirabayashi was born in the U.S., became a Quaker in 1940, and was a student at the University of Washington at the beginning of WWII. After President Roosevelt's EO 9066 went into effect, Hirabayashi thought his birthright citizenship would protect him from the forced evacuation. Then, General John DeWitt, the commanding general of the Western Defense Command, announced a curfew for enemy aliens, including Japanese American citizens, between 8 p.m. and 6 a.m. on March 24, 1942. Hirabayashi ignored the curfew and moved around as a law-abiding citizen. He also quit school and volunteered with the American Friends Service Committee to arrange storage for the belongings of Japanese families before their departure to concentration camps. When it was his turn to register for forced "relocation," Hirabayashi turned himself in to the FBI. Representing Hirabayashi, his legal team challenged the government's legality to incarcerate Japanese Americans without the due process of law through a lawsuit. Unfortunately, FBI agents learned through Hirabayashi's diary that he didn't follow the curfew rule. Since violating curfew was a federal crime, Hirabayashi was arraigned on June 1, 1942. He pleaded "not guilty" on the basis that both the exclusion law and curfew were racially discriminatory and unconstitutional. Judge Black sentenced him to 90 days at the Dupont Road camp outside Tacoma, Washington, for violating curfew and refusing to comply with exclusion orders.

Meanwhile, Hirabayashi's legal team took his case, challenging the constitutionality of President Roosevelt's EO, to the U.S. Supreme Court. Despite the efforts of Hirabayashi's legal team, the U.S. Supreme Court declined to rule on President Roosevelt's EO's constitutionality. Instead, the Court focused solely on the curfew. Viewing the curfew as a necessary wartime "protective measure," the nine Justices unanimously sided with the government. They found Hirabayashi guilty of disobeying the wartime curfew and upheld his 90-day jail sentence. This decision, which ignored the more significant issue of the EO's constitutionality, was a stark reminder of the injustices faced by Japanese Americans during this dark period of history. How Hirabayashi chose to serve his jail sentence was legendary:

Hirabayashi was living in Spokane, Washington, working for the American Friends Service Committee when two FBI agents picked him up and delivered him to District Attorney Edward Connelly's office to begin his ninety-day sentence. D.A. Connelly informed Hirabayashi that because Dupont was located inside the exclusion zone, he would have to serve his sentence out in the Spokane County Jail. Distraught at the possibility of serving more time in such confinement, Hirabayashi asked if there was not another road camp he could be assigned to as he had accepted an extra-long sentence with the understanding, he would be allowed to serve his sentence outside. When the D.A. mentioned that the government could not provide transportation to the nearest road camp, the Tucson Federal Prison, otherwise known as the Catalina Federal Honor Camp, **Hirabayashi suggested that he could get himself there**. D.A. Connelly agreed, and Hirabayashi set off on his next big adventure. **He hitchhiked over the next several weeks from Spokane, through Weiser, Idaho, to visit his parents, through Salt Lake City, Utah, where he visited** *Pacific Citizen* **editor Larry Tajiri, and on down to Tucson, Arizona, where he had to convince officials, he had a legitimate order to be accepted into the prison** [emphasis added].[18]

Yasui v. United States

Minoru Yasui was born in Portland, Oregon. As a young Japanese American lawyer, his employment opportunity was limited due to the prevalent discrimination against Asian Americans at the time. He eventually found a job working for the Japanese consulate in Chicago. As soon as he heard of Japan's attack on Pearl Harbor, he resigned from his post and went back to Portland. After President Roosevelt signed EO 9066, Yasui wanted to challenge it in court. Initially, he tried to find someone else as a plaintiff because he was concerned that the court might not look at him favorably, given his previous employer was the Japanese consulate. But he ultimately decided to challenge the law by risking himself after being unable to find anyone else.

Just like Gordon Hirabayashi, Yasui had refused to obey General John DeWitt's curfew for enemy aliens on March 28, 1942, and was subsequently arrested. An American lawyer friend later bailed him out. Yasui also ignored the government's relocation order. He was quickly found and sent to the Portland Assembly Center. From there, Yasui wrote a letter to General DeWitt on April 4, 1942, about the government's forceful relocation of all Japanese Americans, "without regard to their citizenship status and loyalty to the United States of America, is to effectively deprive them of certain fundamental and inalienable rights of a human being."[19] Unfortunately, the American Civil Liberties Union (ACLU), known for defending civil rights, declined to help Yasui due to his previous employment with the Japanese consulate.

Yasui's trial took place on June 12, 1942. Even before a verdict was rendered, he was sent to the concentration camp at Minidoka, Idaho. The camp was located in a remote desert area, and the internees had to endure extreme weather conditions and limited resources. Yasui, like many others, lived in crowded barracks and had to adapt to a new way of life while waiting for the verdict. A few months later, on November 14, the presiding District Court Judge Alger Fee found Yasui guilty and deemed his employment at the Japanese consulate an act of renouncing his U.S. citizenship.

Judge Fee sentenced Yasui to the maximum penalty of one year in jail and ordered him to pay a fine of $5,000. Yasui and his lawyer appealed. His case eventually landed in the U.S. Supreme Court, about the same time as Hirabayashi's case. Therefore, the Supreme Court heard the two cases on May 10 and 11, 1943.

Despite the Supreme Court's acknowledgment that Judge Fee's decision was flawed, they unanimously ruled against Yasui on June 21, 1943. This ruling, which upheld Yasui's conviction and the legality of the curfew, was a heavy blow to Yasui and his supporters. The court sent Yasui's case back to Judge Fee for sentencing. Given that Yasui had already served nine months in jail, Judge Fee suspended the fine and ordered Yasui to be released. On August 19, 1943, Yasui was "released" from one prison, only to be immediately escorted by a U.S. marshal back to the concentration camp at Minidoka, Idaho.

Korematsu v. United States

Fred Korematsu was born in Oakland, California. He was only 22 when Japan attacked Pearl Harbor. Due to the attack, Korematsu was fired from his employment at a shipyard. On May 9, 1942, Korematsu's parents and three brothers reported to the Tanforan Assembly Center, a concentration camp for Japanese Americans in San Bruno. Korematsu stayed behind at home with his American girlfriend. He took the drastic action of disguising himself: "he had plastic surgery on his eyes to alter his appearance; changed his name to Clyde Sarah; and claimed that he was of Spanish and Hawaiian descent."[20] Still, he was arrested on May 30 for violating the evacuation order. He was tried and convicted of violating a military order issued under Executive Order 9066. He was tried in San Francisco's federal court, given five years on probation, and sent to the Tanforan Assembly Center in San Bruno, California. The ACLU of Northern California filed a legal challenge on his behalf. Later, the U.S. government forced Korematsu and his family to relocate from Tanforan to an internment camp in Topaz, Utah. Korematsu and his lawyers appealed his case to the U.S.

Supreme Court.

After the U.S. Supreme Court agreed to hear Korematsu's case, the U.S. government offered to release him early. Although Korematsu accepted the offer, the U.S. Supreme Court went ahead and heard his case anyway. Unfortunately, the High Court's majority sided with the government in a 6–3 decision. In his dissenting opinion, Justice Robert Jackson wrote, "Korematsu...has been convicted of an act not commonly thought a crime. It consists merely of being present in the state whereof he is a citizen, near the place where he was born, and where all his life he has lived."[21] Wartime national security concern, according to Justice Jackson, was insufficient justification for the government to violate Japanese Americans' constitutional rights. Another dissenting justice was Frank Murphy. Justice Murphy called Roosevelt's EO "the legalization of racism" that violated the Equal Protection Clause of the Fourteenth Amendment. He contended that "Racial discrimination in any form and any degree has no justifiable part whatever in our democratic way of life. It is unattractive in any setting, but it is utterly revolting among a free people who have embraced the principles set forth in the Constitution of the United States."[22]

Endo v. United States

Mitsuye Endo, a 22-year-old state employee from Sacramento, California, found her life turned upside down after the attack on Pearl Harbor. The California State Personnel Board, in a move that would later be deemed unjust, laid off all Japanese American state employees, including Endo. The personal impact of this decision was profound, as Endo later described: "We were given a piece of paper saying we were suspended because we were of Japanese ancestry."[23] This personal tragedy was echoed in the stories of several dozens of fired Japanese American employees, including Endo, who sought to challenge their firing with the assistance of the JACL and retained James C. Purcell as their attorney. Meanwhile, Endo and her family followed the evacuation order and were first sent to the Sacramento Assembly Center and later to the concentration camp in Tule Lake, California.

Besides the employment case, Purcell planned to file a habeas corpus petition to challenge the U.S. government's order and needed a suitable plaintiff. He reached out to Endo because her family background looked appealing to mainstream American society: Endo was a Christian with one brother in the U.S. Army, and she had never been to Japan. Endo initially hesitated because she was a very private person. She told an interviewer years later that she only agreed to do it because she was told it was for the good of everybody. Purcell filed the petition on July 12, 1942. By the time the case ended up at the U.S. Supreme Court, Endo had been sent to the concentration camp in Topaz, Utah. One of her fellow campmates was Fred Korematsu. The U.S. government offered to release Endo and Korematsu early in light of their pending Supreme Court cases. Korematsu accepted the offer, but Endo refused because Purcell advised that remaining in the camp would increase the likelihood of a favorable ruling. Endo's refusal to accept the offer, despite the hardships she faced, made her a symbol of hope and resilience.

On December 18, 1944, the Supreme Court issued two rulings. It denied Fred Korematsu's petition by 6–3. But the justices ruled in Endo's favor unanimously. On behalf of the entire Court, Justice William O. Douglas wrote:

> We are of the view that Mitsuye Endo should be given her liberty. In reaching that conclusion we do not come to the underlying constitutional issues which have been argued. For we conclude that, whatever power the War Relocation Authority may have to detain other classes of citizens, it has no authority to subject citizens who are concededly loyal to its leave procedure.[24]

The day before the ruling, the U.S. government was tipped off that Endo's case would likely prevail. The War Relocation Authority took preemptive action by announcing before the court's ruling that all incarcerated Japanese Americans were to be released from the camps starting in January 1945. Of the four Japanese Americans' cases challenging the forced evacuation order, only Endo's was successful. She was often called the quiet lady who ended the internment camps. These four cases significantly raised awareness about the experiences of Japanese Americans during WWII, enlightening the public about this dark chapter in history.

While the four Supreme Court cases drew the most attention, a lesser-known resistance and legal challenge unfolded in Cheyenne, Wyoming, centered around the Heart Mountain Concentration camp. This camp, with its significant historical weight, was situated between Cody and Powell, Wyoming. More than 10,000 Japanese Americans from California, Oregon, and Washington were forced to relocate to Heart Mountain during WWII.

In October 1942, U.S. military police monitored the camp population and arrested 32 young kids for playing outside of the camp boundaries. The children were later released back to their parents, but the incident deeply disturbed the people inside the camp. The unjust arrest of their children was a stark reminder of the emotional toll of the internment on families. To prevent such incidents and ensure both adults and children would stay within the camp's boundary, the military police asked for volunteers to build a barbed-wire fence around the camp. However, people refused to participate in the project, and more than three thousand of them signed a petition "charging that the fence proved that Heart Mountain was indeed a 'concentration camp' and that the evacuees were 'prisoners of war.'"

As the United States expanded its involvement in WWII, the U.S. Army needed all the men it could get. So, ironically, after putting young Japanese Americans (Nisei) in concentration camps, less than a year later, the U.S. government asked them to register for military service "voluntarily." Adding insult to injury, the War Department, with the Office of Naval Intelligence's (ONI) assistance, created a "Statement of United States Citizen of Japanese

Ancestry," also called Selective Service Form 304A, to determine the likelihood that a U.S.-born Japanese American (Nisei) being considered for military service would be loyal to the United States or to Japan. This form, known among Japanese Americans as a "loyalty questionnaire," had caused great resentment.

The most problematic question on the loyalty questionnaire asked the Nisei to "swear unqualified allegiance to the United States and forswear any form of allegiance to the Emperor of Japan."[25] Nisei asked: "I am a born U.S. citizen. Why should I renounce loyalty to the Emperor of Japan when I never pledged allegiance to the Emperor of Japan in the first place? Why should I pledge unqualified allegiance to the U.S. when it violated my constitutional rights by keeping me locked up without due process?" Even the seemingly innocent questions were problematic. For example, "speaking Japanese well, or belonging to a judo or kendo club would result in negative points, but being Christian, or belonging to the Boy Scouts of America would result in points being added."[26]

The Nisei's organized resistance to filling out the loyalty questionnaires compelled the War Department to modify the form and make some of the questions less provocative. Still, even after the form was modified, only a tiny percentage of Nisei registered for military service. The U.S. government stopped asking for volunteers. It imposed a draft.

Frank Inouye, one of the Japanese Americans in the Heart Mountain camp, established the Heart Mountain Congress of American Citizens. The organization "demanded the U.S. government re-establish Nisei's civil rights, guarantee their citizenship, and eliminate race-based discrimination in the military as a prerequisite to enlistment."[27] Some drafted Nisei filed a lawsuit at the Federal District Court in Cheyenne:

> They [Nisei] refused to go until their people were turned loose from Heart Mountain. They went to the Federal District Court in Cheyenne... They lost of course, and they

all were drafted. They said, "Okay, we love America, we don't even know Japan, but let my mother and my little brother out of Heart Mountain."[28]

In the end, 63 Nisei of the Heart Mountain resisted the draft, and the group leaders were sentenced to federal prison. Mike Masaoka, executive secretary of the JACL, called these legal challengers "self-styled martyrs who are willing to be jailed in order that they might fight for the rights of citizenship."[29]

The JACL, a highly influential organization in the United States, collaborated with the federal government to encourage Nisei to answer the draft. Most Nisei accepted the military draft, driven by a burning desire to prove their loyalty and regain the trust of the American government and the general public. They also hoped that their victory on the battlefield would secure better treatment or even early release of their families from America's concentration camps.

The 18,000 Nisei from the Hawaiian Islands and the mainland U.S. formed an all-Japanese American unit, the 442nd Regimental Combat Team (RCT), almost exactly a year after President Roosevelt signed EO 9066. They were deployed to Europe, a decision influenced by the lingering doubts about these Americans' loyalty. The 442nd RCT's motto, "Go for Broke," symbolized their readiness to put everything on the line to win big. They lived up to that motto.

Not long after the 442nd RCT arrived in Italy, they fought with such valor against the Germans that the Germans called them "the little iron men." Since it was one of the best fighting units in the U.S. Army, the 442nd RCT was often asked to fight in impossible battles and take on missions that seemed almost suicidal. One of their best-known battles was to rescue the "Lost Battalion," the Texas infantrymen trapped by the German army in the Vosges Mountains between France and Germany. The 442nd RCT accomplished its mission but paid for it in blood. Out of 180 men in K Company, only 17 were still alive after the battle.

Daniel James Brown, author of *Face the Mountain: A True Story of Japanese Americans in World War II*, wrote that whether on the battle-fields or in courtrooms, those young Nisei men "were the living embodiments of the spirit that has always animated America – the striving, the yearning, the courage, the relentless optimism, the will-ingness to chip in and lend a hand, the fair-mindedness, the inclu-siveness. They knew they had been called upon to defend a set of simple but profound ideas – the highest ideal of America and the Western democracies – and having heard the call, they answered it, as did millions of young men in the first half of the 1940s."[30] Many laid down their lives for it, so today, we can live in a far better country than the one they were in. Their sacrifices have shaped the America we know and love today, and for that, we are eternally grateful.

After he lost his brother Calvin on the battlefield, George Saito, a Nisei of the 442nd RCT, wrote to his father in 1944: "In spite of Cal's supreme sacrifice, don't let anyone tell you that he was foolish or made a mistake to volunteer. Of what I've seen in my travels on our mission, I am more than convinced that we've done the right thing in spite of what's happened in the past. America is a damn good country and don't let anyone tell you otherwise."[31] George made the ultimate sacrifice himself shortly after penning this letter.

The 442nd RCT became the most decorated in the U.S. Army during WWII, and earned a staggering number of awards and honors. Despite representing just 0.11% of the U.S. military, they earned "over 4,000 Purple Hearts, 4,000 Bronze Stars, 560 Silver Star Medals, 21 Medals of Honor, and seven Presidential Unit Cita-tions," and more. Their exceptional recognition led to Texas Gov. John Connally making the entire 442nd RCT honorary Texans on October 21, 1963.[32] In 2000, when President Clinton awarded Medals of Honor to 20 members of the 442nd RCT, he acknowl-edged that "Rarely has a nation been so well served by people it has so ill-served." In total, about 3,600 Japanese Americans from the internment camps, along with 22,000 others living outside of those camps (i.e., in Hawaii), joined various units within the U.S. armed forces during World War II.

After the U.S. victory, Japanese Americans were allowed to leave the camps and return to their original homes, but many found that they had nothing to return to. The last Japanese concentration camp was closed in 1946. The four Japanese Americans whose cases reached the U.S. Supreme Court lived different lives. Hirabayashi continued his education at the University of Washington and eventually earned a Ph.D. in sociology. He taught at various universities and retired from teaching at the University of Alberta in 1983.

Korematsu moved around and eventually returned to the San Francisco Bay area in 1949. Due to his felony conviction in 1942, he was ineligible for employment at government agencies, and large firms shied away from him, too. Korematsu devoted the rest of his life to ensure what happened to Japanese Americans will never happen again to any American citizen of any race, creed, or color.

Yasui settled in Denver, Colorado. He had a successful law practice and became a well-respected civil rights activist and community leader. He co-founded the Urban League of Denver, an African American organization, in 1946. He was credited with preventing Denver from experiencing the race riots during the 1960s.[33]

Endo was the most low-key person out of the four. After her release from the camp, Endo moved to Chicago and stayed out of the public eye after the war. She rarely discussed her landmark lawsuit and only accepted one interview. Even her daughter didn't know what Endo had accomplished until the interview, a fact that adds a layer of intrigue to her story.

Post WWII, the United States saw a significant shift in its immigration policy with the enactment of the Immigration Act of 1952. This legislation, while retaining the 1924 Act's national-origin quota system, marked a crucial breakthrough by eliminating the racial qualifications that had previously barred Asian immigrants from U.S. citizenship. This pivotal change in the 1952 Act, which was the first time our nation's immigration law became "color-blind," had a profound impact on U.S. history.

A few years later, the U.S. Congress passed the Immigration Act of 1965. This pivotal legislation abolished the national-origin quotas and replaced them with a single annual quota on the total number of immigration visas to be issued annually: 170,000. Immediate relatives of U.S. citizens were exempt from the quota. When President Lyndon Johnson signed the Immigration Act of 1965 into law on October 3, with the Statue of Liberty in the background, he celebrated the new immigration law: "For it does repair a very deep and painful flaw in the fabric of American justice. It corrects a cruel and enduring wrong in the conduct of the American Nation."

Encouraged by the changing macro-political environment, Japanese Americans, led by the JACL, launched a Redress Movement. Their relentless efforts over the six decades that followed the World War II mass removal and confinement of Japanese Americans, seeking the restitution of civil rights, an apology, and/or monetary compensation from the U.S. government, stand as a powerful testament to their unwavering determination for justice:

> The former inmates were required to provide sworn testimony and to produce receipts and other proofs of their losses. If their claim amounted to over $2,500, they were required in effect to sue the government for damages, and await fresh appropriation of funds to pay claims. The Justice Department strongly contested each claim, using a legalistic definition of what could be counted as a 'loss.'[34]

In 1971, the efforts of the Redress Movement led to the repeal of Title II of the Internal Security Act of 1950, which authorized the mass detention of suspected subversives without trial. In 1976, President Gerald Ford, formally terminating President Franklin Roosevelt's notorious Executive Order 9066 and apologizing for the internment, stated:

We now know what we should have known then—not only was that evacuation wrong but Japanese-Americans were and are loyal Americans. On the battlefield and at home the names of Japanese-Americans have been and continue to be written in history for the sacrifices and the contributions they have made to the well-being and to the security of this, our common Nation.[35]

In 1980, pushed by the Redress Movement, the U.S. Congress and President Jimmy Carter approved the creation of a Commission on Wartime Relocation and Internment of Civilians (CWRIC). The Commission held almost three weeks of hearings, during which more than 700 witnesses testified, sharing their personal stories of suffering and loss. These testimonies were instrumental in urging the Commission to recommend that Congress provide an apology and compensation of $25,000 to each person who suffered exclusion and detention.

The final report delivered by the Commission, a significant milestone in the quest for justice, acknowledged that the injustice of U.S. government policies toward Japanese Americans during WWII was caused not by "military necessity" but by "race prejudice, war hysteria, and a failure of political leadership."[36] The commission recommended Congress and the president issue a national apology, establish a foundation to educate the public, and provide $20,000 to each surviving detainee.

In 1983, a group of young lawyers, mostly Japanese Americans, filed a writ *coram nobis* ("before us") petition and re-opened cases for Korematsu, Yasui, and Hirabayashi in three federal district courts: San Francisco for Korematsu, Portland for Yasui, and Seattle for Hirabayashi. Endo wasn't involved because she won her Supreme Court case back in 1944. These presented new evidence showing "that the government's legal team had intentionally suppressed or destroyed evidence from government intelligence agencies reporting that Japanese Americans posed no military threat to the U.S."[37] Federal judge Marylyn Hall Patel overturned

Korematsu's conviction in the same San Francisco courthouse where he had been convicted as a young man four decades previously. Judge Patel said the Supreme Court's *Korematsu* decision should:

> stand a caution that in times of distress the shield of military necessity or national security must not be used to protect governmental actions from close scrutiny and accountability, and that in times of international hostility and antagonisms our institutions must take the leadership, whether those institutions be the legislative branch, the executive branch or the judicial branch, to protect all citizens from the petty fears and prejudices that are so easily stirred up during those times.[38]

In Portland, Judge Belloni vacated Yasui's conviction but refused to address the allegations of government misconduct. Unsatisfied with "a hollow personal victory," Yasui asked his attorneys to appeal to the Ninth Circuit Court of Appeals. On November 12, 1986, Yasui passed away. The appellate court agreed with the government and moved to dismiss the case. Yasui's family appealed to the U.S. Supreme Court, but the court declined to hear their case.

In Seattle, Judge Voorhees vacated Hirabayashi's conviction for violating the forced removal order. But he didn't overturn Hirabayashi's conviction for violating the curfew order. Both sides of the lawsuit appealed to the Ninth Circuit Court of Appeals. The three-judge panel of the appeal court issued a unanimous decision: upholding Judge Voorhees's decision vacating Hirabayashi's forced removal conviction and overturning Hirabayashi's curfew conviction.

Finally on August 10, 1988: President Reagan signed into law a bill to award restitution payments of $20,000 to Japanese American survivors of World War II civilian concentration camps.[39] In his remarks upon signing the bill, President Reagan explained, "What is most important in this bill has less to do with property than with honor. For here we admit a wrong; here we reaffirm our commitment as a nation to equal justice under the law."[40]

In 1998, President Bill Clinton awarded Fred Korematsu the Presidential Medal of Freedom, the nation's highest civilian award given in the U.S. Korematsu's daughter, Dr. Karen Korematsu, established the Fred T. Korematsu Institute in 2009 to carry on her father's legacy as a civil rights advocate. The state of California commemorated Korematsu's journey as a civil rights activist posthumously, by observing the "Fred Korematsu Day of Civil Liberties and the Constitution" for the first time on his 92nd birthday, January 30, 2011. Four years later, the state of Virgina became the second state in the union to permanently recognize each January 30 as Fred Korematsu Day.

President Barack Obama bestowed the Presidential Medal of Freedom, posthumously, to Gordon Hirabayashi and Minoru Yasui in 2012 and 2015, respectively. Endo passed away at her home in Chicago in 2005. Although she was the only one out of the four who won her case, she never got her recognition and had largely been forgotten. Endo was at peace for the rest of her life, not because she sought fame or glory, but because she knew she had done the right thing. She put herself out there at one of the most challenging times in our nation's history because it was the right thing to do, and it was for the good of everyone, including Japanese and non-Japanese Americans. Reflecting on his experiences, Gordon Hirabayashi said in an interview:

When my case was before the Supreme Court in 1943, I fully expected that as a citizen the Constitution would protect me. Surprisingly, even though I lost, I did not abandon my beliefs and values. And I never look at my case as just my own, or just as a Japanese American case. It is an American case, with principles that affect the fundamental human rights of all Americans.[41]

The legacy of these patriotic Japanese Americans continues to impact America today in various meaningful ways. In my hometown, Denver, Colorado, Spark the Change Colorado, a non-profit organization, awards the Minoru Yasui Community Volunteer Award (MYCVA) 10 times a year to men and women who make unique contributions to the Denver metropolitan community. This award, which recognizes the often-unsung heroes of our communities, provides the recipient with a $2,000 cash award to designate to a nonprofit agency of their choice. As of 2024, MYCVA has distributed 1 million dollars to 523 nonprofits since its inception.[42] The MYCVA award is one of the many examples of how Yasui and his fellow Japanese Americans' political activism during WWII continues to inspire Americans to strive to make the world a better place.

CHAPTER 4

• • •

"Our Blood Is the Same" – How the Murder
of Vincent Chin Reunited the Pan-Asian
Civil Rights Movement

In 2004, I left my job at Citibank and went to work for Daimler-Chrysler's Financial Services Americas at their its headquarters in Detroit, Michigan. I was a novice, knowing little about either Detroit or the auto industry. But I was young and ready for a new adventure. My coworkers at Citibank threw me a going-away party. After we said our final goodbye at the parking lot, one of my coworkers looked at my car, a Toyota Corolla, and warned me: "You may want to get a different car in Detroit. The UAW (United Auto Workers) doesn't like Japanese cars very much." I didn't understand why he said what he said, so I said: "But I love my Corolla. Why should I change?" He half-jokingly and half-seriously answered my question with a question: "Have you heard of Vincent Chin?" Seeing me shake my head, he added: "You may want to look him up before you go to Detroit." That was the first time I heard of the name Vincent Chin. Little did I know his story would profoundly impact my perception of Detroit and the auto industry.

Vincent Chin, born on May 18, 1955, was a child of innocence. His parents, Lily and "David" C.W. Hing Chin, were immigrants from China. David, the first to arrive in the U.S., was able to bring his wife, Lily, to America due to his service in the U.S. Army during World War II.[1] Tragically, Lily suffered a miscarriage in 1949 and was unable to have any children. In 1961, the couple adopted Vincent from an orphanage in China when he was only six years old. Vincent was their only child.

The Chin family settled in Highland Park, Michigan. Only six miles north of Downtown Detroit, Highland Park, a working-class neighborhood, is often called "the city within the city of Detroit." Even though Detroit was the home of the headquarters and mass factories of the Big Three American auto companies, Lily and David worked in Chinese laundries and restaurants – the few places that would employ Asian Americans. Later, the Chin family moved to Oak Park, Michigan. Vincent graduated from Oak Park High School in 1973. His profile picture shows a good-looking young man with thick dark hair and a broad smile.[2]

While Vincent was growing up, his hometown, Detroit, was experiencing growing pains as the Big Three American automakers started to face severe challenges from a once unthinkable source, Japan. During WWII, the Allies' heavy bombing of Japan's mainland almost erased the nation's industrial and manufacturing sectors. Yet, within three decades, the Japanese people, aided by the Japanese government's favorable industrial policies, managed to rebuild Japan's manufacturing sectors from the ashes. Japanese automakers, including Toyota, could make high-quality and fuel-efficient cars at a fraction of the cost of American automakers.

Between 1970 and 1976, Japanese car exports to the U.S. saw a staggering growth, tripling to more than one million units.[3] This rapid expansion was partially due to a geopolitical event. Egypt and

Syria attacked Israel on the Jewish holy day of Yom Kippur in 1973. After learning that the Soviet Union had sent arms to Egypt and Syria, then U.S. President Richard Nixon, in a bid to assist Israel's defense, began to send weapons. In retaliation, members of the Organization of Arab Petroleum Exporting Countries (OAPEC) imposed an oil embargo on the United States. The embargo triggered an oil shortage and an energy crisis in America. A few states, including California and New York, responded by rationing gasoline: people could only purchase gas every other day, based on whether the last digit of their license plate number was even or odd.[4]

American consumers reacted to the gasoline shortage by switching from American "gas guzzlers" to smaller, fuel-efficient Japanese-made cars. The changing consumer preference had a significant impact on the U.S. auto industry. In 1980, Japanese carmakers exported close to 2 million vehicles to the U.S. and captured a 21% market share. The sales of the Big Three American automakers plummeted 30% and suffered a $6.2 billion loss, a blow that deeply affected the American auto industry. More than 100,000 auto-factory workers were laid off, and Chrysler, one of the Big Three American carmakers, sought a government bailout to avoid filing for bankruptcy. Some American auto-factory workers blamed Japanese carmakers and anyone who was of Japanese descent for their economic misfortune. The hatred toward anyone with Japanese ancestry was quickly extended to include all other Asian Americans.

We'll never know how much Vincent was aware of these changes happening around him. The early 1980s was a bittersweet period for him. In 1981, when Vincent was 26, his father, David, passed away. Vincent became the man of the family. As a good son, he was responsible for caring for his mother, Lily, and driving her around. Vincent's life got busier in other ways, too. He worked two jobs: as a draftsman in Oak Park and a waiter at a Chinese restaurant in Ferndale on weekends. He also attended Lawrence Tech at night to learn computer operations. He was "well-liked by coworkers and supervisors for his friendly, easy-going nature as well as his strong work ethic and skills."[5] On the personal front, Vincent fell in love and got engaged to Vicki Wong. In the first half of 1982, he and his fiancée were busy preparing for their wedding and looking for a new home to share with Lily.

On the fateful day, June 19, 1982, Vincent went to the Fancy Pants Club in Highland Park with friends to celebrate his upcoming wedding. Two dancers, one white and one Black, performed strip-teases on stage. On the other side of the stage sat two white men: Ronald Ebens, a plant supervisor of a Chrysler plant, and his step-son, Michael Nitz, who had been laid off from an auto factory but was employed at a large furniture company.[6]

There are some disputes of what exactly took place next. It's probably better to quote what Detroit-based filmmaker Michael Moore wrote for the *Detroit Free Press* in 1987:

> After watching Chin give a generous tip to the white dancer, Ebens becomes agitated. "Hey, you little m————!" he shouts at Chin, telling the black dancer, "Don't pay any attention to those little f————, they wouldn't know a good dancer if they'd seen one." At that point, Chin gets up from his seat and starts towards Ebens. "Little f————, big f————, we're all the same," Ebens says to Chin. Chin apparently does not appreciate the comment and hauls off and slugs him. A fight ensues, the black dancer hears Ebens or Nitz say something about "you guys [referring to Chin and Choi] are the reason we're all laid off," and Ebens lifts a chair to strike Chin. He cracks his stepson's head instead. The owner breaks it up and tosses everyone out.

In the parking lot, words are exchanged again. Chin calls Ebens a "chicken s——" and Nitz goes to his car trunk, opens it, and pulls out a Louisville Slugger baseball bat. Chin and his friends run down the street, as Ebens and Nitz, according to the indictment, offer James Perry $20 to help them go find the "Chinaman."

After cruising Woodward for about 10 minutes, they spot Chin sitting outside the McDonald's restaurant on the wooden railroad ties which pass for landscaping at the popular Highland Park hangout. Nitz pulls into the lot and, before he stops the car, Ebens swings the door open and jumps out. The rear tire of Nitz's Plymouth Horizon accidentally runs over Ebens' foot and comes to rest on top of it. "Either pull up or back off 'cause you're sitting on my foot!" Ebens yells. He pries loose his foot and starts running towards Chin, bat in hand.

Chin sees him coming and runs out into the street. Nitz has joined the chase, and within seconds catches Chin and holds him while Ebens cocks the bat and smashes it into Chin's legs. Chin screams in pain, and as he falls to the pavement, Ebens' second swing scores a direct hit to his chest, breaking a number of ribs. Now bleeding and crumpled in the middle of Woodward Avenue, Chin looks up into the light from the golden Arches as Ronald Ebens strikes a third time, this time on the skull. Vincent Chin does not move.

Two dozen people eating their Big Macs and Quarter-Pounders, including two off-duty Detroit police officers, watch the entire scene as Ebens continues to bash the unconscious Chin. Chin's friends have long since fled, leaving him alone to face Ebens and his bat. The officers run out and break things up. Realizing what he had just done, Ebens tells the policemen, "I didn't mean to hurt him that bad."

He and his stepson are taken to the Highland Park police station and later released without being charged.[7]

Vincent was taken to Henry Ford Hospital. He was in a coma and never woke up again. After four days, his mother, Lily, had to agree to remove the life support. Vincent died on June 23, 1982, at the age of 27. Instead of having a wedding, about 400 guests attended his funeral.

Ebens and Nitz insisted that their attack against Vincent Chin was not racially motivated. They accepted a plea bargain to reduce their charge from second-degree murder to manslaughter. Wayne County Circuit Judge Charles Kaufman presided over the trial. On the day of the sentencing, Ebens was ready for the worst. In an interview a few years later, Ebens said: "I told my wife that morning she might as well put a stamp on my a– 'cause they were going to be sending me away. [When Kaufman announced the sentence] you could have knocked me over with a feather."[8] Judge Kaufman sentenced Ebens and Nitz to three years' probation and ordered each to pay a $3,000 fine plus $780 court fees. Neither of them would serve any jail time.[9] Strangely, the prosecutor of the case didn't bother to show up at the sentencing proceeding to argue for a harsher sentence. Even the *Detroit Free Press* found that "the overall handling of the Chin case seems disturbingly casual", and the "result was a process that made Vincent Chin's life seem cheap and the criminal justice system either callous or perverse."[10]

If there was anything more infuriating than such light sentences for two people who beat an innocent young man to death, it was Judge Kaufman's rationale for his leniency. He blamed Vincent Chin for initiating the physical altercation. He didn't think a murder was committed because Chin survived for four days on life support before he died. Since Ebens and Nitz had no prior criminal records, Judge Kaufman was confident the two wouldn't harm anyone in the future because he believed that Ebens and Nitz "weren't the kind of men you send to jail... You don't make the punishment fit the crime; you make the punishment fit the criminal."[11] In a ruling that was as shocking as it was unexpected, Judge Kaufman inadvertently sounded a wake-up call to the Asian American community with his rationale on Vincent Chin's murder.

Between WWII and the early 1980s, while Japanese Americans were seeking justice for their internment during the war, the rest of the Asian American community had remained relatively inactive on America's political scene. Other than a few labor strikes in the 1980s,[12] Asian Americans largely stayed out of political movements while focusing on realizing their American Dream through hard work and educational attainment. However, the Asian American communities in Detroit and the rest of the country were outraged over Vincent Chin's murder and the light sentence of his killers. For many Asian Americans, the kid-glove treatment of Chin's murderer was essentially a license to "kill Asian Americans." Everyone in the Asian American community felt they could be the next Vincent Chin. His death became a rallying cry that reignited Asian Americans' political activism.

Protests erupted in Detroit and beyond, with protestors from diverse racial and ethnic backgrounds uniting under the banner of "Justice for Vincent Chin." In response to the sentencing, Asian American activists banded together to form American Citizen for Justice (ACJ), a group committed to challenging the injustice and pursuing a judicial appeal.

Thanks to ACJ's effort, the U.S. Department of Justice filed civil rights charges against Ebens and Nitz. In 1984, a federal court jury in Detroit convicted Ebens of violating Vincent Chin's civil rights. Ebens was acquitted on the second charge of conspiring to deprive Chin of his civil rights. Nitz was acquitted on both charges. U.S. District Court Judge Anna Diggs Taylor sentenced Ebens to 25 years in prison. The U.S. Sixth Circuit Court of Appeal overturned the conviction in 1986 after finding that an ACJ attorney had inappropriately coached witnesses. Judge Taylor ordered a second trial and reheard the case in Cincinnati, Ohio. The second jury acquitted Ebens on all charges, thus ending any criminal prosecution of him. The outcome was an enormous letdown for the Asian American community.

The Chin family and the ACJ continued to pursue civil charges against Ebens and Nitz and seek financial compensation. In 1987, Nitz was ordered to pay the Chin family $50,000, and Ebens was ordered to pay $1.5 million, at $200/month for the first two years and 25% of his income or $200/month thereafter, whichever was greater. Ebens couldn't have been happier about this outcome. He explained in an interview that he believed he would not have to pay a dime to the Chin family due to his unemployment. He was fired by Chrysler in 1982 after he was charged with murdering Vincent Chin, and he has been unemployed since. He told the interviewer that the Chin family "can't get blood from a stone."[13]

In 1987, Chinese American filmmaker Christine Choy co-directed a documentary, *Who Killed Vincent Chin?*[14] This film not only recounts Vincent's murder and the subsequent trials of Ronald Ebens and Michael Nitz, but also highlights how this case united Asian American communities of Detroit for the first time, transforming them from a grassroots advocacy group into a national movement. The film's impact on the Asian American community was so profound that it was nominated for an Oscar for Best Documentary Feature.

Ebens continued doing everything he could to avoid paying the Chin family financial compensation even after he found employment again. Ebens made only a few payments before he moved to Nevada and abruptly ceased all payments to the Chin estate. In 2015, he sought to remove the lien on his home in Nevada, claiming the lien was placed "with malice…to annoy and harass" him. Nevada's Homestead Act allows individuals to protect up to $550,000 of assets from creditors in their homes. At the time, the money Ebens owed to the Chin estate exceeded $8 million, a significant blow to the estate.[15] Helen Zia, a journalist and an executor of the Chin estate, said: "It's not about the money. It's about him [Ebens] being able to live his life outside of jail for all these years and him never taking full responsibility for what he's done."[16]

Today, Vincent Chin's case is recognized as a turning point in the Asian American civil rights movement and a pivotal moment in America's civil rights history, particularly in the fight against hate crimes and discrimination. The case's profound impact has led to significant legal reforms that benefit all Americans:

> Because of Chin and other similar cases, families of victims are now allowed to deliver victim impact statements at hearings before the judge. At the time of Ebens' and Nitz's first sentencing before Judge Kaufman, Wayne County prosecutors were not required to attend sentencing proceedings. Now, prosecutors are required to be at all hearings.[26] Further, less than one year after Chin's murder, the Wayne County Prosecutor's office barred future reductions of second-degree murder charges to manslaughter. This had the effect of eliminating probation as a sentencing option. Finally, the Supreme Court and the Legislature addressed the wide latitude judges had in sentencing with mandatory minimum sentencing guidelines.[17]

In 2010, the city government of Ferndale, Michigan, erected a milestone marker at the intersection of Woodward Avenue and 9 Mile Road in memory of Vincent Chin. The Chin estate established the Vincent Chin Institute, a beacon of hope and empowerment for the Asian American community. This institute has since played a crucial role in uniting Asian American organizers, fostering a collective effort to fight anti-Asian hate and advance the ideals of equal justice.

Vincent's mother, Lily, was deeply affected by her son's tragic death. She couldn't bear to continue to live in the home she had shared with Vincent in Oakwood, Michigan, because everything there reminded her of loss. Thus, Lily moved back to China. In 2001, Lily returned to the U.S. for medical treatment. Despite her health struggles, she was unwavering in her determination to honor her son's memory. She established a scholarship in his name. One of the most memorable moments of Lily's was her impassioned plea for justice for her son on national television, "Our skin color may be different, but our blood is the same." Lily passed away in Farmington Hills, Michigan, in 2002. She was laid to rest next to her husband, David, and her son, Vincent Chin.

Two years later, I arrived at Farmington Hills in my Toyota Corolla. I kept driving the same car while working for Daimler-Chrysler between 2004 and 2008. No one ever harassed me for driving a Japanese-brand automobile, and I felt a sense of safety. I knew that I had the Chin family and many Asian Americans' political activism to thank.

CHAPTER 5

• • •

"We Were Targeted and Isolated"
– How the 1992 LA Riots Changed Korean
Americans Forever

One of the early galvanizing moments of the 1990s was the 1992 Los Angeles Riots. On the morning of March 3, 1991, Rodney King, a Black motorist, was driving under the influence and led the police on a high-speed car chase before they stopped him. He was brutally beaten by the police officers who arrested him. The beating was captured on video by a resident, George Holliday. Holliday shared his footage with a local television station. Within days, an edited video was played nationwide, and many Americans were shocked and outraged by what they saw.[1] On March 15, four LAPD officers, Sergeant Stacey Koon and officers Laurence Powell, Timothy Wind, and Theodore Briseno, were indicted for assault in the King beating.

A year later, on April 29, 1992, the jury of the case acquitted all four officers of all charges except one – the jury was deadlocked on the charge against Officer Laurence Powell of excessive force. Nearly two decades later, Powell's attorney, Michael Stone, said in 2011: "Most of the nation only saw a few snippets where it's the most violent. They didn't see [King] get up and run at Powell" in the unedited video. According to Stone, the unedited video helped the officers' case at the trial. But back in 1992, right after the jury announced their verdict, hundreds of angry people gathered outside police headquarters in downtown Los Angeles, chanting, "No justice, no peace."

In a predominantly Black neighborhood in South Central Los Angeles, an agitated crowd pulled Reginald Denny, a white truck driver, from his vehicle, beat him, and smashed his truck. The whole scene was captured by live television. Good Samaritans who saw what happened to him on television later rescued Denny from the neighborhood. Another mob smashed the door to a Payless liquor store, beat up the store owner, and took whatever they wanted. Thus began one of the worst riots in America's history.[2]

Over the next few days and nights, violence, looting, and arson spread throughout Los Angeles. The riot's impact on LA's Korean community was profound and lasting, which wasn't coincidental. The riot was inflamed by the existing resentment, fear, and mistrust between the Black and the Korean communities, underscoring the crucial need for cross-cultural understanding and empathy.

Compared to Chinese and Japanese immigrants, Korean immigrants were relative newcomers. Although small groups of Korean immigrants came to the U.S. in the late 19th century, a significant wave of Korean immigrants started arriving in the United States during the Korean War (1950–1953), a pivotal event that shaped Korean immigration to the U.S. This wave included Korean wives of American soldiers, orphans adopted by American families, and students, businesspeople, and intellectuals. These Koreans benefited from several new immigration laws at the time: The War Bride Act of 1946, which allowed the U.S. servicemen to bring their Asian brides to the U.S., and the McCarran and Walter Act of 1952, which repealed the 1924 Immigration Act's ban on Asian immigrants by allotting 100 immigration visas to each Asian nation. The 1952 Act offered a path to citizenship to eligible Asian immigrants and established a preferential system to prioritize immigration applications for those with families already residing in the U.S.

Immigration from Asia, including Korea, increased even more after the passage of the 1965 Immigration and Naturalization Act, a landmark piece of legislation that significantly shaped the demographic landscape of the United States. The 1965 Act kept the preference system introduced in the Immigration Act of 1952, prioritizing family reunions for relatives of U.S. citizens and permanent residents. The Immigration Act of 1965 opened the door for immigrants from Asia and Latin America by removing the national-origin quota system. The act imposed a numeric cap on the total number of immigration visas to be issued yearly: 170,000, exempting immediate relatives of U.S. citizens and "special immigrants." Many immigrants from Asia and Latin America took advantage of the family reunion preference and sponsored their families to become legal immigrants in the United States. Between 1960 and 1980, the percentage of total immigrants from Asia and Latin America increased from 13.3% to 47.4%. The Korean diaspora community was the third largest group of new immigrants to the U.S., right after the Mexicans and the Filipinos.[3]

LA had experienced large-scale racial unrest before. Back in 1965, thousands of Blacks in LA's Watts district, angered by what they perceived as social and racial injustice, started riots on August 11. By the time the government finally restored order on August 16, about 34 people had been killed, nearly 4,000 arrested, more than 1,000 injured, and hundreds of buildings were burned to the ground. Many white-owned businesses moved out of predominately Black neighborhoods in South and Central LA, opening up opportunities for Korean immigrants looking for affordable real estate to start businesses and chase their American Dream.

Numerous Korean immigrants had set up mom-and-pop shops,

including grocery and liquor stores, in predominantly Black neighborhoods. These Korean immigrant-operated stores were often the only ones available in those communities, providing essential goods and services. Despite these Korean immigrants contributing to the local economy, there were growing tensions between the Black communities and the Korean communities. Some Black community members complained that Korean shops extended employment opportunities only to other Koreans, not Blacks from the community. However, due to cultural and language barriers, Korean shop owners felt more comfortable working with fellow Korean immigrants.

Some Blacks perceived, without credible evidence, that Korean immigrants became economically better off through price gouging of impoverished and marginalized Blacks. Rev. J. Edgar Boyd, pastor of Bethel African Methodist Episcopal Church of Los Angeles, commented on *NBC News* about the tension between Black and Korean communities in LA by stating, "There became areas and moments of frustration and tension between those who were marginalized and those who seemed to be surviving – and surviving from the resources of those who were pinched and who were impoverished."[4] Korean business owners, however, denied the price gouging allegation. Instead, they pointed out that they took significant personal and business risks to operate stores and provide services needed in tough neighborhoods. Koreans and their businesses and employees were often victims of various crimes, including thefts, robberies, and violent attacks, and the perpetrators were often Blacks. Yet, Koreans felt that Black residents in the neighborhood did not appreciate their efforts and the risks they had to endure.

The constant crimes put many Korean shop owners and employees on edge. As people who take great pride in their cultural heritage, Koreans believe they work hard and have every right to protect themselves and their businesses. However, this cultural pride sometimes led to misunderstandings as they struggled to differentiate between good and bad customers, so sometimes they treated all customers with some level of suspicion, which led to some Black customers feeling that Korean store owners and employees were rude and made customers feel constantly watched and treated disrespectfully. Consequently, the resentment and distrust between some in the Black and Korean communities kept growing, and sometimes, these feelings led to deadly consequences.

Soon Ja Du and her husband emigrated to America with their three kids to seek their American Dream. The couple invested their life savings in a run-down Empire Liquor Market in South LA, a neighborhood plagued by crimes. In 1990 alone, "936 felonies were reported, including five murders, nine rapes, 184 robberies and 254 assaults." Working in such an environment was highly stressful for the couple. In early 1992, the store was robbed by three gang members. Given the persistent violence and crimes outside of their store, the couple always kept an M-1 carbine rifle and a handgun near their cash register. On March 16, 1991, the day after four LAPD officers were indicted for assault in the Rodney King beating, Latasha Harlins, a 15-year-old girl, walked into Du's liquor store. She put a bottle of orange juice in her backpack and walked to the counter. Here's what happened next, according to an eyewitness:

> Believing that Harlins was stealing from her, too, Du reached over the counter to grab at her backpack. Harlins pushed Du back. But Du got up and tried to grab at Harlins' backpack again, only to be knocked over one more time. "When [Du] comes up the second time, she's got a gun in her hand," Stevenson said: "Then, as Latasha turns around to walk out of the store, she shoots Latasha." Point blank in the back of the head. Harlins' body lay motionless in a pool of blood. When the police arrived on the scene, they found $2 in her hand.[5]

Du's family and lawyer insisted that she shot and killed Latasha mistakenly because she had never fired a gun before. Later, Du was convicted of voluntary manslaughter, but she received only five years of probation, 400 hours of community service, and a fine. LA's Black community was outraged by the light sentence.

In the three months following Du's shooting, several more shootings took place in South Central LA. On May 25, two Korean American employees at a liquor store were killed after complying with robbery demands made by a Black assailant. Less than a week later, "an African-American man suspected of committing a robbery in an auto parts store on Manchester Avenue was fatally wounded by his accomplice, who accidentally fired a shotgun round during a struggle with the shop's Korean-American owner."[6]

Then, on June 15, 1991, Lee Arthur Mitchell, an African American, walked into a Korean-owned liquor store. He offered to buy a wine cooler at less than the listed price. After the store owner's wife, Kumoch Park, rejected Mitchell's offer twice, Mitchell "went behind the store counter and tried to remove money from the cash register, he began scuffling with store owner Tae Sam Park. The merchant drew a pistol from under the counter and fired several shots, striking Mitchell five times."[7] Tae Sam Park suffered three broken ribs during the scuffle with Mitchell. However, Park wasn't charged because the police concluded that Park had acted out of self-defense.

All these incidents only stressed the already tense race relationships between the Black and the Korean communities. Both sides took every incident as new evidence to indict an entire group on the other side. Some Black residents began to regard the Korean immigrants as part of the unjust system that oppressed the Black community. After the verdict of Rodney King's ruling, riots erupted in LA almost immediately. The rioters said they were against what they perceived as an unfair and racially biased system. But rather than burning down federal buildings or targeting government employees, rioters first aimed their anger at vulnerable civilians passing by and then quickly turned their anger toward Korean immigrants. Chaos, looting, and violence spread to Koreatown like wildfire. Eyewitnesses described Koreatown as looking like a war zone, with buildings on fire. Mayor Tom Bradley, the first Black mayor of LA, declared a state of emergency and instituted a curfew. The overwhelmed LAPD left Korean immigrants to defend themselves and their businesses. Sonny Kang, a young Korean immigrant, later told *NBC News*: "We felt betrayed by our local law enforcement that's supposed to protect and serve. They literally abandoned us and left us pretty much on our own."[8]

Korean immigrants took action to save themselves and their businesses. When rioters approached Richard Pak's gun store, he and his employees fired their guns, causing the rioters to quickly retreat. This incident affirmed Korean store owners' belief that they must fight back to protect the safety of their businesses, employees, and themselves. One thing that worked to their advantage was that due to South Korea's Conscription law, many Korean men were skilled in the use of firearms. A group of Korean men, including a dozen Korean Marine Corps veterans, carried guns either they owned or could find and formed a task force to patrol in front of Korean-owned businesses under rioters' attack. Radio Korea, a community radio station, became Koreatown's de facto 911 center, further showcasing the community's resourcefulness. Frightened Korean store owners, especially those who were women, would call Radio Korea for help, as they didn't have enough people to protect their stores. The station would then notify the task force where to go to assist distressed Korean-owned stores.

Since the local TV stations were broadcasting the riots live, audiences throughout the city and the nation saw images of gun-toting Korean men. Some were patrolling in front of their stores, some were hiding behind barriers, and some were engaged in gunfights with looters. The most iconic image was of a group of Korean men standing on the rooftop of a grocery store, all carrying rifles. They mostly fired blanks or warning shots to scare looters.[9] Some

Korean Americans later blamed the media for overplaying the images of gun-toting Korean men, portraying them as vigilantes when, in fact, they saw the entire Korean community in South LA as victims of the riots. Only a small group of Korean men were armed. Many Korean stores, especially those run by women, were defenseless and were looted and burned to the ground.

The jury verdict, the beating of Reginald Denny, and the 1992 LA riots caused King to say on May 1, 1992, "Can we just get along?" But the riots didn't end until May 4th, after President George H.W. Bush dispatched several thousand troops and Marines, along with 1,000 riot-trained federal law officers, to help restore order. The final tally of the damages of the LA riots included more than 50 deaths, more than 2,300 people injured, and 12,000 arrests. About 1,100 buildings were damaged, and the estimated property damage was about $1 billion. Notably, Koreatown suffered about 40% of the total damage.[10] Since many storeowners had tried to save money by not purchasing insurance policies for their businesses beforehand, they didn't have the money to rebuild what had been destroyed. The riots shattered their American Dream. Still, Koreatown would have suffered even more damage, and more people could have been injured or killed if not for armed Korean men standing up and defending their community when they were "targeted and abandoned." The LA riots would go down as one of the worst civil disruptions in U.S. history, leaving a lasting impact on LA and especially the Korean community.

In the collective memory of Korean Americans, the LA riots are remembered as "Saigu," a term that signifies the date the riots erupted. This unique name, as Shelley Lee, associate professor of history and comparative American studies at Oberlin College, points out, underscores the profound trauma it inflicted at the time, its pivotal role as a turning point, and its enduring presence in the collective immigrant and diasporic consciousness of Koreans in America and beyond.[11] Post-riots, many Korean business owners sold their grocery and liquor stores to a new wave of immigrants from Latin America and the Middle East and departed permanently.

The legacy of the LA riots is different for different people. It was the birth of a unique identity and a wake-up call for Korean Americans. Before the riots, the label "Korean American" wasn't widely used. Korean immigrants were lumped into the generic term "Asian Americans." The LA riots, especially the images of gun-toting Korean immigrants defending their stores, gave birth to a distinct "Korean American" identity. The riots also served as a wake-up call. Korean Americans learned that their American Dream would be incomplete if they were only better off economically. They never wanted to feel "targeted and abandoned" again. Therefore, Korean Americans learned that they must become more engaged civically and politically in America.

Participation in a civil society takes on diverse forms. Since the riot, Korean Churches for Community Development ("KCCD") has partnered with groups of different cultural and ethnic backgrounds, including the California African American Museum, to establish culture dialogues and tackle issues such as affordable housing and job training for low-income individuals. Hyepin Im, a pioneer in dispelling myths and misunderstandings about the Korean American community, founded the Faith and Community Empowerment Corp. Her work has enlightened and informed many about the true nature of the Korean American community.[12] The achievements of Korean Americans in politics and business are also noteworthy. Jay Chang Kim (R–CA) became the first Korean American elected to the House of Representatives in 1992. LA voters elected David Ryu as its first Korean American city council member in 2003. In the 117th U.S. Congress, four Korean Americans served: Andy Kim (D–NJ), Young Kim (R–CA), Michele Park Steel (R–CA), and Marilyn Strickland (D–WA). These individuals served as inspiring examples of the potential and success of the Korean American community.

The new Koreatown in Los Angeles is full of trendy and hip

restaurants, bars, and coffee shops, many owned and operated by second-generation Korean Americans who speak fluent English and are comfortable living and thriving in a diverse and multi-cultural environment. The Korean American community has played a significant role in this transformation, contributing to the vibrant culture and economic growth of Koreatown. Real estate prices in Koreatown have appreciated faster than in many LA neighbor-hoods.

The second half of the 20th century saw Asian Americans make tremendous progress. From once being excluded from becoming U.S. citizens to being welcomed with open arms and quickly becoming one of the fastest-growing immigrant groups in the U.S.; from once being treated as suspicious enemy aliens during WWII to winning the Presidential Medal of Freedom; from scapegoating for America's economic woes and racial tensions to playing a significant role in civil discourse and even running for political office. Every step forward for Asian Americans has not only bene-fited them but also enriched the rest of America, making them an integral part of the nation's social fabric.

PART III

• • •

*The Third Wave of Asian
American Political Activism:
From the 2010s to the Present*

INTRODUCTION

At the turn of the 21ˢᵗ century, many Asian Americans, myself included, felt a sense of pride and optimism. Asian Americans have been the fastest-growing racial or ethnic group in the United States (see Appendix 2). Our community's overall educational attainment and economic achievement have consistently surpassed the national average.[1] Asian cultures, from food to movies, have gradually become part of the mainstream: even my favorite wholesale store, Costco, started to stock more Asian foods that were once only found in Asian food marts. In 2000, a kung fu movie, *Crouching Tiger, Hidden Dragon,* directed by Asian American Ang Lee with an all-Asian cast, was the first foreign-language film to break the $100 million mark in the United States. The film also clinched four Academy Awards, including Best Foreign Language Film. Many American teens became fans of Korean pop music bands. Asian holidays, such as the Chinese New Year, were celebrated by numerous American cities, businesses, and school districts. President Barack Obama even designated May as Asian Heritage Month in 2010. It truly felt like a moment of arrival for Asian Americans. Or did it?

Unfortunately, discrimination against Asian Americans has not vanished. It only has manifested itself in various other forms, from elite colleges' admission offices practices to hate crimes against Asians on the streets of San Francisco and New York, and to social media. However, the more than 150 years of political activism have empowered Asian Americans to combat discrimination and champion equality through civil, legal, and political engagement. This section highlights some significant events from 2010 to the present, including how the so-called "Asian Penalty" incorporated in college admissions led Asian Americans to challenge Harvard University's affirmative action through a landmark case; how Asian voters defeated the progressives' war on merit at the ballot box; how Chinese and Indian Americans recalled progressive school board members and the progressive DA in San Francisco; and the inspiring journey of a few Asian Americans who sought the highest office in the nation during the 2024 presidential campaign. All these examples underscore the crucial role of activism in Asian Americans' ongoing fight for equality.

CHAPTER 6

* * *

How "The Asian Penalty" Motivated a New Generation of Political Activists and a Supreme Court Case

On the morning of June 29, 2023, I eagerly awaited the U.S. Supreme Court's decision on the constitutionality of affirmative action–based admission policies at the University of North Carolina and Harvard University. The lawsuit, brought by Students for Fair Admissions (SFFA) and mainly representing Asian American plaintiffs, was a pivotal moment. By mid-morning, the long-awaited news arrived: the Supreme Court ruled in favor of the plaintiffs. This decision, which many saw as a landmark victory, sparked a flurry of text messages from my Asian American friends. One message read, "No more Asian penalty!" To fully understand the implications of this ruling, we must explore the historical context of affirmative action.

When the term "affirmative action" first emerged in the American political landscape, it was not primarily about racial preference. In 1935, the U.S. Congress passed "the Wagner Act," which established the National Labor Relations Board (NLRB) and collective bargaining power. The act also required that employers treat all employees fairly and "take such affirmative action including reinstatement of employees with or without back pay." [1] It was President John F. Kennedy who significantly shaped the history of affirmative action. He signed Executive Order 10925, which mandated government contractors to "take affirmative action to ensure that applicants are employed and that employees are treated during employment, without regard to their race, creed, color or national origin." President Kennedy also established the Committee on Equal Employment Opportunity, which laid the groundwork for affirmative action.

President Lyndon Johnson's 1965 executive order put the Secretary of Labor in charge of administering affirmative action and created the Office of Federal Contract Compliance within the U.S. Department of Labor. When President Richard Nixon came into office, he called for unilateral affirmative action in all government employment through Executive Order 11478 on August 8, 1969. The majority of Asian Americans supported affirmative action because it opened up numerous employment opportunities within the U.S. government that previously were denied to Asian Americans.

After affirmative action became acceptable in government employment, the call to expand it to education grew louder. Allan Bloom, author of *The Closing of the American Mind*, wrote:

> Since the end of World War II, there was in most major universities an effort—ever increasing in intensity—to educate more blacks, in the sincere American belief that education is good and the inclusion of blacks at the highest levels of intellectual achievement would be decisive in the resolving of the American dilemma. Practically nobody hesitated, and there were private discussions about whether,

at least in the beginning, the standard should be informally lowered for talented but deprived blacks in order to help them catch up.[2]

During the 1960s Civil Rights movement, especially after the assassination of the Rev. Dr. Martin Luther King, Jr., civil rights activists called upon American colleges and universities to increase the enrollment of Black students as a remedy for the racial discrimination Black Americans have suffered. Many schools felt the urgency, and they answered the call to action by incorporating a race-based quota system as part of their admissions process, trying to admit more Black students. Allan Bloom was teaching at Cornell in 1967. He observed that:

In order to get to many, particularly poor blacks, standards of admission had silently and drastically been altered. Nothing has been done to prepare these students for the great intellectual and social challenges awaiting them in the university. Cornell now had a large number of students who were manifestly unqualified and unprepared, and therefore, it faced an inevitable choice: fail most of them or pass them without their having learned. Moralism and press relations made the former intolerable; the latter was only partially possible (it required consenting faculty and employers after college who expected and would accept incompetence) and was unbearably shameful to black students and university alike.[3]

Bloom predicted that affirmative action in universities would be the source of "a long-term deterioration of the relations between the races in America." Bloom's prophecy quickly became true.

The 1970s witnessed the first major legal challenge to racial quotas in college admissions, with the case of Allan Bakke at the forefront. Bakke, a white applicant, applied twice to the University of California Medical School at Davis and was twice rejected. The

UC Davis affirmative action program, which set aside 16 spots in each freshman class of one hundred for "qualified" minorities, was the subject of heated debate. Bakke filed a lawsuit against the UC, arguing that his academic qualifications were superior to any minority students admitted in the two years he applied, suggesting that UC Davis had turned him down solely based on his race.

The *Regents of the University of California v. Bakke* case, a landmark case that eventually reached the U.S. Supreme Court, had a profound impact on affirmative action policies. In its 1978 5–4 ruling, the Supreme Court declared that race-based quotas violated the Fourteenth Amendment's Equal Protection Clause. Justice Lewis Powell, in his decisive opinion, stated, "Preferring members of any one group for no reason other than race or ethnic origin is discrimination for its own sake. This the Constitution forbids."[4] Yet, the majority also made a significant attempt to promote diversity in education. They tried to fit a round peg into a square hole by insisting that universities could use race as a factor (not a dominant one) in their admissions processes. This decision, while controversial, was an apparent effort to cave to progressives' insistence that affirmative action is necessary to foster a more inclusive educational environment.

The court's decision in the *Regents of the University of California v. Bakke* case, while attempting to provide a framework for affirmative action, also created confusion. Both supporters and opponents of affirmative action could find passages in the court opinion that seemed to support their positions. The court upheld the use of race as a factor in admissions but also ruled against a specific university's affirmative action policy. This apparent contradiction left room for those seeking clarity to challenge affirmative action in college admissions, leading to the emergence of new cases.

Not surprisingly, the legal debate continued with the emergence of two cases related to the University of Michigan's affirmative action admissions policies in the late 1990s. In *Gratz v. Bollinger,* Jennifer Gratz and Patrick Hamacher, two white students rejected by the U-M's College of Literature and Science, sued the U-M. They alleged the university's race-based undergraduate admissions policy was unconstitutional. At the time, an applicant to the U-M needed to score at least 100 out of the school's 150-point scoring system to gain admission. However, the U-M automatically assigned applicants of underrepresented groups, including Blacks and Hispanics (note Asian students were excluded), a 20-point bonus "without consideration of the particular background, experiences, or qualities of each individual applicant."[5]

The U.S. Supreme Court took up the *Gratz v. Bollinger* case in 2002 when it reviewed another case related to the U-M, *Grutter v. Bollinger*. Barbara Grutter, a white woman who was rejected by the University of Michigan's Law School, argued that the law school's admissions process, while not using a racial quota system, regarded race as a "predominant" factor. This, she contended, gave "applicants belonging to certain minority groups a significantly greater chance of admission than students with similar credentials from disfavored racial groups."

The U.S. Supreme Court's rulings in 2003 were marked by a significant conflict. In *Gratz v. Bollinger*, the High Court invalidated the University of Michigan's undergraduate admissions system, stating that the university's practice of "setting up automatic, predetermined point allocations for the soft variables, ensures that the diversity contributions of applicants cannot be individually assessed." However, in the decision regarding *Grutter v. Bollinger*, the Court, with a 5–4 vote, upheld the U-M Law School's admissions policy based on Justice Powell's opinion in *Bakke*. The Court's decision to allow the U-M Law School to use race as merely a "potential 'plus' factor" during its admission evaluations, while emphasizing that racial "classifications are constitutional only if they are narrowly tailored to further compelling governmental interests,"[6] highlights the complexity of the issue.

Justice Sandra O'Connor, the first female justice appointed to the U.S. Supreme Court, was the swing vote in *Grutter v. Bollinger*. A moderate conservative, O'Connor had expressed her reservations about affirmative action in the past but also recognized its potential benefits. Andrew McBride, one of O'Connor's former law clerks, lamented, "She [Justice O'Connor] didn't like affirmative action, though she was the one to save it." [7] Justice O'Connor saved affirmative action by choosing a compromise between liberals and conservatives. As McBride explained, "A liberal justice might say, 'Affirmative action now; affirmative action forever.'" Lindquist explains, "A conservative justice would say, 'Never affirmative action.' What she said was, 'OK, affirmative action, but we expect to see it over in 25 years,' again finding a middle ground." [8]

Instead of settling the legality of affirmative action, the contradictory rulings of *Gratz v. Bollinger* and *Grutter v. Bollinger* have fueled an ongoing legal debate. The discussion's persistent and significant nature opened the door to future legal challenges, underscoring the issue's urgency.

Less than a decade after *Grutter*, another white woman, Abigail Fisher, sued the University of Texas at Austin after her application was rejected in 2008. At the time, the UT's admissions policy was to fill the first-year class first under the Top Ten plan, which guarantees admittance to in-state students who graduated within the top 10% of the class. The remainder of the class would be applicants who passed "holistic reviews," which included race as one of the factors. Fisher, who graduated in the top 12% of her class, alleged that the UT's consideration of race in admissions violated the Equal Protection Clause. A U.S. District Court upheld the UT's admissions policy, referring to the U.S. Supreme Court's rulings in both *Bakke* and *Grutter* as precedents. A Fifth Circuit court affirmed its ruling. Fisher and her lawyer appealed to the U.S. Supreme Court.

In a 7–1 decision, the Supreme Court vacated and remanded the Fifth Circuit's ruling. The court found that the Fifth Circuit failed to apply *strict scrutiny* in its decision, affirming the UT's admissions policy. The Fifth Circuit court, after a thorough review, heard

Fisher's case again and decided that the UT's admissions policy was constitutional because it was "narrowly tailored" to achieve the only interest (a diverse student body brings educational benefits to all) that the U.S. Supreme Court approved in the *Bakke* and *Grutter* cases. Unsatisfied, Fisher and her lawyer appealed to the U.S. Supreme Court again, and her case was referred to as "Fisher II," a significant case in the legal history of affirmative action in college admissions. This time, the high court ruled in favor of the UT, stating that the "university has thus met its burden of showing that the admissions policy it used at the time it rejected petitioner's application was narrowly tailored."[9]

Some of the most robust objections to affirmative action came from prominent Black scholars, including Thomas Sowell and Walter Williams; both have written at length about how the history of affirmative action has been a history of broken promises, and especially in education, affirmative action has created a vicious cycle. This "vicious cycle" refers to the situation where Black students, despite the benefits of affirmative action, continue to struggle academically, leading to a sense of failure and resentment among both the Black and white communities.[10]

Interestingly, many Asian Americans initially didn't see race-based college admissions as a threat or regard themselves as victims. The long history of discrimination that Asian Americans had endured in the U.S. made them sympathetic to public policies that sought to address the legacy of historical wrongdoings through government interventions. Although Asian American parents knew that affirmative action didn't apply to their kids, they were convinced that accepting affirmative action in college admissions was a temporary measure to achieve equality and diversity.

Asian Americans also have a deep-rooted cultural confidence in the meritocracy system. They believe that as long as college admissions remain based on merit, their children will be accepted at good schools. This unwavering belief in meritocracy is a key aspect that distinguishes the diverse Asian American communities from other racial groups in the U.S. The emphasis on education is another distinguishing factor. Compared to different ethnic and racial groups in America, Asian Americans have the highest educational attainment. More than 54% of Asian Americans have a bachelor's degree or higher, while 33% of the general population in the U.S. does.[11] High educational attainment is one of the critical drivers of why Asian Americans are doing well economically as a group. Indian Americans especially stood out, as the average household annual income of Indian families was around $120,000 in 2019.[12]

However, Asian Americans do not regard the goal of pursuing education as all about economic outcomes. My friend Sosamma Samuel-Burnett, an Indian immigrant with three children and a law degree, told me that besides economic benefits, "Education is considered a noble pursuit—expanding the mind and capacities." This cultural perspective is deeply rooted in Asian societies, where education is seen as a means of personal and societal advancement. Asian cultures' reverence for education begins at home. Asian parents usually start reading books to their kids and teaching them numbers and simple arithmetic early on. My mom often quizzed me with math questions such as "What does 2+2 equal?" at the dinner table. Every Sunday, my dad would ask me to recite the poems he taught me during the week. We learned from our parents that doing well at school, finishing homework on time, and respecting teachers were some of the most important things expected of us and were not negotiable. Whenever I told my American friends that an "A-" was an Asian "F," they always took it as a joke. But to many Asian kids, it's nothing funny but a fact of life and a reflection of our parents' expectations. One of the worst ways kids could dishonor their parents was to fail the year-end exams and not be able to move up to the next grade.

Asian parents do not merely talk about the importance of education; they prioritize education-related spending in their household budgets, often at the expense of denying themselves material comforts. I grew up poor in Communist China. My siblings and I rarely had new clothes. As the youngest child in the family, I often wore hand-me-down clothing from my older sister. But the tiny apartment we lived in always had many books. My parents would pinch pennies on groceries but never hesitated to buy books, send us kids on school field trips, or travel for academic competitions. I realize these sacrifices were not just about the books or the trips but about instilling in us a love for learning and a belief in the power of education. I have observed a similar approach in Asian American households, especially low-income ones. This universal dedication to education is a testament to the shared values of Asian cultures. Asian parents often work multiple jobs to afford to send their kids to piano lessons or get additional tutoring, and the impact of these sacrifices on the children's lives is profound.

The emphasis on education starts at home but doesn't end there. Asian American families have a plethora of community support. The dominance of Scripps National Spelling Bee competitions by students of Southeast Asian descent – Bangladesh, Pakistan, and India – is a telling example. In the last two decades, Indian American kids have won all but four Scripps National Spelling Bee championships. Their dominance today makes it hard to believe that Indian American kids hadn't always been good at spelling. Once upon a time, they consistently outperformed in every subject *except* English.

After Balu Natarajan became the first Indian American to win the Scripps National Spelling Bee in 1985, Indian Americans like Ratnam Chitturi, who founded the North South Foundation (NSF) in 1989, believed that getting kids excited about spelling bee competitions would be an excellent way to improve their English language skills. NSF organized its first spelling bee competition in 1993. Today, NSF has more than 90 chapters in the United States. These chapters organize annual Regional Education Contests in spelling, vocabulary, math, essay writing, public speaking, and geography. Winners of these contests are invited to the NSF's National Finals, where champions receive scholarships to college.

The 2002 documentary *Spellbound*, which follows eight competitors in the 1999 Scripps National Spelling Bee, had a profound impact on the Indian American community. The victory of Nupur Lala, an Indian American girl, over David Lewandowski to win the 1999 national title ignited a wave of enthusiasm and pride. Lala's triumph made her a household name among Indian Americans, inspiring many kids to follow in her footsteps. To meet the growing demand, Rahul Walia launched the South Asian Spelling Bee in 2008, a platform focusing on spelling bee training and organizing annual competitions in the United States for children of South Asian descent. South Asian–focused news media cover its regional and national competitions, further amplifying its impact.

Parents in the community have played a crucial role in this journey, setting up tutoring centers, summer camps, software, and study materials and raising the competition's bar. Their unwavering support and dedication have been instrumental in the success of many kids of South Asian descent who have qualified for the Scripps National Spelling Bee finals, many of whom are alumni of NSF and South Asian Spelling Bee competitions. These parents' role is not just crucial; it is indispensable, and their efforts are not just appreciated but celebrated.

These community-level competitions (nicknamed "minor league") and the media coverage have turned spelling bees into a popular sport within South Asian American communities. Kids who win national titles are not just celebrities, they are symbols of our cultural acceptance and inclusivity. Their achievements are not laughed at, but respected and admired, much like Olympic gold medalists or Nobel laureates. Their performances are not just watched, they are celebrated. Their success becomes a beacon for more kids to join the spelling bee competitions, and they are inspired to put in the hard work.

Rishik Gandhasri, one of the eight co-champions of the 2020 Scripps National Spelling Bee competition, spent between one and four hours each day learning new words, in addition to his homework and various after-school activities such as swimming and piano lessons. The secret sauce of American kids of South Asian descent's dominance in the Scripps National Spelling Bee competition is no secret. It results from personal dedication, family commitment, cultural acceptance, and the unwavering support of our community.

I often have to explain to my American friends repeatedly that most Asian students were not born with good math and science skills or a penchant for homework and study. They are like kids everywhere. If it were left to them, Asian American kids would like to spend more time doing fun things rather than studying. However, it's the Asian culture that demands, motivates, and incentivizes Asian kids to do the hard work and excel at school. This cultural influence on academic success is a fascinating aspect that often goes unnoticed, but it's a significant factor in the achievements of Asian students.

Therefore, when American colleges began to incorporate race-based admissions policies, almost everyone understood that the special treatment created by affirmative action didn't apply to Asian Americans because of the perception that Asian students didn't need any extra "help" and they had already been well-represented on college campuses based on their own effort. While this perception is problematic, the Asian community largely accepted it. Asian parents, faced with this challenge, responded the only way they knew how: with unwavering dedication. Their relentless commitment, born out of love and care for their children, is truly commendable. When the bar is raised, they motivate their kids to jump higher. It's the depth of their commitment that has pushed Asian students to study harder, score higher, and do more extracurricular activities in order to stand out in the college admissions process. Asian students continued to make impressive academic gains. For example, "Asians were less than 10% of U.S. Math Olympiad winners during the 1980s but rose to a striking 58% of the total during the last thirteen years, 2000–2012. For the Computing

Olympiad, Asian winners averaged about 20% of the total during most of the 1990s and 2000s, but grew to 50% during 2009–2010 and a remarkable 75% during 2011–2012."[13]

Then, in 2011, Amy Chua, a Yale Law professor, published her controversial memoir, *The Battle Hymn of a Tiger Mother.* She took pride in being a strict parent who demanded her two daughters devote "every single afternoon, 365 days a year, to homework and music practice, with no sleepovers, playdates, TV or computer. And when they refused to obey her, she made them stand in the cold, or threatened to give their toys to the Salvation Army."[14] Chua pointed out that her daughters were straight-A students and music prodigies, proving that her tiger parenting worked. While some Asian parents found either validation or inspiration from Chua, many were shocked by her severe parenting style and felt she misrepresented or exaggerated Asian cultures' emphasis on education. Unfortunately, Chua's book probably also reinforces the stereotype of Asian students: someone who is obedient, quiet, and not interested in anything other than spending all their time doing homework and practicing music. Future lawsuits would reveal that such a stereotype would have a severe negative effect on Asian students' admissions at American elite universities including Harvard.

Some Asian parents were alarmed by Chua's book's revelation of how competitive elite college admissions could be. For a long time, ignorance of how elite colleges apply affirmative action in college admissions also played a role in why Asian Americans initially accepted affirmative action with few complaints. Few Asian Americans knew how much Asian students had been disadvantaged by race-based college admissions until Princeton University published a study titled "Admission Preferences for Minority Students, Athletes, and Legacies at Elite Universities."[15] The study uses the term "bonus" to describe the additional SAT points an applicant's race is worth. For instance, the study shows African Americans received a "bonus" of 230 points, and Hispanics received a 185-

point bonus. However, for an Asian student, 50 points were *deducted*. This deduction, often referred to as the "Asian penalty," is a form of discrimination in college admissions, as it requires Asian students to achieve significantly higher scores than their peers to compensate for their race.

It didn't take long for Asian communities to realize the "Asian penalty" had extended far beyond bonus points for standard test scores. With this revelation, people looked at Amy Chua's book and her parenting in a different light. Chua had pushed her daughters unreasonably hard, probably due to her inside knowledge (she and her husband were both professors at Yale) about the "penalty" Asian students faced during college admissions processes. The shift in perception of Chua's book and parenting style was profound, as it was no longer seen as a triumph or vindication of Asian parenting but as a desperate response to higher education's discrimination against Asian students.

Seeking to minimize the harm of the "Asian penalty," high school counselors began to tell anxious Asian American parents and students that a student could appear to be "too Asian" on the college application if he had a high test score, perfect GPA, played one or more musical instruments, and didn't play any sports. To gain admission to elite universities, Asian American students must appear "less Asian" on their college applications.[16] A cottage industry of college consultants has emerged to advise Asian American students how to deemphasize their "Asian-ness." Some of their advice included: Asian students should not mention their immigrant stories in their college essays; instead of declaring they desire to become scientists, Asian students should claim they like social science; instead of saying that they play musical instruments, Asian students are better off joining a theater group or playing sports. In addition, some Asian youths who have one non-Asian parent choose not to check "Asian" as their race on their college applications, hoping to avoid discrimination.

However, in 2012, Ron Unz, a Harvard alumnus, brought to

light a disturbing truth in his article titled "The Myth of American Meritocracy." He revealed that elite colleges, including Harvard, have established a bamboo ceiling to limit the admission of Asian students, regardless of their qualifications. This discrimination against Asians is not a new phenomenon. It's a chilling echo of the disgraceful treatment of Jewish students in the early 20th century, a historical context that underscores the weight of this issue and the urgent need for action.

In 1922, Jews comprised 21.5% of Harvard's freshman class, a level surpassed only by Columbia and the University of Pennsylvania among the Ivy League. However, Harvard's then-president, A. Lawrence Lowell, was concerned that too many Jews would "ruin the college." According to Harvard's website, Lowell "masterminded" Harvard's well-documented efforts to exclude Jewish students in the early 20th century. He did this in various ways: first, by privately tilting the admissions scale against Jewish transfer applicants, adopting a national recruitment strategy focused on regions of the country with smaller Jewish populations, and then by capping the number of Jewish students admitted and introducing new admissions criteria. These criteria, including personal interviews and the requirement that all candidates submit photographs with their application materials, were approved by the faculty in January 1926. And, at Lowell's behest, the Committee on Admission was granted discretion to execute, in his words, a "discrimination among individuals."[17] These practices had a long-lasting impact, successfully suppressing the number of Jewish students at Harvard for the next three decades.

Other Ivy League colleges adopted similar practices to limit the number of Jewish students on their campuses. Finally, in 2022, Stanford University President Marc Tessier-Lavigne made a significant step toward reconciliation by apologizing on behalf of the university for its efforts to limit the admission of Jewish students in the 1950s.[18] This apology, a beacon of hope for the future, stands in stark contrast to Harvard University's silence on the matter.

After reminding readers of Harvard's past discrimination against Jews, Unz went on to call Asian Americans the "new Jews." He pointed to Harvard's admissions data, which shows "the share of Asians at Harvard peaked at over 20% in 1993, then immediately declined and after that remained roughly constant at a level 3–5 points lower, and the sheer constancy of these percentages, with almost every year from 1995–2011 showing an Asian enrollment within a single point of the 16.5% average, despite huge fluctuations in the number of applications and the inevitable uncertainty surrounding which students will accept admission." Unz also found all the other Ivy League universities seem to "have gone through similar shifts in Asian enrollment at similar times and reached a similar plateau over the last couple of decades." Given that Asian Americans have been the fastest-growing racial group in America during the same period and Asian students' academic performance continued to improve, Unz concluded that elite colleges, including Harvard, essentially deployed a *de facto* Asian quota system to keep the share of Asian students at the schools flat.[19]

Unz's bombshell article initially didn't receive much attention since it was published in *The American Conservative*, which is not a mainstream media outlet. However, once the *New York Times* started to share similar statistics to those Unz used and raised a similar question about whether Harvard intentionally discriminated against Asian students,[20] some Asian Americans began to panic because they finally realized that no matter how high Asian students were willing to jump, how hard they had worked, and how much they'd accomplished in their young lives, some of them would be denied a fair shot at the elite colleges because of their race.

The discussion of the "Asian penalty" in mainstream media was significantly influenced by Edward Blum. Blum, a long-time activist opposing race-based public policies, founded the Project on Fair Representation in 2005. The organization has provided counsel in several race-related U.S. Supreme Court cases. Blum's initiative to collect stories from students who claimed they were not admitted to Harvard due to their race, launched in 2014, further fueled the debate.

One of the students who came forward was Calvin Yang, who had "a 3.9 GPA, a 1550 SAT score, two varsity sports, a political policy startup, and a spot on Canada's 30 Under 30 list."[21] He also admitted that he did everything he could to appear "less Asian" on his college applications in 2020, including glossing over the fact that he was a very talented piano player because he was afraid "it might strike an admissions officer as too stereotypical." Yang was still not accepted by Harvard, his dream school. In an interview, Yang expressed his shock: "I remember just sitting in my room reading that letter over and over again and making sure that I hadn't mistaken anything."[22] Yang initially didn't think he was a victim of the "Asian penalty" until he talked to other Asian classmates and friends and learned they all shared similar disappointments and frustrations. Yang realized that being Asian had something to do with Harvard's rejection. Yang went to the University of California, Berkeley, instead. Still, he decided to work with Blum, not out of bitterness nor resentment, but as part of a mission to fight for fair admissions on behalf of the Asian American community.

Jon Wang, an Asian American student, achieved a remarkable 1590 out of 1600 on his SAT and a 4.65 high school grade point average. Despite his exceptional academic record, he faced rejection from six top schools, including Harvard, MIT, CalTech, Princeton, Carnegie-Mellon, and UC Berkeley.[23] Powerful stories, like Yang's and Wang's, underscored the urgent need to address the issue of fair admissions policies. Blum soon launched similar sites for students who were rejected by the University of North Carolina (UNC) at Chapel Hill and the University of Wisconsin–Madison.

In 2014, Blum founded SFFA, a membership-based non-profit organization seeking to eliminate affirmative action in school admissions. The movement's strength is evident from the fact that more than 20,000 parents and students joined SFFA in the group's fight against race-conscious admissions practices. On November 17,

2014, SFFA filed a lawsuit in the United States District Court for the District of Massachusetts under the Civil Rights Act of 1964 against Harvard University. SFFA also filed a similar federal lawsuit against, the University of North Carolina, Chapel Hill, the UNC System, and the UNC Board of Governors.

The *SFFA v Harvard* case got the most attention. Most of the plaintiffs were Asian Americans, including Yang and Wang. The lawsuit alleged that Harvard's admissions policy "held Asian American students to a higher standard based on their race and intentionally limited the number of Asian Americans admitted each year," which violated the Equal Protection Clause and Title VI of The Civil Rights Act.[24] Harvard vehemently denied the charge and asked the court to stay the proceeding pending the Supreme Court's resolution of *Fisher v. University of Texas.* Presiding Judge Allison Burroughs granted Harvard's request.

After the Supreme Court's pivotal decision in favor of the University of Texas at Austin, deeming its undergraduate race-conscious admissions program lawful under the Equal Protection Clause, the legal landscape of the case shifted. Judge Burroughs ordered SFFA and Harvard to resume their discovery proceeding, a significant development influenced by the highest court in the land. Judge Burroughs also granted SFFA's request to compel Harvard to produce "comprehensive data from its admissions database from the past six complete admissions cycles from 2009–2015 as well as limited admissions data for the 2007–2009 cycles."[25] Meanwhile, 64 Asian American organizations, led by the Asian American Coalition for Education, filed a discrimination complaint against several elite universities, including Harvard, Princeton, and Yale, with the Justice and Education Departments. Under President Obama, neither the DOJ nor the Education Department did anything about it.

Of course, given the diversity of the Asian American community, it was not surprising that some Asian Americans, including dozens of Asian American student associations on college campuses, announced their opposition to the SFFA lawsuits. Those who opposed the lawsuits are mostly the second or third generation of immigrant families and are more receptive to leftist political views than both their parents' and grandparents' generations and newly arrived immigrants. These progressive Asian Americans argued that the SFFA lawsuit affirms the "model minority" myth. Progressive Asians believe the "model minority" label is harmful to Asian Americans because it ignores the diversity within Asian American communities, erases individuality, and reenforces the myth that Asian Americans are perpetual outsiders of American society. Additionally, they believe holding Asian Americans up as the "model minority" hurts racial justice for other minorities, hoping to drive a wedge and divide and conquer people of color.

Asian Democratic representatives in the U.S. Congress, such as representative Ted Lieu (D–CA) and Mazi Hirono (D–HI), voiced their support for affirmative action in college admissions while dismissing other Asian Americans' concern about the "Asian penalty." The irony of these progressive Asian Americans' argument is that they acknowledge that not all Asian Americans have achieved economic success and educational attainment. Yet, they accept that Asian Americans as a whole, including those who are still struggling economically and counting on educational attainment as their only way out, should be collectively punished by affirmative action. It is important to note non-progressive Asian Americans continue to see the "model minority" label as a badge of honor and affirmative action in college admissions as unfair and unjust.

Upon SFFA's commission, Peter Arcidiacono, a distinguished professor of labor economics at Duke University, comprehensively analyzed Harvard's admissions data. His findings unveiled a glaring injustice—that "Asian American applicants would likely be admitted at a higher rate than applicants of all other racial/ethnic backgrounds if admissions decisions were made based solely on academic and extracurricular ratings."[26] However, Asian applicants have been unfairly disadvantaged by the "personal rating," a score an admissions officer assigns based on interviews with alumni, application essays, and teacher recommendations. This rating, which evaluates an applicant's qualities such as integrity, courage, empathy, helpfulness, and leadership, among other things, is a critical factor in the admissions process. The admissions office staff ranks applicants on a scale of one to four, with one being the highest and four the lowest score. Arcidiacono's analysis revealed that Asian Americans in the top academic deciles often received lower "personal ratings" than applicants from other racial groups with similar academic qualifications. This injustice has led to Asian American students' overall rating being dragged down, significantly reducing their chances of being admitted to Harvard.

SFFA's discovery process uncovered some derogatory comments from Harvard's admissions officers regarding Asian applicants. These comments referred to the "reoccurring characterization" of Asian American students, describing them as being "quiet/shy, math/science-oriented, and hard workers." Examples include comments such as, "Applicant seems like a reserved, hardworking, aspiring woman scientist/doctor," or "He's quiet and, of course, wants to be a doctor," or the applicant is a "classic V.N. [Vietnamese] bootstrap case," or "a classic BC/NC [blue collar/non-college background] Asian American from the inner-city."[27] These comments reflected "recurring characterizations of Asian American applicants that were broadly consistent with stereotypes." In addition to constantly associating Asian students with adjectives such as "bright," "hardworking," "bland," and "not exciting," SFFA's analysis also shows admissions officers were statistically more likely to use "standard strong" to describe Asian American applicants, which means "a strong applicant who is nonetheless unlikely to be admitted because he or she is not sufficiently distinguished within Harvard's exceptional applicant pool." These comments not only reinforced the stereotypes of Asian Americans but also likely contributed to lower "personal ratings" assigned to Asian students and thus affected their admissions.

The trial officially began in the fall of 2018. SFFA had a strong case. In addition to evidence that Asian students had statistically received lower personal scores, William Fitzsimmons, dean of admissions at Harvard University, testified that the school has different SAT cutoff scores for prospective students based on factors including race. The school would send recruitment letters to African American, Native American, and Hispanic high school seniors with mid-range SAT scores (around 1100 on math and verbal combined). However, Asian Americans must score at least 1350 for women and 1380 for men to get a recruitment letter from Harvard. Fitzsimmons insisted such a race-based approach wasn't discriminatory but merely an effort to "break the cycle" and try to get more diverse students who wouldn't otherwise consider Harvard to apply to the school.[28]

However, even some Black students at elite schools including Harvard opposed affirmative action in college admissions. Daniel Idfresne, a 19-year-old first-generation Haitian American and a student at Syracuse University, explained in an interview:

> As a student, I take extreme pride in the work that I've done. [Race-conscious admissions] take away from that narrative that you have for yourself: that I'm the hero of my story and I got into a school because I worked for it. If African Americans have this idea that there's a possibility that they're in Harvard because of affirmative action and not because they know their ABCs and 123s, that could hurt their self-image and their belief about being able to leave their mark on the world.[29]

In October 2019, Judge Allison Burroughs ruled that Harvard University's affirmative action approach to college admissions does not discriminate against Asian American applicants. In her ruling, she acknowledged that implied racial bias in the "personal rating" of Asian Americans was evident. Still, she insisted that "the statistics [SFFA presents] perhaps tell 'what,' they do not tell 'why,' and here the 'why' is critically important." But to many Asian Americans, that "why" had already been answered. What's even more disappointing was that Judge Burroughs stated in her opinion that since Asians represent only 6% of the U.S. population but close to 24% of Harvard's admitted class, Asian Americans are already "overrepresented," a stance that further fueled the controversy.

Asian Americans have heard the "overrepresentation" accusation before. The progressives have long insisted that an organization or institution is not diverse if its membership or personnel composition does not reflect a similar racial proportion of the community. Such an illogical argument ignores that individuals have different aspirations, work ethics, and God-given talents. As free people, we choose what we want to do in our lives, and our paths to success aren't and shouldn't merely reflect how many intersectional racial or ethnic boxes we check. Perhaps even the proponents of the "proportional representation" argument knew the absurdity of their "proportional representation" argument. Therefore, they avoided demanding affirmative action for specific organizations. For example, even though Asians are underrepresented in the NBA, a professional basketball league, the left hasn't demanded at least six percent of the NBA players be Asians. The progressives only demand proportional representation when either Asians or whites dominate an institution, such as elite colleges and high schools.

Undeterred by Judge Burroughs's ruling, the SFFA and its lawyers bypassed appellate review and directly appealed to the U.S. Supreme Court to hear both the Harvard and the UNC cases. The Supreme Court announced in January 2022 that it would consider the cases during its term beginning in October. This decision carried significant weight, as it could potentially reshape the future of admissions processes in higher education. Asian Americans and SFFA were hopeful for a favorable ruling. At the same time, Harvard President Lawrence Bacow claimed the court's decision to take the cases "put at risk the ability of schools to create diverse campus communities, which strengthens the learning environment for all." UNC's spokesperson said the school would defend its "holistic" admissions process, which is "consistent with long-standing Supreme Court precedent."[30]

Meanwhile, the DOJ under President Donald Trump began to investigate Yale's "race-based discrimination" in 2018, based on the complaint filed by several dozens of Asian organizations but ignored by former President Obama's DOJ. In October 2020, the DOJ filed a lawsuit against Yale University, alleging the school violated federal civil rights law by discriminating against Asian American and white applicants in undergraduate admissions. Yale's "oversized, standardless, intentional use of race has subjected domestic, non-transfer applicants to Yale College to discrimination on the ground of race." The DOJ's complaint also pointed out that Yale's race-based admissions perpetuate racial stereotypes. "Because Yale claims that its race discrimination is necessary to admit sufficient numbers of racially-favored applicants, mostly Black and Hispanic applicants, Yale signals that racially-favored applicants cannot compete against Asian and White applicants. This kind of race discrimination relies upon and reinforces damaging race-based stereotypes."[31] Yale denied any wrongdoings and it dragged its feet to respond to the DOJ's complaint, trying to buy itself time and hoping the problem would go away if the Supreme Court ruled in favor of Harvard and the UNC.

The Supreme Court finally heard the *SFFA v. Harvard* and *UNC* cases in late 2022. The hearing was sometimes tense, and justices asked both sides tough questions. Lawyers representing both schools and the U.S. Solicitor General, Elizabeth Prelogar, struggled to answer three key questions. When Justice Clarence Thomas asked Ryan Park, North Carolina's Solicitor General who defends UNC, "what diversity is," Park had difficulty coming up with a clear and concise definition other than saying it is about a "broadly diverse set of criteria that extends to all different backgrounds and perspectives and not solely limited to race."[32] When Justice Kavanaugh asked Park whether UNC would consider an applicant's religion under his diversity definition, Park admitted that, unlike the race question, there is no box to check for one's religion on the application form. Harvard's lawyer, Seth Waxman, also acknowledged that Harvard's holistic admissions process doesn't consider an applicant's religious beliefs. Park and Waxman had difficulty defining diversity because they know it is politically correct to speak of diversity in broad terms. But in practice, the schools they represent care about only one diversity aspect: racial quotas.

Justice Neil Gorsuch pressed Park, "How do you distinguish between what this Court has said is impermissible, a quota, with what you argue should be permissible going forward, which is diversity. How can you do diversity without taking account of numbers?"[33] Park wasn't able to provide a satisfactory answer other than insisting that the UNC achieves "diversity" by looking at the individual applicant through its holistic process, which includes race as one of many factors. Justice Gorsuch responded that diversity had been used "as a subterfuge for racial quotas" on college campuses. Elizabeth Prelogar, the U.S. Solicitor General, proved Justice Gorsuch was right when she warned the Court that "a blanket ban on race-conscious admissions would cause racial diversity to plummet at many of our nation's leading educational institutions."[34]

None of these diversity advocates were interested in discussing that college campuses, including UNC and Harvard, lack intellectual and ideological diversity. For example, Harvard's own survey shows that less than two percent of its faculty identified as conservatives.[35] Responding to the survey, Alan Dershowitz, a professor emeritus at Harvard Law School and a life-long Democrat, said in an interview that Harvard's "emphasis on race and gender may well reduce academic diversity." Harvard is not diverse in many other ways either. Cameron Norris, an attorney for SFFA, states that about "9 percent of incoming freshmen at Harvard are conservatives. Harvard is 82 percent wealthy. There are 23 rich students for every one low-income student on campus."[36] Yet to those in charge of elite institutions like Harvard, none of these other diversity measures matter as long as they can demonstrate racial diversity on campuses.

Justice Thomas drilled Park on the educational benefits of diversity. Unable to provide any quantitative measures, Park focused on some qualitative "feel good" measures: "diversity of all kinds leads to 'a deeper and richer learning environment,' leads to more creative thinking and exchange of ideas, and, critically, reduced bias between people of different backgrounds and not solely for racial backgrounds."[37] Justice Thomas clearly wasn't satisfied with such an answer, and told Park, "I didn't go to racially diverse schools, but there were educational benefits." Furthermore, Justice Thomas reminded Park that parents do not necessarily send their kids to college "to have fun or feel good or anything like that; they send them there to learn physics or chemistry or whatever they're studying." After Justice Thomas pressed Park again to explain the educational benefits of diversity, Park mentioned a study showing racially diverse groups make more efficient trading decisions.[38] Justice Thomas replied, "I don't put much stock in that because I've heard similar arguments in favor of segregation too."

The one question that defenders of Harvard and UNC struggled with most was when several justices, including Justice Barrett and Justice Alito, asked when both schools' race-based admissions would end: "When is your sunset? When will you know?" In her majority opinion in *Grutter v. Bollinger* (2003), Justice Sandra Day O'Connor famously said that affirmative action in college admissions was permissible but not in perpetuity, and "We expect that 25 years from now, the use of racial preferences will no longer be necessary to further the interest" in student-body diversity.[39] Almost 20 years had passed since *Grutter*, but none of the defenders of Harvard and UNC was willing to commit to a target date or a set of measures to end race-based admissions policies.

Park saw no end because "the compelling interest in diversity" will never expire. Prelogar didn't think *Grutter* provided a timetable. Instead, she believed the schools should consider race as part of their admission policies until they achieve "meaningful representation and meaningful diversity on those campuses." But she couldn't define what "meaningful representation" is. Harvard's leading attorney, Seth Waxman, admitted that "Harvard does not currently, based on its data, expect that in 2028 it will have achieved—been able to use—only race-neutral alternatives."

Justice Kavanaugh asked, "If you don't have something measurable, it's going to be very hard for this Court. If we're called upon ten years from now or 20 years from now, it's going to be—you know, this is a bit of a replay of the *Grutter* argument, but if we come back to it, okay, are we there yet? What do we look at?" No one could offer him a clear answer. As Patrick Strawbridge, lawyer for the SFFA, pointed out, at these schools, "There was no plan ever to consider sunsetting their use of race."

The oral arguments of these two cases revealed the fundamental objective of affirmative action supporters. They want affirmative action to remain perpetually. Under cover of vaguely defined "diversity," they can get away with favoring some races while discriminating against other races consequence-free. They feel justified in their approach because they see America as systemically racist and no compromise from the right will ever satisfy them.

Before the Supreme Court ruled, Pew Research found that the issue of selective colleges and universities taking prospective students' racial and ethnic backgrounds into account when making admissions decisions is one that stirs strong emotions. A significant 50% of Americans disapprove of this practice, while only 33% approve. The remaining 16% are unsure. The same research also found that Americans are nearly three times as likely to *strongly* disapprove of this (29%) than they are to strongly approve (11%).[40] Across racial and ethnic groups, close to half (47%) of Black Americans support affirmative action in college admissions, compared with 29% who disapprove (24% are not sure). Among Hispanic

Americans, identical shares approve and disapprove of these practices (39% each). Most whites (57%) disapprove, compared to 29% who approve.

Asian Americans' attitude toward affirmative action is more mixed. On the one hand, a slight majority (53%) of Asians say affirmative action is a good thing, 19% say it is a bad thing, and 27% say they are unsure. The reasons for these attitudes are varied, with some citing the need for diversity and others expressing concerns about fairness. On the other hand, the majority of Asian Americans (76%) say race or ethnicity should not factor into college admissions decisions. This belief is often rooted in the principle of meritocracy. There is a clear partisan divide. About two thirds (64%) of Asian Democrats or Democrat leaners say affirmative action is good. Not surprisingly, progressive Asian American civil rights organizations such as the Asian American Legal Defense and Education Fund and Asian Americans Advancing Justice (AAJC) have filed briefs supporting race-conscious admissions. By contrast, only one third (32%) of Asian Republicans or Republican leaners support affirmative action.[41]

On June 29, 2023, the U.S. Supreme Court delivered its ruling on these two landmark cases. The court deemed race-based college admissions unconstitutional, a decision that will have a profound impact on higher education policies. Chief Justice Roberts, who wrote the opinion on behalf of the majority, stated, "For too long, [universities] have wrongly concluded that the touchstone of an individual's identity is not challenges bested, skills built, or lessons learned but the color of their skin. Our constitutional history does not tolerate that choice."[42] His ruling was a clear indication that the court found such affirmative action discriminatory. Both Harvard and UNC's race-based admissions were found to violate the Fourteenth Amendment's Equal Protection Clause's twin commands that "race may never be used as a 'negative' and that it may not operate as a stereotype."

The court found that the Harvard admissions office consistently "rated Asian-American applicants lower than others on traits like 'positive personality,'" likability, courage, kindness, and being "widely respected...often without even meeting them."[43] These low personal ratings not only reflect but also reinforce historical stereotypes of Asian Americans. Harvard's consideration of race had also led to an 11.1% decrease in the number of Asian Americans admitted to Harvard, a clear injustice that needed to be addressed.

The chief justice was joined by Justices Clarence Thomas, Samuel Alito, Neil Gorsuch, Brett Kavanaugh, and Amy Coney Barrett. The court's three liberal justices, Justices Elena Kagan, Sonia Sotomayor, and Ketanji Brown Jackson, were the dissenters. They argued that affirmative action is a necessary equalizer to right the historical wrongs of racial discrimination in America. Justice Sotomayor wrote in her dissenting opinion:

> In a society where race continues to matter, there is no constitutional requirement that institutions attempting to remedy their legacies of racial exclusion must operate with a blindfold... The opinion today will serve only to highlight the Court's own impotence in the face of an America whose cries for equality resound.

Similarly, Justice Jackson wrote:

> Our country has never been colorblind. Given the lengthy history of state-sponsored race-based preferences in America, to say that anyone is now victimized if a college considers whether that legacy of discrimination has unequally advantaged its applicants fails to acknowledge the well-documented "intergenerational transmission of inequality" that still plagues our citizenry... But deeming race irrelevant in law does not make it so in life.

Justice Thomas responded to the dissenters, especially Justice Jackson, with his opinion concurring to the chief justice's. Justice

Thomas deemed the Fourteenth Amendment affirming that:

> Equality and racial discrimination cannot coexist. Under that Amendment, the color of a person's skin is irrelevant to that individual's equal status as a citizen of this Nation. To treat him differently on the basis of such a legally irrelevant trait is therefore a deviation from the equality principle and a constitutional injury... All racial stereotypes harm and demean individuals.

I especially appreciate Justice Thomas for recounting the racial discriminations Asian Americans have endured historically. He wrote:

> Asian Americans can hardly be described as the beneficiaries of historical racial advantages...our Nation's first immigration ban targeted the Chinese, in part, based on "worker resentment of the low wage rates accepted by Chinese workers"...strong anti-Asian sentiments in the Western States led to the adoption of many discriminatory laws at the State and local levels, similar to those aimed at blacks in the South, and segregation in public facilities, including schools, was quite common until after the Second World War...it seems particularly incongruous to suggest that a past history of segregationist policies toward blacks should be remedied at the expense of Asian American college applicants.

Justice Thomas challenged Justice Jackson's dissenting opinion directly:

> Would JUSTICE JACKSON explain the need for race-based preferences to the Chinese student who has worked hard his whole life, only to be denied college admission in part because of his skin color? If such a burden would seem difficult to impose on a bright-eyed young person, that's because it should be. History has taught us to abhor theo-

ries that call for elites to pick racial winners and losers in the name of sociological experimentation.

My favorite passage of Justice Thomas's opinion is:

> Individuals are the sum of their unique experiences, challenges, and accomplishments. What matters is not the barriers they face, but how they choose to confront them. And their race is not to blame for everything—good or bad—that happens in their lives. A contrary, myopic world view based on individuals' skin color to the total exclusion of their personal choices is nothing short of racial determinism.

Edward Blum, the founder and president of SFFA, responded to the ruling:

> The opinion issued today by the United States Supreme Court marks the beginning of the restoration of the color-blind legal covenant that binds together our multi-racial, multi-ethnic nation. The polarizing, stigmatizing and unfair jurisprudence that allowed colleges and universities to use a student's race and ethnicity as a factor to admit or reject them has been overruled. These discriminatory admission practices undermined the integrity of our country's civil rights laws. Ending racial preferences in college admissions is an outcome that the vast majority of all races and ethnicities will celebrate.[44]

The ruling and the majority's opinion were a cause for jubilation and relief within the Asian American community. My phone was flooded with group text messages from other Asian Americans, all sharing the sentiment, "It's about time." One person wrote, "Our kids have worked hard and should never have been penalized by affirmative action." Another replied, "No more Asian penalty!" We all knew that discrimination against Asian kids wouldn't vanish overnight. Still, we were thankful for the wisdom of our founders, for our nation's colorblind Constitution, for the countless Americans who have fought for equal protection for all, and for our Supreme Court justices who had the courage to stand for individual liberty and dignity and the Constitution. As a nation, we still have a journey ahead to achieve a truly colorblind society, but this ruling has given us hope and inspiration. June 29, 2023, was a significant milestone in our struggle for equality, and it is a reminder that our journey continues.

Calvin Yang, one of the plaintiffs, who was rejected by Harvard but was thriving at UC Berkeley, shared his thoughts in an interview with *The New York Post*:

> "The court has sided with us and affirmed that Asian Americans are routinely being penalized because their last name is Kim or Lee. The fact that our skin color is a disadvantage in the application process is just an open secret in their admissions prospects because of their ethnicity… Every online forum or parent group chat for families in the college application process is filled with tips on how to make your application seem less Asian. That's just so sad. But all of that is going to change now, thanks to the Supreme Court… One day I hope to have kids, and I'm glad they'll grow up in a society that judges them based on their character rather than their last name or the color of their skin."[45]

Many Americans celebrated the end of affirmative action as an essential step toward eliminating racial discrimination and achieving equality for all in the United States. Yet, the progressive left has targeted Asian Americans who supported the ruling with the most racially charged rhetoric and outlandish false accusations. For instance, Yiatin Chu, an immigrant parent of New York City public school students, was viciously attacked on Twitter after she shared a celebratory message with her daughter on X.com (formerly known as Twitter). She wrote, "I told my daughter that today is a big day. They've ended affirmative action. 'Isn't it what you've been fighting for?' she asked. I said yes." The *Atlantic* writer Jemele Hill replied, "Can't wait until she reads that you gladly carried the water for white supremacy and stabbed the folks in the back whose people fought diligently for Asian American rights in America."[46]

Of course, not all Asian Americans were thrilled by the Supreme Court's decision. Some progressive Asians denigrated Asian American plaintiffs in the two Supreme Court cases on affirmative action as "pawns" or "tools" used by white supremacists because both cases were led by the conservative activist Ed Blum, who is white. Progressive Asians, including *Star Trek* actor George Takei, also attacked fellow Asian Americans who supported the ending of affirmative action as being motivated by "the promise of proximity to whiteness and power." The *Nation's* contributor Promise Li denounced Asian American conservatives as "key allies" and "militant co-conspirators" of white supremacists.[47]

By ridiculing Asian Americans as "pawns," "tools," or as people who "carry water" for white supremacists or are being radicalized by "the promise of proximity to whiteness and power," the progressive left treat Asian Americans as second-class citizens and inferior human beings who have no agency, cannot think independently, nor act on our own free will. How is this progressive racism any different from white supremacy, which believes that white people are superior to other racial groups and should lord over them? California Democratic Rep. Ted Lieu, a supporter of affirmative action in college admissions, added insult to injury with a statement denouncing the Supreme Court's decision:

> I strongly oppose the Supreme Court's decision in *Students for Fair Admissions, Inc. v. President and Fellows of Harvard College*. The ruling deals an unnecessary blow to efforts to increase diversity across higher education. The majority

opinion, however, contains a critical exception that I urge all colleges and universities to utilize: "nothing in this opinion should be construed as prohibiting universities from considering an applicant's discussion of how race affected his or her life, be it through discrimination, inspiration, or otherwise."[48]

Congressman Lieu wasn't the only prominent Democrat who encouraged colleges to find workarounds, especially exploiting Chief Justice Roberts's "loophole." Kristen Clarke, the Biden administration's Assistant Attorney General for Civil Rights, has been a key figure in the administration's efforts to uphold and expand affirmative action. She urged college leaders to heed Justice Ketanji Brown Jackson's dissent and "remain free to consider any characteristic of a student that bears on the institution's admissions decision, including "his or her lived experience with race."

Congressman Ted Lieu didn't have to remind universities to look for workarounds. Anticipating the Supreme Court might strike down affirmative action in college admissions, some universities had already proactively eliminated objective criteria such as SAT scores from their admissions, as early as 2020, and substituted subjective factors as surrogates for race (I will discuss this more in a later chapter). In an email response to the Supreme Court's ruling, Harvard University also announced it would continue to consider race in its admissions policy, despite Chief Justice Roberts explicitly pointing out in his majority opinion that "**universities may not simply establish through application essays or other means the regime we hold unlawful today** [emphasis added]." Within days after the ruling, Stanford law professor Richard Thompson Ford wrote in the *Chronicle of Higher Education* that colleges "need not volunteer to help promote the covert segregationist agenda of a reactionary faction of the court."[49]

A report published in spring 2024 found 43 out of the top 65 of the *U.S. News and World Report*'s top colleges and universities used essay prompts as a proxy for race by asking students to address cultural backgrounds, identity, or adversity in their admissions, and 31 of which mandated responses from students.[50] Columbia Law School asked applicants to submit a 90-second video statement, a move many critics said was a "thinly veiled attempt" to defy the Supreme Court's ruling.[51] With many colleges gaming the system, the Supreme Court's ban on affirmative action had "minimal" influence on the class of 2028's admissions process.[52]

Still, Asian Americans who support the affirmative action ban remain hopeful because there have been signs that positive changes are coming. One month after the Supreme Court's landmark decision, one of the defendants, the UNC at Chapel Hill, announced it would prohibit the consideration of race, sex, or ethnicity in both admissions and hiring decisions. UNC Chapel Hill became the first institution to outlaw affirmative action in hiring, an indication that the Supreme Court's ruling would have implications far beyond college admissions.

Within days of the Supreme Court's ruling, a civil rights group filed a federal complaint, challenging legacy admissions at Harvard. Legacy admissions programs have fast-tracked prospective students who have family members who are alumni or donors. The lawsuit argues that a legacy admissions program is affirmative action for white, wealthy students. Interestingly, the lawsuit relied on admissions data uncovered during the *SFFA v. Harvard* lawsuit, which showed about 70% of Harvard's donor-related or legacy applicants were white and close to half of the white students Harvard admitted came through legacy admissions. A month later, another study found "Legacy students that come from families in the top 1% are *five times* as likely to be admitted to the schools studied as the average applicant that has similar test scores, demographic characteristics, and admissions office ratings. Additionally, legacy students that come from families below the 90th percentile are still *three times* as likely to be admitted as peers with similar credentials."[53]

The compelling data, along with the legal pressure from lawsuits, have prompted several elite schools, including Virginia Tech and the University of Virginia, to announce the ending of their legacy admissions programs. As Wesleyan President Michael Roth explained in a blog post about his decision to end the legacy admissions at his school, "We still value the ongoing relationships that come from multi-generational Wesleyan attendance, but there will be no 'bump' in the selection process...family members of alumni will be admitted on their own merits."[54]

The Supreme Court's ruling against affirmative action has also given Asian Americans more confidence in defending their children's equal rights to education through the legal system. Yiatin Chu, an immigrant mother who was viciously attacked online for posting her support for the Supreme Court's ban on affirmative action, has shown remarkable courage in her fight for equality in education. She decided to continue her fight in the K–12 school system by filing a lawsuit against New York's Science and Technology Entry Program (STEP) initiatives.

The STEP initiatives offer resources such as hands-on training and exam preparation to 7th–12th-grade students who are economically disadvantaged or belong to a minority group. However, the STEP's guidelines define minorities as Black, Hispanic, Native American, or Alaskan Native, not Asian. The Pacific Legal Foundation (PLF), which filed the lawsuit on behalf of Chu, pointed out the irony of the STEP's minority definition: "This means that a child of billionaires who happens to identify as black is eligible for the STEP program. But a Chinese American student whose parents barely top the poverty line is not."[55] Chu explained why she decided to challenge the legality of the STEP guidelines: "I'm not asking us to be treated differently. Just don't treat us any different than you would treat a black student, Hispanic student, or a white student. That's all I want, no favors, no priority, just to be treated equal."[56] This shared desire for equality is what unites us all, regardless of our background or circumstances. That's what the plaintiffs of the Harvard and UNC cases wanted, too. The winning of the landmark cases ensure that America is one giant step closer to equality for all.

CHAPTER 7

. . .

Asian Americans Fought Back Against the
War on Merit

Introduction

Not all wars are being fought on battlefields. In the last couple of years, especially since 2020, America's progressives have been waging a war on merit in this country. The battle cry is that a person's race, ethnicity, and how many intersectionality boxes they can check matter much more than their knowledge and skills. The lethal weapons of this war are various acronyms, such as DEI and CRT. The war has been fought in classrooms, workplaces, government agencies, newsrooms, and many more places. The war on merit has affected the quality of products and services Americans rely on, and casualties of this war on merit are many, including but not limited to straight white males and Asian Americans. Since many Asian Americans firmly believe that meritocracy is why so many of us reach our American Dream, Asian Americans have been at the vanguard, leading the charge to fight the war on merit.

7.1 The Acronyms

On December 15, 2023, tech billionaire Elon Musk made a thought-provoking post on his social media platform, X.com (formerly known as Twitter), "DEI must DIE." His post sparked a significant debate among both supporters and detractors. This post not only generated heated discussions but also raised important questions. What is DEI, and why did Musk feel so strongly about it? The impact of his post was felt far and wide, drawing attention to a topic that is often overlooked.

DEI, which stands for "Diversity, Equity, and Inclusion," is more than just an acronym; it's an ideology. Since the 1960s, when equal employment laws and affirmative action mandates were introduced, many corporations and institutions have implemented diversity training programs. These programs initially aimed to integrate a workforce from different racial backgrounds and protect employers from discrimination-related lawsuits. However, in the '80s and '90s, these trainings evolved to celebrate multiculturalism and create a more welcoming workplace for an increasingly diverse workforce. This shift expanded the dimension of diversity to include observable characteristics like age, gender, race, and ethnicity, as well as invisible attributes such as religious beliefs and sexual orientation. Yet, one crucial element was missing: the diversity of ideas.

These trainings, which were mandatory, often left employees feeling frustrated as they sat through tedious workshops that simply listed dos and don'ts. Instead of fostering better understanding and communication among different racial and ethnic groups, these sessions often reinforced racial stereotypes and were largely ineffective. The resentment toward these mandatory diversity trainings was widespread, even among the human resources staff who were tasked with organizing them. The advent of the internet in the '90s provided a welcome relief, allowing employees to navigate through training modules at their own pace and pass a relatively simple test.

Then, starting in 2015, McKinsey & Company, a consulting company, published a series of studies claiming there was a direct link between diversity and profitability. Dame Vivian Hunt, McKinsey's managing partner, a coauthor on all four of McKinsey's studies, said in an interview: "What our data shows is that companies that have more diverse leadership teams are more successful. And so, the leading companies in our datasets are pursuing diversity because it's a business imperative and driving actual business results."[1] It is worth noting that in 2024, McKinsey's findings' credibility was questioned. Two economists, Professors Jeremiah Green and John R. M. Hand, conducted a study that failed to replicate McKinsey's results and highlighted severe flaws in McKinsey's methodology.[2] But since 2015, these McKinsey studies convinced corporations and many public and private institutions to invest in diversity initiatives, became a gospel of the progressives, led to the creation of new departments and programs on college campuses, and served as the basis for well-paying corporate consulting jobs.

Those who promoted and made a living off of diversity-related initiatives quickly persuaded companies and organizations that the emphasis on diversity alone was insufficient; there must be "Inclusion." They argued that diversity and inclusion are not interchangeable. According to a Gallup definition, inclusion is "a cultural and environmental feeling of belonging. It can be assessed as the extent to which employees are valued, respected, accepted, and encouraged to fully participate in the organization."[3] Inclusion, as its advocates see it, is about acceptance, about embracing every individual for who they are. They believe that without inclusion, diversity initiatives would fall flat. This belief gave birth to a new acronym, D&I (Diversity & Inclusion), which was at the forefront of workplace transformation.

Soon after, however, advocates argued that "Equity" must be added to the D&I mix. That's how we got "Diversity, Equity, and Inclusion," or DEI. Equity is different from equality. The Civil Rights Movement in the 1960s, led by Martin Luther King, Jr. and others, fought to end racial discrimination and instead to have equality for all, regardless of people's inner and external differences, personal backgrounds, historical grievances, etc. Equality is about ensuring everyone has the same opportunity. The DEI advocates claim, however, that equality doesn't fix the disparities in outcomes among different racial and ethnic groups. DEI advocates believe that unequal outcomes are the result of certain racial/ethnic groups facing more challenges in our society due to historical and systemic factors. Rather than seeking equal opportunities, DEI advocates believe in treating people differently (or reverse discrimination is acceptable) to make up for historic and systemic issues to achieve equal outcomes. They use two side-by-side cartoons to visually illustrate the distinction between equality and equity (Figure 1).

Figure 1. Equality vs. Equity (created by Interaction Institute for Social Changes).

EQUALITY   EQUITY

The scene depicts three kids attempting to watch a ball game over a fence. In the "Equality" cartoon, all three kids, varying in height, stand on the same size boxes. The two taller ones can see over the fence, while the shortest one can't. In the "Equity" cartoon, the tallest kid stands on the ground, the middle-height kid stands on one box, and the shortest kid stands on two stacked boxes. This arrangement allows all three kids to easily watch the ball game over the fence. These images were so compelling that during the 2020 presidential election, the Democratic Party's vice-presidential candidate, Kamala Harris, shared them on Twitter.

However, these images and the equity advocates' argument are problematic. It is clear that one of the two stacked boxes the shortest kid is standing on was taken from the tallest kid. Who decides how many boxes (a metaphor for resources and opportunities) someone or some group should or shouldn't have? What if the fence was high enough that the tallest kid couldn't look over it without standing on a box? What if he didn't want to give up his box, but someone forcefully took it away from him and gave it to others? It is unjust that the tallest kid lost his opportunity or that he's been punished for something he has no control over, which was to be born tall. The noble desire to help the shortest kid, while commendable, led to an injustice where an opportunity was taken away from the tallest kid, creating not an equal outcome but a new set of winners and losers. As Bari Weiss, founder and editor of the *Free Press*, said about DEI:

> In theory, all three of these words represent noble causes. They are in fact all causes to which American Jews in particular have long been devoted, both individually and collectively. But in reality, these words are now metaphors for an ideological movement bent on recategorizing every American not as an individual, but as an avatar of an identity group, his or her behavior prejudged accordingly, setting all of us up in a kind of zero-sum game.[4]

Regrettably, the true essence of DEI is often misconstrued, leading to its widespread adoption by schools, universities, human resources departments at companies, public and private institutions, and government agencies. This has resulted in significant societal impacts, particularly in education, where DEI proponents frequently and unfairly single out Asian Americans.

New York City is the proud home of eight specialty high schools, including Stuyvesant High School, the Bronx High School of Science, and Brooklyn Tech, all renowned for their academic excellence and among the nation's best high schools. These eight specialty high schools, with their rigorous academic programs, required applicants to take the Specialized High School Admissions Test (SHSAT), a three-hour exam that has been the sole basis for admission to these schools. The SHSAT is a standardized test that assesses students' math and verbal skills. Only those who passed the test could be admitted. In 2019, New York City's Democratic Mayor Bill de Blasio and his progressive allies argued that Asians were overrepresented at the city's elite high schools, meaning that the proportion of Asian American students at these schools is higher than their proportion in the city's overall student population. At the time, Asian Americans accounted for more than 60% of the student bodies at these elite schools but only 14% of the city's student population. Meanwhile, Black and Hispanic students accounted for just 10% of the student bodies at these schools, although they made up close to 70% of the city's overall student population.

Mayor de Blasio didn't have the power to cancel the SHSAT on his own because the state law established the test, meaning that canceling the SHSAT requires the state legislature's approval. Democrats in the New York State Assembly had introduced several bills to cancel the SHSAT. However, these bills and Mayor de Blasio's proposal faced fierce opposition from many minority communities in the city, including Asian Americans. They regarded de Blasio's proposal and the supporting arguments as "racist." Some found it "offensive" to accuse these elite high schools dominated by Asians of lacking diversity. They said these schools are already diverse because Asian Americans are not a monolith but a diverse group that "trace[s] their roots to more than 20 countries in East and Southeast Asia and the Indian subcontinent, each with unique histories, cultures, languages and other characteristics," according to Pew Research.[5] Many Asians also questioned de Blasio and other progressives' assertion that those high schools are racially "segregated" by pointing out the majority of the student body at these schools is non-white.

Some Black and Hispanic students and alumni of these top high schools also opposed de Blasio's proposal to cancel the SHSAT test, concerned the mayor and his progressive allies were reinforcing the racial stereotype that Black and Hispanic students couldn't learn. Horace Davis, a Black and a Brooklyn Tech graduate, pointed out that many Black and Latino students who are now successful professionals passed the SHSAT and attended those specialized high schools in the '70s, '80s, and even '90s. Their success is a testament to how merit-based admissions worked. Therefore, Davis saw that "underrepresentation of blacks and Hispanics at specialized high schools [today] is a symptom of a much larger problem" and the city's school system "has been failing black and Hispanic students long before they get to high school."[6] Had the school system done an excellent job educating all students in the first place, expensive test preps wouldn't even be necessary.

A study done by the New York City Independent Budget Office projected that should de Blasio's proposal go into effect, Black students would make up around 19% and Hispanic students 27% of all specialized high schools, but Asian American students' share at these schools would be cut about in half, from 61% to about 30%. While Asian Americans want to see more Black and Hispanic students in top high schools, they say it shouldn't come at the expense of qualified Asian students, especially those who come from disadvantaged backgrounds. A *New York Times* analysis states, "Fully 63 percent of Brooklyn Tech's students are classified as economically disadvantaged. Census data shows that Asians have the lowest median income in the city and that a majority speak a language other than English at home."[7] For these Asian students and their families, academic success is their only lifeline to get out of poverty, and using a single test to determine who gets to attend a top public school is the only fair way to level the playing fields between the well-to-do and the poor, because "However stressful a high-stakes test, it means a surname is no obstacle. No one knows they are Bengali, Tibetan, Nigerian or Tajik."[8]

Recognizing the pushback from Asian Americans and their allies, de Blasio recanted his proposal after his failed presidential bid in 2019. But the progressives' war on merit-based tests had only begun, and it would gain tremendous momentum a year later.

For many people, 2020 was a year they would rather forget or wish it never happened because so many things changed and so many lives were affected. The year began with news about the COVID-19 outbreak in China. The Chinese Communist Party, more concerned about its reputation than the welfare of the people, downplayed the severity of the epidemic and delayed sharing what it knew with its own people and the rest of the world. Governments worldwide initially thought the outbreak was contained in China and urged their citizens to go about their lives as usual. However, once the virus was confirmed to be contagious between humans, and images of overcrowded hospitals in the Chinese city of Wuhan (where the COVID-19 outbreak started) surfaced on the internet, it became clear that the initial underestimation of the pandemic had led to a global crisis. Many governments made a 180-degree shift from "It's not a big deal" to "We must shut down almost everything to save lives." In the United States, 49 states imposed lockdowns and kept all "non-essential" businesses, including schools, closed for various lengths of time. I never got why politicians and public health officials regarded schools, which are so crucial to children's development and well-being, as "non-essential."

Then, in May 2020, the image of Minneapolis policeman Derek Chauvin kneeling on the neck of 46-year-old African American George Floyd, and Floyd's subsequent tragic death, shocked not only America but the whole world. Floyd's death sparked nationwide mass protests and riots. Black Lives Matter (BLM), a decentralized political and racial justice group cofounded by three Black activists in 2013, rose to prominence, raising $90 million in 2020 alone.[9] BLM became the leading voice in demanding America take radical steps to address what it calls systemic racism, including defunding the police, and paying reparations to Black people who are descendants of slavery, among other things.

Another leading figure who called for radical racial reckoning in America was Ibram X. Kendi. Born Ibram Henry Rogers, Kendi rose to fame when his book *How to Be an Antiracist* became a best-seller in 2019. He became a highly sought-after guru on racism in America, particularly after the tragic death of George Floyd. Kendi's central message is that all disparities result from racism, and he believes "The only way to undo racism is to identify and describe it consistently—and then dismantle it." Kendi divides all people into two categories: racists and anti-racists, and there is no middle ground. He believes racial discrimination is a viable solution to past discrimination, and he argues that the idea of colorblindness, which suggests that race should not be a factor in social inter-actions, is just another form of white supremacy as it ignores the systemic inequalities that exist.

The idea that Kendi promotes, that America is still plagued by systemic racism and white supremacy, is nothing new. He claims that the intellectual foundation of his brand of antiracism is the Critical Race Theory (CRT). According to Christopher Rufo, a fellow at the Manhattan Institute who has written a book and numerous articles on CRT, CRT originated from Marxism. Classic Marxism believes the world is comprised of the oppressor and the oppressed, divided by economic class. Marxists use class division and class struggles to explain away all the social ills and call for armed revolution. However, after several communist regimes, including the former Soviet Union and Communist China, caused economic disasters that led to some of the worst suffering in human history, "Marxist scholars in the West simply adapted their revolutionary theory to the social and racial unrest of the 1960s. Abandoning Marx's economic dialectic of capitalists and workers, they substituted race for class and sought to create a revolutionary coalition of the dispossessed based on racial and ethnic cate-gories."[10] Thus, CRT was born. Once a fringe, far-left discipline found primarily within academia, since the summer of 2020, CRT has come to dominate our culture and society, significantly influencing our social and political landscape.

CRT declares racism in America is a systemic problem. Some of CRT's professed core beliefs are:

- "All unequal outcomes by race – inequity for short – are the result of racial oppression.

- All Blacks are oppressed and all whites are oppressors. This is systemic: never ask whether oppression occurred, only how it occurred. Everyone and everything white is complicit.

- If you are white and won't admit you are racist, you are racist by implicit bias. To reduce implicit bias, you must self-criticize, confess to privilege, apologize to the oppressed race.

- Whiteness is belief in, among others: achievement, delayed gratification, progress, schedules and deadlines, meritocracy, race-blindness, the written word, facts and objectivity (they deny lived experience), logic and reason (they deny empathy), mathematics and science (until they are de-colonized and humanized)."[11]

Since CRT is rooted in Marxism, it adopted classic Marxism verbiage such as "oppression" and "struggle." CRT also shares classic Marxism's ultimate goal to overthrow capitalism. Ibram X. Kendi insisted that "you can't separate capitalism from racism," therefore, "To be an anti-racist is to be anti-capitalist." The irony is that as a self-identified anti-racist and anti-capitalist, Kendi has demonstrated that he has no problem taking advantage of a system he critiques and achieving enormous financial success. His book, *How to Be an Antiracist*, was a *New York Times* bestseller and featured on reading lists from Fortune 500 companies to the U.S. military.[12] Netflix turned one of Kendi's books, *Stamped from the Beginning*, into a documentary. Kendi popularized the term "anti-racist" and sold merchandise branded with it. Despite Kendi's lack of any scholarly research or publication of any research paper on racism apart from his articles and three books, Boston University established the Center for Antiracist Research under his name just days after George Floyd's death. Kendi also received generous funding from Corporate America, including a substantial $10 million donation from former Twitter CEO Jack Dorsey.

Kendi frequently speaks on TV and at conferences, making at least $300,000 annually in speaking fees. For example, the University of Virginia paid Kendi $32,500 (for less than an hour) for telling students and faculty how racist America. That's approximately $541.67 per minute. No wonder that since 2020, Kendi has been the highest-paid activist in the world, reportedly pulling in $75 million between July 2023 and July 2024 alone. It's a paradox that Kendi, the staunch anti-capitalist, has found success in the capitalist system.

For Kendi and other CRT promoters, their accomplishments don't invalidate their belief that America remains a racist nation and Black people have no chance of succeeding without government intervention. They insist that the only way to remedy past racial discrimination is "anti-racist discrimination" through government policies, including affirmative action and reparations. Kendi's proposal for an anti-racist constitutional amendment is a significant one, as it "enshrines two guiding anti-racist principles: Racial inequity is evidence of racist policy and the different racial groups are equals. The amendment would make unconstitutional racial inequity over a certain threshold, as well as racist ideas by public officials (with "racist ideas" and "public official" clearly defined). It would establish and permanently fund the Department of Anti-racism (DOA), comprised of formally trained experts on racism and no political appointees. This proposal carries a weighty significance in the ongoing discourse about race in America."[13] It is clear that CRT is not about racial healing but about sowing divisions and deepening resentment.

CRT has also unjustly established a new racial hierarchy, with Blacks, Hispanics, and Native Americans placed at the top and

Asians and whites relegated to the bottom. This is exemplified by a whistleblower at Coca-Cola, who revealed that the company enforces anti-racism training taught by Robin DiAngelo, author of *White Fragility*. The training includes the directive for employees to learn "how to be less white" because "nothing exempts any white person from the forces of racism."[14] This hierarchy is not only divisive but also inherently unfair.

One of the corrosive effects of CRT is the influence of progressives like the *New York Times'* Nikole Hannah-Jones, who publicly declared that Asian Americans are not part of people of color (POC) but are "white by adjacency" due to their academic achievement and economic mobility being more similar to that of white people. This narrative, along with the core beliefs of CRT, has had a negative impact on Asian Americans. They quickly became alarmed at how they were being excluded. A wake-up call for David Lee, a Chinese American in New York City, came when his son applied for a high-school program to help minority students interested in Science, Technology, Engineering, and Math (STEM). In this field, minority representation is traditionally low. However, a representative turned him away and explained, "Oh, you're Chinese. You're not a minority."[15]

Not surprisingly, the CACAGNY delivered one of the most vigorous rebuttals to CRT on February 23, 2021, calling it "a hateful, divisive, manipulative fraud." The rebuttal was significant because it was still at the height of the racial justice movement after the death of George Floyd, and very few people or organizations dared to criticize the CRT out of fear of being labeled as "white supremacists." However, it would be difficult to discredit CACAGNY as "white supremacist" because CACAGNY is one of the oldest chapters of the CACA, whose mission has been not only fighting discrimination against Chinese Americans but also fighting for racial equality for all people of all ethnicities.

According to CACAGNY, education is the area where Chinese and other Asian American groups have felt the most negative impact from CRT. For instance, at R.I. Meyerholz Elementary

School in Cupertino, California, where a median home price is $2.3 million, a math teacher compelled third graders (most of them are non-white) to deconstruct their racial and sexual identities, then rank themselves according to their "power and privilege." The lesson was shut down after outraged Asian American parents pushed back. One parent said in an interview that CRT reminded him of ideas promoted by the Cultural Revolution in China: "[It divides society between] the oppressor and the oppressed, and since these identities are inborn characteristics people cannot change, the only way to change it is via violent revolution," the parent said. "Growing up in China, I had learned it many times. The outcome is the family will be ripped apart; husband hates wife, children hate parents. I think it is already happening here." [16] Examples such as this were why CACAGNY felt compelled to speak up against CRT.

CRT shouldn't be confused with DEI. CRT and DEI are closely related and help sustain each other, but they are not ideologically identical twins; they are more like fraternal twins. CRT focuses on racial justice, looks at everything through the lens of oppression and systemic racism, and lends the DEI bureaucracy theoretical and ideological justifications as to why different racial and ethnic groups should be treated differently. The term "DEI bureaucracy" refers to the institutional structures and processes that are put in place to implement DEI policies. These policies are all about giving preference to certain historically disadvantaged racial and ethnic groups and ensuring equal outcomes. DEI is affirmative action on steroids.

7.2 "Meritocracy is Racist"

The widespread proliferation of CRT and DEI since the summer of 2020 have led to the progressives' war on merit. Journalist and founder of the *Free Press*, Bari Weiss, observed, "People were to be given authority in this new order not in recognition of their gifts, hard work, accomplishments, or contributions to society, but in inverse proportion to the disadvantages their group had suffered, as defined by radical ideologues."[17]

The war on merit has been visible in the corporate world. A plethora of companies have installed chief diversity officers responsible for hitting DEI hiring goals, being compliant with state and federal DEI-related laws and regulations, and reporting directly to the CEO and the board of directors. In 2018, California was the first state that passed a law with an explicit DEI quota for corporate boards. The law required "publicly traded companies headquartered in California to have one member who identifies as a woman on their boards of directors by the end of 2019. By January 2020, boards with five directors must have two women, and boards with six or more members must have three women. Companies that do not include the required number of female board members would have to pay a fine of $100,000 for first violations and $300,000 for subsequent violations."[18] California's Democrat-led legislature passed this law despite the findings from a study of the effect of a similar policy in Europe that "Gender quotas at board level in Europe have done little to boost corporate performance or to help women lower down."[19]

California's gender quotas on corporate boards were only one of many examples of the tremendous pressures American companies were under from various stakeholders to do more for social justice and racial diversity in the workplace. One leading voice pushing for the DEI ideology in the corporate world is Larry Fink, chief executive officer of BlackRock, a trillion-dollar asset management firm. Weaponizing BlackRock's enormous financial power, Fink has coerced many other American companies to adopt the "environmental, social, and governance" (ESG) agenda, including specific DEI hiring goals. For example, in its 2020 annual reports, BlackRock bragged that it had "voted against management more than 1,500 times for 'insufficient diversity'" in company management.

Responding to these external demands and corporate executives' eagerness to signal virtue, American companies rushed to hire DEI professionals. The Society for Human Resource Management reported in 2020 that DEI roles in the workplace increased by 55% following Floyd's death. In a recent report titled "The Rise and Fall of the Chief Diversity Officer," *The Wall Street Journal* found, "In 2018, less than half the companies in the S&P 500 employed someone in the role, and by 2022, three out of four companies had created a position."[20]

The fever of embracing the DEI hiring goal reached the highest level of the U.S. government between 2020 and 2021. While running for president in 2020, Democratic presidential nominee Joe Biden promised he would pick a Black woman as his running mate, which significantly narrowed the pool of candidates. Biden eventually picked California Democratic Senator Kamala Harris, the daughter of a Jamaican and an Indian immigrant. Harris's senate career was unremarkable. She ran against Biden during the 2020 Democratic primary, and her campaign was a disaster. She had difficulty running a campaign effectively or keeping her staff. During the second primary debate, Harris was torched by criticism of her records in the Senate and when she served as the attorney general of California. After that, her polling was so poor that she did not even make it to Iowa. However, for Joe Biden, picking Harris as a running mate allowed him to claim that he had fulfilled his campaign promise. After Biden narrowly won the presidential election in 2020, the Democrats and liberal media hailed Harris as a history-making first Black female vice president of the United States of America, largely overlooking her Asian heritage.

President Biden was very public about his commitment to DEI. He once said, "To me, the values of diversity, equality, inclusion are literally…the core strengths of America. That's why I'm proud to have the most diverse administration in history that taps into the full talents of our country. And it starts at the top, with the vice president."[21] Under the Biden-Harris leadership, various government agencies made promoting DEI one of their core missions. For example, Secretary of State Antony Blinken established an

Office of Diversity, Equity, and Inclusion in 2021, led by a new chief diversity and inclusion officer (CDIO), and devised an "Equity Action Plan" to redirect U.S. diplomacy. In 2022, the U.S. Securities and Exchange Commission approved the Nasdaq stock exchange's proposal that most of the nearly 3,000 companies listed on the exchange should have at least one woman on their boards, along with one person from a racial minority or who identifies as gay, lesbian, bisexual, transgender, or queer. This rule came into effect even though, in May of that year, a Los Angeles judge ruled the law in California requiring women on corporate boards was unconstitutional.

Besides having specific DEI quotas, many companies and public institutions updated their DEI education and training materials with controversial ideas. In the fall of 2020, the National Museum of African American History and Culture (NMAAHC) published a chart as part of the museum's "talking about race" education material. The chart links characteristics including delayed gratification, emphasis on the scientific method, hardworking, nuclear family, respect for authority, and self-reliance to whiteness.[22] The museum later removed the chart after receiving widespread criticism. As Clifford Asness, founder and managing principal of AQR Capital Management, noticed, "At the core of today's progressivism is the idea that success comes only from plunder and that failure is the ultimate sign of virtue,"[23] and such a harmful idea could potentially have a significant impact on corporate culture and employee morale.

CRT gurus such as Robin DiAngelo charged tens of thousands of dollars for presenting at corporate DEI trainings with explicit CRT beliefs and verbiage such as "white supremacy," "systemic racism," "implicit bias," and "intersectionality."[24] In 2021, screenshots of Coca-Cola Company's mandatory "Confronting Racism" course, part of the company's DEI training, were leaked to the media. The course was based on an interview with Robin DiAngelo and was offered by LinkedIn Education. Some of the leaked slides suggested that employees "try to be less white" with tips including "be less oppressive," "listen," "believe," and "break with white solidarity."[25] LinkedIn removed the training material amidst public backlash.

Of course, CRT and DEI have the most influence in education. From K–12 schools to colleges, educational institutions have devoted enormous resources to build up DEI bureaucracies on campuses and indoctrinate America's youth with CRT and DEI ideas, often at the expense of academic excellence. For example, the number of DEI employees at The Ohio State University grew from 88 in 2018 to 189 in 2023, costing taxpayers $20.38 million annually.[26] Duke University created a Racial Equity Advisory Council in 2020, aiming to propose "measures to assess and foster racial equity" to the university's leadership.

Many colleges and universities also started requiring anyone applying for a faculty position to provide a DEI statement, which must have three elements: affirming their belief in DEI, demonstrating their past commitment to DEI through examples, and pledging to do more for DEI in the future. DEI statements have become litmus tests for employment in higher education. Several universities, including the University of California at Berkeley, even prescreened candidates solely based on their diversity scores derived from their diversity statements. According to a National Association of Scholars (NAS) report, the UC Berkeley approach reduced the pool of applicants from 893 to 214, and "finalists also were asked to describe their DEI efforts [again] during their job talks." Similarly, the hiring committee at the Department of Psychology and Human Development at Vanderbilt University used the DEI statements as a prescreening tool and "reduced the initial applicant pool by around 85 percent, from 400 to around 60."[27]

Students at more than two-thirds of colleges and universities must take DEI-related coursework to meet their graduation requirements.[28] Furthermore, a DEI "credentialing explosion" has occurred on college campuses. *USA Today* reported early in 2024 that "[a]t least a half-dozen colleges across the country either offer

DEI degree programs or soon will. ... Dozens of colleges, from Texas State University to Michigan Tech to the U.S. Military Academy at West Point, New York, offer minors or concentrations with titles such as 'diversity studies.' And more than 100 schools offered programs categorized as intercultural or multicultural diversity studies, up from about 50 in 2012."[29]

The most significant change at the university level that affected Asian American students was the removal of standardized tests such as the SAT and ACT from the admissions process. This change initially presented as a temporary pandemic-related relief for students applying for colleges in the fall of 2020, but has evolved into a widespread practice. Close to 1900 colleges and universities have adopted a test-optional or test-flexible policy, allowing students to choose whether to submit test scores based on their GPA or other requirements.[30]

Dropping SAT and ACT from college admissions was a significant win for progressives after they'd pushed for it for years. Progressives' opposition to standardized tests is usually threefold. First, they claim the SAT is useless and doesn't predict a student's future academic or career success, ignoring multiple studies that have demonstrated that SAT scores do an excellent job of predicting grades and other important educational and social outcomes. The SAT's predictability makes sense because in order to get a good score, a student must be willing to study hard and master cognitive skills, such as reading comprehension, quantitative reasoning, memorizing, and maintaining attention – all essential for success in school and life. There is a clear correlation between SAT scores and career accomplishments.[31]

Second, progressives claimed that standardized tests are unjust barriers to keeping minority children from good schools. Opponents of standardized tests insist that Asian and white kids, on average, had better test scores than Black and brown kids because the former could afford to attend costly testing preparation programs or their families were able to hire private tutors. Third, after the U.S. Supreme Court ruled affirmative action as unconstitutional in the *SFFA v. Harvard* and *UNC* cases, the ACLU called on universities to eliminate the "use of standardized test scores in admissions" and broaden their "recruitment efforts to underserved communities."[32] Even without the ACLU's urging, many colleges and universities already knew that they could circumvent the Supreme Court's ban on affirmative action and continue to consider an applicant's race by removing objective measures such as the standardized tests from the admissions process and focusing on more subjective measures such as essays and recommendation letters.

Contrary to the progressives' assertions, there is much evidence that Black and Hispanic children from poor and disadvantaged backgrounds can excel in standardized testing despite lacking material means. This challenges the assumptions we may have about the impact of socioeconomic status on academic performance. For example, Success Academy, a free public charter school network in New York City known for its rigorous academic program, high expectations, and strong discipline policies, serves 20,000 students, all of whom are admitted on a lottery basis. About 53% of students are Black, and 30% are Hispanic; 78% are from low-income households, and 15% are current and former special-needs students. In 2019's state-run standardized tests, 99% of Success Academy's students passed the math exam, and 90% passed the English exam, compared to only 46% of students in traditional public schools in the city.[33] Success Academy's impressive results should debunk progressives' claims that there is "cultural bias" in standardized tests and that standardized testing is "racist."

Not surprisingly, one of the loudest voices supporting the cancellation of standardized tests is teachers' unions. Randi Weingarten, president of the American Federation of Teachers, asserted in a social media post in 2021: "Standardized testing doesn't help kids learn, and it doesn't help teachers teach." Instead, she argued, "we need to measure what matters."[34] Her tweet was mocked because it was so obviously self-serving. Teachers' unions have long opposed tying teachers' compensation to testing results. However, without an objective measure such as standardized testing, evaluating teachers' performance and holding bad teachers accountable for poor outcomes is difficult. Thomas Chatterton Williams, an author and contributor to *The New York Times Magazine*, responded to Weingarten's tweet with his own: "As a young black kid with no family connections or intergenerational wealth, I had a father who instilled the value of study. I can look you in the eye and say that standardized testing changed the course of my life. Measuring how hard someone is willing to study does matter."[35] His personal experiences, including the SAT being a lifeline for those without a legacy to fall back on and the GRE making grad school possible for him, make a compelling case for the value of standardized testing.

I couldn't agree more with Williams because my own experience mirrors his. More than two decades ago, I came to the United States alone, with no family wealth, connections, or legacy to fall back on. I took the Graduate Management Admissions Test, or GMAT, a standardized test for business schools, which gave me a lifeline and allowed me to compete against others on a level playing field. It was this standardized test that opened the door to opportunities for me. I scored well enough that the University of Wyoming's business school accepted me and awarded me a scholarship. The MBA degree that I then earned helped launch me into a successful career in banking and finance.

It is true that standardized testing is far from perfect. For example, some teachers emphasize "teaching to the test" and do not pay enough attention to students' overall learning and development. It is also true that standardized tests are usually overly focused on evaluating cognitive skills; evidence suggests that other core competencies, such as emotional intelligence and creativity, are also essential for success in today's economy. Furthermore, we must not overlook the importance of grit, resilience, and work ethic in education. These qualities are crucial for success and should be given more emphasis. It is easy to find examples of those who performed poorly on standardized testing but still became wildly successful later in life. Still, many progressives' criticisms of standardized testing are exaggerated or misleading. Despite its flaws, standardized testing is still the best way to objectively evaluate and predict education outcomes. It levels the playing field for poor immigrant youths like me, and it helps us achieve upward economic mobility through our own efforts and merit. Getting rid of standardized testing will do a disservice to students with nothing else to fall back on.

Of course, progressives such as Weingarten do not want to discuss how each student can improve their lot with discipline, grit, resilience, and a sound work ethic, regardless of material circumstances. Instead, they condemn these attributes as "white privilege," and Weingarten calls for the outright elimination of standardized testing. Black writer Chatterton Williams lamented: "It is peak white privilege to tell minorities they don't need grit or metrics."[36] Armstrong Williams, a Black entrepreneur, called "white privilege" the biggest "white lie" of all.[37]

It is also crucial to highlight that those advocating for the elimination of standardized testing have not yet proposed a fair and effective alternative. With widespread grade inflation, a student's GPA has become an unreliable metric nowadays. Research also suggests that college admissions essays and personal statements do not necessarily predict a student's performance on campus.[38] The Stanford Center for Education Policy Analysis suggests that essays correlate to family wealth.[39] Therefore, a college admissions system that disregards SAT or ACT scores but prioritizes personal essays will unfairly favor wealthy students, undermining the principle of equity in education.

Just as the North Pole theory posits, every direction you look is south at the North Pole. Similarly, for the proponents of CRT and DEI, systemic racism and white supremacy seem to pervade every aspect of the education system. This has led to significant changes not only in America's higher education system but also in the K–12 system. Any programs that recognize merit, any expectations of good behavior, and any knowledge passed down by white men, no matter how valuable, have been labeled as problematic and even "racist." This shift in perspective is reshaping our education system.

The Seattle school district voted to dismantle its gifted-and-talented programs, accusing these programs of exacerbating racial and economic segregation because these programs were "over-saturated" with white and Asian students.[40] The Oregon Department of Education (ODE) instructed math teachers to focus on dismantling racism in mathematics instruction because "white supremacy culture can show up in the classroom in various ways," such as when "the focus is on getting the 'right' answer," or when "students are required to 'show their work.'"[41]

The San Diego Unified School District (SDUSD) overhauled its grading system to combat racism and achieve grade "equity" after data showed more Black and brown kids received D or F grades than white kids. Vice President Richard Barrera of SDUSD said, "If we're actually going to be an anti-racist school district, we have to confront practices like this that have gone on for years and years."[42] The new "anti-racist" grading system wouldn't account for factors including tardiness of homework and classroom behavior toward a student's overall academic grade.

There has been a renewed push to cancel merit-based admissions to elite high schools nationwide. San Francisco's school board voted to replace Lowell High School's merit-based admissions system with a lottery system (more on this will be discussed in the next chapter). The Boston School Committee unanimously voted to suspend the admissions test for the city's three prestigious schools and replace it with a zip-code quota for the incoming fall class to address racial equity. The move was backed by the city's Democratic officials, including Congresswoman Ayanna Pressley, who applauded the committee's decision through a statement:

> In this moment of national reckoning on systemic racism and racial injustice, we must continue to be unapologetic in our efforts to examine and address the ways in which our institutions contribute to and exacerbate our gravest inequities and disparities—our education system is no exception.[43]

Backed by the PLF, the Boston Parent Coalition for Academic Excellence Corp., a nonprofit, has shown unwavering devotion to merit-based admissions by filing a federal lawsuit, alleging the Boston School Committee had violated the equal protection rights of its parent members.

The fight to cancel merit-based admissions to elite high schools in New York City opened a new front. A state law that predated Mayor de Blasio created the Discovery Program, mandating New York City's elite high schools to accept about 5% of low-income students from anywhere in the city who scored below the cutoff score of the Specialized High Schools Admissions Test (SHSAT), but completed the required summer coursework. After former Mayor Bill de Blasio's 2019 plan to cancel SHSAT failed due to pushback from the city's Asian American population, de Blasio found a workaround by increasing the Discovery Program's acceptance rate from 5% to 20% mandatory at each specialized high school. This change has disproportionately affected Asian American students because the expanded program now only admits students from schools with a 60% or higher poverty rate, a rule specifically targeting Asian students because most poor Asian students do not attend schools that meet the 60% poverty rate.

In 2022, New York City voters elected a new Democratic mayor, Eric Adams. Mayor Adams vowed to bring positive changes to the city. However, on the education front, he maintained former Mayor Bill de Blasio's expansion of a Discovery Program. In response, the CACAGNY filed a lawsuit with the backing of the PLF. They alleged that the mayor's Discovery Program modifications were "violating the Constitution's equal protection guarantee because it was adopted with a discriminatory purpose—to limit the number of Asian American students at the Specialized High Schools."[44]

One of the most high-profile cases over elite high schools' merit-based admissions occurred in Fairfax County, Virginia. Fairfax is one of America's top 10 wealthiest counties, with a median household income of more than $105,000. The county's Thomas Jefferson High School for Science and Technology (TJ) was ranked the number-one high school nationwide and known for its academic rigor before 2020. Its admissions process, historically race-blind and merit-based, has been a cornerstone of its success. Applicants must undergo a multi-stage evaluation process and meet criteria, including passing three competitive standardized tests. For the 2020–2021 school year, the racial makeup of TJ was 71.97% Asian American, 18.34% white, 3.05% Hispanic, and 1.77% Black.

The school closures during the COVID-19 pandemic in 2020 affected the academic performance of many students, especially those from the most vulnerable backgrounds. "The percentage of middle-school students failing has increased by 300 percent this year compared to last year, with Hispanic middle-schoolers and middle-schoolers with disabilities failing at an increased rate of 400 percent and economically disadvantaged students failing at an increased rate of 375 percent."[45] The school board, however, chose to focus its attention on the district's best high school in the name of "racial equity."

Following George Floyd's tragic death in 2020, the Fairfax County school board deemed the "overrepresentation" of Asian American students and the underrepresentation of Black and Hispanic students at TJ "unacceptable." This sentiment was echoed by some school leaders and racial justice activists who, in their pursuit of equity, saw the need for a more diverse student body at TJ. However, they ignored the diversity among Asian American students, instead referring to TJ's majority-Asian student body as "racist" and even comparing test preparation to illegal "performance-enhancement drugs."[46] The school board insisted it must change TJ's admissions process and criteria to "counter racism and discrimination in our society."

In December 2020, the school board voted to replace TJ's merit-based admissions with a "holistic" evaluation, a decision that significantly altered the school's student-body composition. The aim was to bring in more Black and Hispanic students by reducing the number of Asian American students and making the TJ student body closely mimic the racial demographics of Fairfax County. At the time, the countywide racial makeup of students was 36.8% white, 27.1% Hispanic, 19.8% Asian, and 10% Black.[47]

The school board eliminated the three competitive entrance exams and altered the minimum academic requirements. TJ's new "holistic" admissions criteria are a point-based system, including essay requirements. Students who meet specific socioeconomic criteria, such as attending a middle school deemed "historically underrepresented at TJ" or being eligible for free and reduced lunches, will receive "experience factors" – bonus points to boost their total score and help them secure admission to TJ. These "experience factors" could include participation in extracurricular activities, community service, or overcoming significant personal challenges. The new admissions process also guarantees seats at TJ for 1.5% of students at each participating public middle school in the district.

The school board claimed that such a holistic admissions process was necessary to "achieve greater equity" and was not about "eliminating merit but reframing our understanding of merit." But text messages and emails from the school board members had demonstrated that they knew from the start that the new admissions process was really about decreasing the representation of qualified Asian American students at TJ to attain the board's desired racial balance in the school's student body.

Furthermore, board members were fully aware that, contrary to their stated objective of achieving educational "equity" for students of color, TJ's new process's biggest beneficiary wouldn't be Black or Hispanic students but white students. In a group text message exchange, school board member Stella Pekarsky wrote that the new proposal "will whiten our schools and kick [out] Asians. How is that achieving the goal of diversity?" Another member, Abrar Omeish, replied, "I mean, there has been an anti-Asian feel underlying some of this, hate to say it, lol!"[48]

After TJ's new admissions process was enacted in 2021, the enrollment data revealed that TJ admitted 56 fewer Asian American students than it did in the prior school year. Asian Americans make up 54% of TJ's 2025 class, significantly dropping from 73% of the 2024 class. When Asian, Black, and other concerned parents voiced unease about the fairness of TJ's new admissions process, the school board used racially charged terms to denounce them, such as telling Asian Americans to check their "privilege" and calling any advocacy for a merit-based admissions process "segregation bullsh*t." This name-calling revealed the school board's bigotry and ignorance of the ethnic diversity and wide income gaps within the Asian American community. Refusing to give up, Asian American parents led a coalition of families and alumni from diverse racial backgrounds to file a lawsuit in 2021, arguing TJ's new admissions policy was designed to reduce the number of Asian students at the school, a violation of Constitutional protections against racial discrimination. The lawsuit was backed by the PLF.

In 2022, federal judge Claude Hilton agreed with the Asian parents who led the TJ coalition that "It is clear that Asian-American students are disproportionately harmed by the [Fairfax County School] Board's decision to overhaul TJ admissions… Currently and in the future, Asian-American applicants are disproportionately deprived of a level playing field in competing for both allocated and unallocated seats." Judge Hilton also noted that the Fairfax County school board's discussion of TJ admissions changes "was infected with racial balancing since inception" and had demonstrated "discriminatory intent." Judge Hilton concluded that "racial balancing for its own sake is 'patently unconstitutional.'"[49] Therefore, he ordered the Fairfax school district to stop using the new non-merit-based admissions process for TJ.

Judge Hilton's ruling had plenty of public support. A 2019 survey by Pew Research shows that most Americans (73%) believe schools should not consider race or ethnicity when making decisions about student admissions.[50] Yet Democrats and their allies continue to ignore public opinions while pushing for racial preference in elite high schools and colleges, all in the name of equity and anti-racism. The CACAGNY issued a statement, congratulating the TJ parents' coalition on their legal victory, while declaring, "Our TJ victory may be appealed; our other cases may frustrate. No matter – we fight on. For America's sake, we must keep fighting until meritocracy is restored, equal rights under the law is reaffirmed, and Justice prevails."[51]

In May 2023, after the Fairfax County school board filed an appeal, a majority of a three-judge panel ruled in favor of the school board's argument that the admissions policy doesn't discriminate against Asian Americans but aims to increase diversity. The majority also deemed the new admissions policy hasn't harmed Asian students because Asian applicants still were admitted at a rate that was higher than their representation in the population. However, in her dissenting opinion, Circuit Judge Allison Rushing pointed out the evidence that the school board's admissions policy change was "passed with discriminatory intent and disproportionately impact a particular racial group," even if they appear race-neutral on paper. This dissenting opinion carries significant weight and challenges the majority ruling.[52] The TJ coalition petitioned the Supreme Court to pick up TJ's case, one month after the majority of the U.S. Supreme Court sided with the SFFA case against Harvard and UNC that race-based admissions are unconstitutional.

Unfortunately, the majority of the Supreme Court declined to take TJ's case. Justice Samuel Alito and Justice Clarence Thomas dissented from the court's decision. In his dissenting opinion, Justice Alito argued that the U.S. Court of Appeals for the 4th Circuit's ruling had been "based on a patently incorrect and dangerous understanding of what a plaintiff must show to prove intentional race discrimination." When the Supreme Court chose not to intervene, Justice Alito suggested, the 4th Circuit's ruling would stand and allow government officials "to discriminate against any racial group with impunity as long as that group continues to perform at a higher rate than other groups."[53]

TJ's progressive leadership and the county school board might have won the legal battle, but reality dealt them a decisive blow. The school's academic performance has suffered since it dropped merit-based admissions. For the first time in the school's history, it had to introduce a remedial math class for its freshman class, suggesting these students aren't as academically prepared as students admitted under merit-based admissions. The *U.S. News & World Report* magazine publishes an annual "Best High School Rankings" list. TJ's ranking, a symbol of its academic excellence, dropped from first on the list to fifth in 2023 and fourteenth in 2024, after the school's last merit-based class graduated in June 2024.[54] This significant drop in ranking underscores the gravity of TJ's decline, a decline that was predictable: when you declare war on merit, you will get mediocrity in return; when you punish success, you will get failure in return. Asian students have been most affected by TJ's changing admissions policy as their enrollment at TJ dropped from 70% of the student body to around 50%. A *Washington Examiner* commentator lamented TJ's DEI-driven admissions policy as "comparable to a swim team selecting athletes who can't swim and require life jackets at the expense of swimmers who are highly proficient in all four strokes."[55]

Many Asian Americans, like me, are immigrants who arrived in the United States without intergenerational wealth or a deeply rooted network. A meritocracy-based education is our only fair chance to succeed in this country. When Democrats and their progressive allies eliminate meritocracy-based education and deny Asian kids an equal opportunity, it's akin to destroying the single ladder Asian Americans rely on for upward mobility. The TJ lawsuit has shown that Asian Americans will not stand for such injustice and bigotry. We will fight with all our strength, resilience, and determination. Despite the disappointment of the Supreme Court's decision, Asian Americans, especially those who led the TJ coalition, have good reasons to be optimistic. The dam of DEI and CRT is beginning to crack, and the impact of the TJ lawsuit on the fight against injustice is empowering and motivating.

7.3 The DEI and CRT Bubble Popped

Clifford Asness, a hedge fund manager and a vocal critic of DEI, warned that "No society that worships failure and abjures success can long endure." [56] Fortunately, the DEI and CRT bubbles started to pop in 2022 before the Supreme Court struck down affirmative action in college admissions in June 2023.

The first sign of the DEI and CRT bubbles starting to pop was the shocking revelation that some of the most well-known racial justice warriors are grifters. In the spring of 2021, reports emerged that Dyane Pascall, who worked for a company founded by BLM co-founder Patrisse Cullors and her partner Janaya Khan, purchased a six-million-dollar mansion in Los Angeles in 2020 two weeks after BLM received $66.5 million in donations. Cullors initially denied the mansion was bought for her and her family and blamed racism for media attention. But later, she admitted that she did use the mansion frequently for personal purposes. This revelation was particularly jarring given Cullors' self-proclaimed Marxist beliefs and her ownership of several million-dollar properties in the U.S. and the Bahamas.

Cullors' million-dollar real estate holdings didn't sit well with activists like Hawk Newsome. Newsome's call for "an independent investigation" was not just a demand, but a necessity to find out how BLM spent millions of dollars it received. This urgency was palpable in his words, "If you go around calling yourself a socialist, you have to ask how much of her own personal money is going to charitable causes. It's unfortunate because it makes people doubt the validity of the movement and overlook the fact that it's the people that carry this movement." [57]

More questions were raised about BLM's finances after California and Washington State threatened legal action against BLM for failing to submit financial disclosures for 2020. Under pressure, BLM released its financial data for the first time, which showed the organization raised more than $90 million in 2020. After excluding $8.4 million in operating expenses and $21.7 million in grants to more than 30 organizations, the group still retained nearly $60 million. The financial disclosure only led to more criticism. Many complained that the leaders of BLM raked in personal financial gains while spending little to support activists and families who lost loved ones to police violence. This financial mismanagement was not just a matter of numbers but a heavy burden on the movement. Lisa Simpson and Samaria Rice, two mothers who lost their children to police violence, asked the BLM and others to stop capitalizing on their sufferings.

Cullors faced more questions after the revelation that she "has been tied to even more charities whose finances raise 'red flags' after the organization donated hundreds of thousands to the non-profits which then made payments to Cullors and her business partners."[58] Cullors resigned from BLM in May 2021 without ever admitting any wrongdoings. Despite all her complaints about systemic racism in America, she raked in an abundance of financial gains from her political activism. In addition to owning multiple million dollars' worth of real estate, she published two books, inked a deal with YouTube, and signed a production deal with Warner Bros. However, the organization she helped found and abruptly left behind was in disarray.

Cullors said she appointed Makani Themba, the chief strategist at a Mississippi social-justice consultancy, and Monifa Bandele, then the chief operating officer at the Time's Up Foundation, as her successors. However, in a social media post, Themba declared that she and Bandele had never accepted the job offers. In January 2022, Washington State and California informed BLM that it was prohibited from soliciting or disbursing funds due to its failure to submit an annual report for the 2020 tax year and threatened to hold leaders of the organization personally accountable. A month later, BLM halted online fundraising activities.

Cullors wasn't the only racial justice warrior who became a racial grifter. Ibram X. Kendi, the self-designed anti-racist prophet, has a history of overpromising and underdelivering. When he ran an anti-racist center at American University, none of his promised projects or research materialized despite his collecting millions of donations and grants from wealthy foundations. This financial aspect of his alleged misuse of funds is a serious concern. Yet, he was never held accountable. Instead, he kept failing. Boston University hired him to run the Center for Antiracist Research in the wake of George Floyd's murder, and individuals, as well as tech billionaires, have given him millions for conducting anti-racism research. In 2023, however, Kendi's Center for Antiracist Research reportedly had squandered more than $43 million in less than three years with nothing to show for it. The center produced minimum research. Almost all of the center's employees were laid off.

Some former employees complained about Kendi's poor leadership, tendency to focus on promoting himself and his work, and inability to guide any project from start to finish. One former employee said, "It was mostly about him, rather than the work."[59] Furthermore, as early as 2021, employees at the center began to file complaints about its toxic work culture, and the issues were, ironically, discrimination. The irony of discrimination in an anti-racist center is not lost on anyone. Others criticized Kendi's gross mismanagement of the center's finances and the lack of transparency about where the money went, a fact that had left many feeling a sense of betrayal. Saida Grundy, an associate professor of sociology who worked at the center, filed a complaint in 2022, alleging that the center was "collecting grant money with no intention of carrying out research projects."[60] Other observers pointed out that many other research centers had produced significantly more studies and papers than Kendi's anti-racist center with a fraction of the funding. After conducting a secret investigation of the anti-racist center, Boston University claimed it didn't find anything inappropriate. Still, the university refused to discuss if its investigation yielded any answers about where the 43 million dollars went. Kendi kept his position at the university, but his anti-racist center essentially ceased to exist.

Christopher Rufo, a fellow at the conservative thinktank the Manhattan Institute, said the implosion of Kendi's anti-racist center proved Rufo's warning in 2021 that Kendi was the "false prophet of a dangerous and lucrative faith."[61] Another false prophet who faced her reckoning is Robin DiAngelo. In August 2024, a complaint was filed with the University of Washington (where DiAngelo received a PhD in multicultural education), alleging DiAngelo committed plagiarism in her doctoral thesis, "Whiteness in Racial Dialogue: A Discourse Analysis." The complaint pointed out that DiAngelo lifted "two paragraphs from an Asian American professor, Northeastern University's Thomas Nakayama, and his co-author, Robert Krizek, without proper attribution, omitting quotation marks and in-text citations."[62] It is important to remember that DiAngelo charged between $30,000 and $40,000 per speech and has made millions in speaking fees alone by lecturing Americans that all white people are racists.

Grifters like Ibram Kendi, Robin DiAngelo, and BLM's Patrisse Cullors are opportunists. They have enriched themselves by exploiting people's and corporations' sympathies for real-life tragedies and their desire for change. The ideology they championed has caused so much harm to our culture and society. The impact of the ideology bubble popping following its champions' disgraceful falls cannot be overstated.

March 2022 marked a significant step in reversing CRT and DEI's war on merit. The Massachusetts Institute of Technology (MIT) made history by becoming the first private elite college in the U.S. to reinstate the SAT/ACT as part of its college admissions process after suspending the test requirement in the 2020 and 2021 school years. MIT's dean of Admissions and Financial Services, Stuart Schmill, explained:

> Our research has shown that, in most cases, we cannot reliably predict students will do well at MIT unless we consider standardized test results alongside grades, coursework, and other factors. These findings are statistically robust and

stable over time, and hold when you control for socio-economic factors and look across demographic groups... Low-income students, underrepresented students of color, and other disadvantaged populations often do not attend schools that offer advanced coursework (and if they do, they are less likely to be able to take it). They often cannot afford expensive enrichment opportunities, cannot expect lengthy letters of recommendation from their overburdened teachers, or cannot otherwise benefit from this kind of educational capital... It turns out the shortest path for many students to demonstrate sufficient preparation — particularly for students with less access to educational capital — is through the SAT/ACT, because most students can study for these exams using free tools at Khan Academy, but they (usually) can't force their high school to offer advanced calculus courses, for example. So, the SAT/ACT can actually open the door to MIT for these students, too.[63]

The Supreme Court's ruling that affirmative action in college admissions is unconstitutional has given many people confidence, courage, and probably some legal cover to push back on policies and ideas advocated by CRT and DEI. An important example was in early 2024, when the *New York Times*, one of the most influential critics of the SAT/ACT, admitted the leftists' war on standardized tests such as the SAT was "misguided." David Leonhardt, a long-time *Times* reporter on higher education, acknowledged the crucial role of evidence in this debate. He pointed out that study after study, including a 2020 study by the University of California and a 2007 study from the journal *Science*, has repeatedly demonstrated a clear correlation between SAT scores and a student's academic and career accomplishments.

After colleges dropped standardized test scores from their admissions process, they have relied heavily on factors such as students' GPAs, extracurricular activities, and essays, which are problematic in their own ways. GPAs are ineffective predictors of academic success due to "grade inflation in recent years." Leonhardt realized, "Affluent students can participate in expensive activities, like music lessons and travel sports teams, that strengthen their applications. These same students often receive extensive editing on their essays from their well-educated parents." Many affluent students attend private schools where counselors polish each student's application. Consequently, by replacing the SAT and ACT with essays and extracurricular activities, the colleges have failed to achieve their equity goal because they "have even larger racial and economic biases."[64]

Without including an objective measure such as the SAT or ACT, "the students who suffer most are those with high grades at relatively unknown high schools, the kind that rarely send kids to the Ivy League," said Harvard economist David Deming.[65] For those talented and hard-working kids from disadvantaged backgrounds, which could include students from low-income families, underfunded schools, or first-generation college students, the SAT or ACT score is the "lifeline" that enables them to pull themselves out of poverty and achieve upward social mobility.

The progressives' assertion that the disparity in SAT and ACT scores results from wealth disparity because affluent families can afford expensive test prep courses has long been debunked. In 2010, the *Princeton Review* company dropped its claim that its "Ultimate Classroom" SAT preparation course would dramatically improve a student's test score. A study by the Fordham Institute found more Asian students from the lowest socioeconomic status (whose mothers didn't graduate from high school) outperformed the highest socioeconomic status Black and Hispanic students in reading and math. This revelation sheds light on the true factors influencing test scores, dispelling misconceptions and promoting a more informed discussion.

The disparities in SAT scores across racial and ethnic groups are consistent with the disparities in the National Assessment of Educational Progress results. This test measures K–12 learning. Some on the left are finally willing to admit that "the disparities in

SAT scores are a symptom, not a cause, of inequality in the US" or, "To put it another way, the existence of racial and economic gaps in SAT and ACT scores doesn't prove that the tests are biased," the *Times* reports.[66] Thus, eliminating SATs and ACTs only hides rather than eliminates the racial gaps in educational outcomes.

The *Times'* conclusion that the progressives' "misguided" war on SATs has failed to make higher education more "equitable" and has done a disservice to students from disadvantaged backgrounds is not surprising. Many conservatives, including myself, warned about it several years ago. What is surprising is that the *Times*, after serving as Democrats' mouthpiece for so long, would raise questions about one of their favorite causes. After the *Times* article came out, several other highly selective colleges, including Dartmouth, Yale, Harvard, and Johns Hopkins, followed MIT's lead to bring back the SAT/ACT scores as part of their admissions process. This positive development, based on similar studies demonstrating the close correlation between standardized test scores and students' first-year grades at their schools, offers hope for a more equitable college admissions process.

Still, many college administrators told the *Times* that despite all the evidence and research, they are still reluctant to reinstate SAT or ACT scores, fearing "the political reaction on their campuses and in the media if they reinstated tests." I'm also disappointed that the *Times* has failed to call out the fundamental objective of eliminating SATs or ACTs in college admissions, which is to discriminate against Asian students. Without standardized tests, college admissions officers can focus on racial quotas and reject academically qualified Asian American applicants without leaving a paper trail.

While some colleges are voluntarily reintroducing SATs/ACTs as part of their admissions process, it's important to note that some changes on college campuses are being driven by legislation. In May 2023, Florida Republican Gov. Ron DeSantis signed Senate Bill 266, the so-called anti-woke law prohibiting institutions from spending federal or state dollars on discriminatory initiatives, such as DEI programs. A month later, Texas Republican Gov. Greg Abbott signed a similar bill into law for the Lone Star State. Several Republican-led states, including Iowa and Kansas, also passed legislation to limit or eliminate DEI programs in public institutions, including state universities. For example, Kansas passed a law prohibiting public universities from requiring prospective students or hires to make any DEI statement. The University of Florida, the state's largest public university, announced in March 2024 that it would fire all DEI staff, shut down its DEI office, and suspend DEI contracts with outside vendors. The university will redistribute its $5 million-a-year DEI budget to a faculty recruitment fund.

The most drastic change in CRT and DEI came from Corporate America. After the Supreme Court struck down affirmative action in college admissions, a group of Republican attorneys general sent a letter to Fortune 100 companies with this warning, "The Supreme Court's recent decision should place every employer and contractor on notice of the illegality of racial quotas and race-based preferences in employment and contracting practices." The letter said, "We urge you to immediately cease any unlawful race-based quotas or preferences your company has adopted for its employment and contracting practices. If you choose not to do so, know you will be held accountable." Not surprisingly, some companies have tried to protect themselves from future legal challenges by scaling back DEI initiatives and laying off DEI-focused employees. Big Tech companies such as Amazon and Twitter have laid off diversity professionals, followed by other well-known corporations including American Airlines and Wells Fargo. The demand for DEI professionals was down 75% in the second half of 2023. The attrition of DEI-focused employees has also accelerated since 2023, including the departures of high-profile Chief Diversity Officers at Netflix and Warner Bros.

Besides the desire to shield themselves from possible legal challenges, companies have experienced buyer's remorse with their DEI hires. In a hurry to fill DEI roles, "some companies moved people into diversity leadership if they were an ethnic minority, even when they weren't qualified,"[67] essentially setting them up for failure and leading to a high turnover rate for DEI professionals.

Even with well-qualified and experienced DEI professionals, many companies' DEI initiatives made no one happy. Research on inclusive workplace practices by Kincentric found that "more than half of white men surveyed by the group felt devalued at work, or not given full credit for their contributions. Roughly 43 percent of ethnically diverse men reported the same."[68] Like in the rest of America, DEI remains a contentious topic in the workplace. A May 2023 Pew Research Center survey found employees' opinions about DEI vary considerably along demographic and political lines. Only 30% of employees place great importance on so-called diversity in their workplace.[69] Rather than creating an inclusive workplace, DEI training at some companies generated controversies, alienated specific segments of employees, reinforced stereotypes, and worsened the division of the workforce.

Despite limited return on investment for their employers, DEI professionals have been generously compensated; the average salary of a DEI director in the United States is $201,770. Between 2022 and 2023, U.S. economic growth slowed down, mainly due to rising inflation and the Federal Reserve's series of interest rate hikes. Businesses have seen their revenues and profits drop significantly. For companies looking to cut costs, DEI-focused employees are an easy target because of their relatively high level of compensation while having little to show for it.

One of the most significant tide-turning events affecting how Americans view DEI was triggered by something that took place outside the United States. On October 7, 2023, Hamas terrorists attacked Israel, tortured and murdered more than 1,200 civilians, and kidnapped more than 250 hostages, including American citizens. In the wake of such a horrific event, some of the most appalling responses came from America's elitist universities.

More than 30 student groups at Harvard University issued a statement that holds "the Israeli regime entirely responsible for all unfolding violence." Students of other elite universities, including the New York University (NYU), quickly followed Harvard's lead with their statements that supported Hamas terrorists while condemning Israel. Even some professors at these prestigious universities also blamed Israel, and openly rejoiced over Hamas' so-called "resistance" on October 7, 2023.

Americans who hadn't paid close attention to universities' march to Marxism have been shocked to see privileged and ignorant American youth chant slogans such as "Long live the intifada; intifada, intifada; globalize the intifada" that call for the elimination of Israel, set up encampments on campus, harass Jewish students, including erecting barriers to prevent Jewish students from entering campus, and causing property damage including broken windows and slogans sprayed on walls. These student protestors' actions, the slogans they chanted, and the moral confusion they demonstrated reflected the CRT and DEI indoctrination they have received through our educational system from K–12 to college, as well as misinformation from social media such as TikTok.[70]

These student protestors support Hamas because they see the terrorist organization as representing the "oppressed." Thus, any action the "oppressed" takes, regardless of how outrageous and despicable, is justified. They publicly denounce countries such as the United States and Israel because they see these nations as oppressors, the very embodiment of capitalism, colonialism, and racism. Ironically, these students have behaved like typical "Champagne Marxists," who embrace Marxist ideas but can't live without the comforts afforded by capitalism. Student protesters at the "Gaza Solidarity Encampment" reportedly sustained their revolutionary zeal with various organic, vegan, and gluten-free food choices, including $12 croissants and $14 avocado toasts.[71] Despite a sign inside the encampment saying, "Resist colonial power by any means necessary," these Champagne Marxists couldn't give up their privileged lifestyle made possible by "colonial power."

It's not just the student protestors' behaviors that have left the American public dismayed. It's the fact that the adults in charge of these elite universities – the administrators and leaders – have failed in their duty to protect students and academic freedom. These adults have chosen to appease the instigators and let the lunatics run the asylum. These university leaders, who have been quick to issue strongly worded statements about every other so-called social justice incident in the past three years, have suddenly decided their institutions shouldn't take sides. They claim to be "neutral" and to let "free speech" flourish, even though these institutions have been known as some of the most hostile environments for free expression. Harvard University, for example, has consistently ranked poorly in the Foundation for Individual Rights in Education's (FIRE) College Free Speech Rankings. In 2023, Harvard ranked dead last, the only school with an "Abysmal" speech climate. It is a sad revelation how far elite colleges such as Harvard have fallen under the spell of the DEI and CRT ideology.

The student protestors' behaviors and leaders at these elite institutions' collective failure to condemn Hamas and antisemitism on college campuses have triggered a donor revolt, a powerful demonstration of the impact of collective action. Billionaire Marc Rowan, a significant donor to the University of Pennsylvania and the chief executive officer of Apollo Global Management, a prominent private equity firm with close to $600 billion in assets under management, urged fellow Penn alumni to "close their checkbooks" until the school's president, Elizabeth Magill, and the chairman of its board of trustees, Scott Bok, stepped down. Rowan blamed Magill and Bok for the school's history of failing to denounce antisemitism, even after the horror committed by Hamas became known.

Several mega-donors answered Rowan's call to action. David Magerman, a Venture Capital investor and significant donor to Penn, said, "I refuse to donate another dollar to Penn." Jon Huntsman, former governor of Utah and U.S. ambassador to China, notified Penn that the "university's silence in the face of reprehensible and historic Hamas evil against the people of Israel…is a new low. Consequently, the Huntsman Foundation will close its checkbook on all future giving to Penn."[72] One day later and a few billion dollars shorter, Penn's Magill issued a statement, claiming she and the university "condemn Hamas's terrorist assault on Israel and their violent atrocities against civilians" and stand "emphatically against antisemitism."

Larry Summers, a former economic official in the Obama and Clinton administrations and former president of Harvard, also criticized the "morally unconscionable" statements of Harvard students and slammed Harvard leaders for their responses. Israeli billionaire Idan Ofer and his wife, Batia, quit a Harvard executive board in protest of the university leaders' timid response to the Hamas terror attack on Israel on October 7. Former Victoria's Secret billionaire Leslie Wexner's foundation ended its relationship and financial support for Harvard University and Harvard's Kennedy School, stating its reason in a letter to the university's board of overseers: "We are stunned and sickened by the dismal failure of Harvard's leadership to take a clear and unequivocal stand against the barbaric murders of innocent Israeli civilians."[73]

On December 5, 2023, Harvard President Dr. Claudine Gay, Penn President Liz Magill, and MIT President Sally Kornbluth were grilled by the House of Representatives in a heated Congressional hearing. While all three presidents denounced Hamas and refuted antisemitism generally, they chose not to renounce or discipline students who called for the genocide of Jews and insisted that such speech was allowed. The most notorious exchange of the hearing was when Rep. Elise Stefanik (R–NY) repeatedly asked when student protestors' chants for Jewish genocide would constitute a violation of these universities' policies on bullying or harassment. Harvard's President Claudine Gay replied: "If the speech becomes conduct, it can be harassment." Rep. Stefanik shot back: "Conduct being committing the act of genocide?" All three presidents said the incidents were "context-based decisions."

The hearing was a disaster for the three university presidents. The calls for their resignations flooded in immediately after the hearing. Penn President Liz Magill quickly resigned. Harvard President Claudine Gay tried to apologize by saying she "failed to convey what is my truth," which wasn't an apology at all. Still, she refused to resign. Then journalists Christopher Rufo of the Manhattan Institute and Aaron Sibarium of *The Washington Free Beacon* reported the allegations of Gay committing plagiarism and provided evidence showing that several dozens passages of text from Gay's academic papers had been duplicated from other scholars' without citations.[74] Gay and the Harvard corporation initially denied the plagiarism charge. Still, new charges of plagiarism kept popping up. Gay announced her resignation in January 2024. She continues teaching at Harvard and retains her more than $900,000 yearly salary.

In May 2024, Cornell University President Martha Pollack announced her resignation.[75] Although she insisted her decision had nothing to do with claims that she inadequately handled anti-semitic demonstrations on campus, her resignation came after Jon Lindseth, a significant donor, threatened to withdraw his funds to Cornell unless Pollack quit. Major donors including Lindseth as well as some alumni criticized Pollack for allowing the DEI dogma "to infiltrate the curricula, [and Pollack] has not done enough to stop rampant antisemitism from festering on campus, and quashed intellectual diversity even while declaring Cornell a safe haven for free speech."[76]

Bari Weiss of the *Free Press* concluded that "nothing has made the dangers of the CRT and DEI more clear than what's happening these days on our college campuses—the places where our future leaders are nurtured."[77] She called for an end of DEI for good: "No more standing by as people are encouraged to segregate themselves. No more forced declarations that you will prioritize identity over excellence. No more compelled speech. No more going along with little lies for the sake of being polite."

Also, in May, MIT announced that it had ceased using diversity statements for faculty hiring. While several public universities in red states have already done the same, MIT was the first elite private college in a blue state to make such a move. MIT's embattled president, Sally Kornbluth, probably made the move to save her job.

More than one year after the U.S. Supreme Court struck down affirmative action in college admissions, MIT released its fall 2024 undergraduate student enrollment data. It showed the percentage of Black students enrolled dropped to 5% from 15%, and the percentage of Hispanic students dropped to 11% from 16%; the percentage of whites dropped to 37% from 38% last year, while the percentage of Asian American students rose to 47% from 40%.[78] This increase of Asian student enrollment is the latest evidence that race-based admissions indeed discriminated against Asian students. Stuart Schmill, MIT's dean of admissions, explained that the university followed the U.S. Supreme Court's affirmative action ban and didn't inquire as to applicants' race or ethnicity information this year (only from those enrolled). Furthermore, the court decision prompted the university to expand its recruitment and financial aid programs that prioritize low-income students from all backgrounds. MIT now looks for diversity through "prospective fields of study and areas of research, extracurricular activities, and accomplishments, as well as economic, geographic, and educational background."[79]

Harvard reported its fall 2024 undergraduate student enrollment data shows that students identifying as African American or Black dropped slightly from 18% last year to 14% for the class of 2028. The percentage of students identifying as Hispanic increased by 2%, while the percentage of students identifying as Asian American stayed the same.[80]

Responding to this latest enrollment data, Edward Blum said in an interview that "every student admitted...will know that they were accepted only based upon their outstanding academic and extracurricular achievements, not the color of their skin."[81]

Even the *New York Times*, a long-time cheerleader for DEI, turned on the ideology. In October 2024, the paper's education reporter, Nicholas Confessore, presented a lengthy investigative report on the University of Michigan's DEI initiative. Between 2016 and 2023, U-M spent nearly a quarter of a billion dollars building the largest DEI bureaucracy in any public university. The number of DEI staff has more than tripled in merely seven years, from 69 at the end of 2017 to 241 as of 2023. For the 2023–2024 school year, U-M's 241 DEI staff cost more than $30 million, enough to fund close to 1,700 in-state students' yearly tuition ($17,736 per student) at the university.

Despite the substantial investment, U-M's DEI initiative has not achieved its intended goals. The university remains far from being a diverse and inclusive institution. The percentage of Black students at the university has stagnated at a low 4–5%, a figure reminiscent of the 1970s, in a state where 14% of residents are Black. A 2022 university survey further revealed that students and faculty of all races and ethnicities "reported a less positive campus climate than at the program's start and less of a sense of belonging. Students were less likely to interact with people of a different race or religion or with different politics – the exact kind of engagement DEI programs, in theory, are meant to foster." The sentiment on campus is best captured by Confessore's observation that almost everyone he spoke to "rolled their eyes," showed "disdain" regarding U-M's DEI initiative, considering it "background noise, like the rote incantations of a state religion."[82]

More troubling was that the DEI bureaucracy helped fuel a culture of grievances at U-M, as "everyday campus complaints and academic disagreements are now cast as crises of inclusion and harm" by students and faculty.[83] "Complaints involving race, religion or national origin increased to almost 400 from a few dozen." A culture of fear accompanies U-M's culture of grievances. One of their regents, Mark Bernstein, admitted to the *Times* reporter that more and more students and professors whispered to him, "'I can't say anything in class anymore. I'm going to get run out of class.' There's an enormous amount of fear."[84] The *New York Times* report is likely to be the final nail in the coffin for DEI's programs on college campuses, leading to their demise.

The DEI ideology has also lost its shine with Corporate America as companies backed away from their DEI initiatives in droves.

Companies including Ford Motor, Deere, Harley-Davidson, and Lowe's announced in the summer of 2024 that they had withdrawn their major DEI initiatives. In an internal email, the distiller Brown-Forman Corp.'s executive leadership team explained that since the company launched its DEI initiatives in 2019, "the world has evolved, our business has changed, and the legal and external landscape has shifted dramatically, particularly within the United States." Therefore, the company declared that it would end "quantitative workforce and supplier diversity ambitions," also known as race-based hiring, contracting, and promotion.[85]

Of course, America still has a long way to go to repair the damage caused by CRT and DEI ideology. Still, the downfall of well-known racial grifters, the Supreme Court's ruling on affirmative action, the news of several states' bans on DEI bureaucracy in their state university systems, the resignations of several elite college presidents, and the reinstating of the SAT and ACT in college admissions are signs that the CRT and DEI ideology bubble has popped.

CHAPTER 8

• • •

Winning at the Ballot Box

Introduction

Asian Americans have advocated for equality for all, and not just in courtrooms through landmark cases. With the support of voters from other ethnic communities, Asian Americans have also become better at pushing back progressive policies at the ballot box in recent years. This chapter highlights a few examples, including the defeat of ballot measures bringing back affirmative action in Washington State and California and the campaigns that recalled San Francisco's progressive school board members and the city's district attorney, all of which have significantly impacted progressive policies that give racial preference in education and law enforcement.

8.1 Not Going Back

Even before 2020, the affirmative action landscape was significantly influenced by Asian Americans. In a remarkable twist, they made a significant impact by rejecting affirmative action at the ballot box in a traditionally liberal state.

In April 2019, Democrat legislators in Washington State approved Initiative 1000 (I-1000), also known as the Affirmative Action and Diversity Commission Measure. This initiative, which allowed the state to implement affirmative action policies for education and employment opportunities, sought to repeal Initiative 200 (I-200). I-200 was a measure co-sponsored by Mary Radcliffe, a Black State Representative who lived through discrimination in the South before the civil rights movement. Rep. Radcliffe's personal perspective, shaped by her experiences, led her to sponsor I-200 because she didn't want her race to be a factor in any part of her success. I-200 "prohibited public institutions from discriminating or granting preferential treatment based on race, sex, color, ethnicity, or national origin in the areas of public education, public employment, and public contracting."[1] Washington voters passed I-200 in 1998 with a wide margin, suggesting that people valued "the principal of equality for all, regardless of race as the foundation for civil rights law," according to radio show host John Carlson.[2]

Nearly two decades later, progressives wanted to bring affirmative action back. They claimed that I-1000 addressed concerns about how affirmative action had often resulted in quotas and preferential treatment in the past. They promised that I-1000 would allow "affirmative action without the use of quotas" and ban preferential treatment. But the devil was in the details. I-1000 only banned *preferential treatment* when "using one of the characteristics listed as the *sole factor* for selecting a lesser-qualified candidate over another" (emphasis added). In other words, as long as these characteristics are considered *along with* qualifications, preferential treatment of particular identity groups was allowed under I-1000. When evaluating a person for education or employment opportunities, I-

1000 allowed consideration of such factors as age, color, disability, ethnicity, national origin, race, sexual orientation, and veteran status. Other provisions of the initiative indicated preferential treatment based on these characteristics was necessary to achieve "goals and timetables, and other measures designed to increase Washington's diversity in public education, public employment, and public contracting." I-1000 was racial discrimination in disguise.

I-1000, with its demand for the creation of the Governor's Commission on Diversity, Equity, and Inclusion, raised significant concerns. How could a university or a government agency ensure compliance with I-1000 and meet its "diversity" goal and timetables without resorting to a quota system or giving preferential treatment based on identity? It was disingenuous for supporters of I-1000 to have claimed that this initiative would create equal opportunities for all Washingtonians. John Carlson, who led the campaign to pass Initiative 200, testified before the legislature against I-1000 because he believed it would abolish "equality for all regardless of race" as required by I-200 and replace it with a system using different rules for people of different races.[3] Such reverse discrimination in the name of equity was a cause for concern.

Yet, the state's public universities were among the loudest progressive subgroups supporting I-1000. After voters banned racial preferences in public education, public employment, and public contracting in 1998, public universities started recruiting more students from economically disadvantaged backgrounds or families where no one had ever attended college. Yet, the state had relatively small Black (3%) and Hispanic populations (7.5%), and not all of them struggle economically. Some of them are doing well financially. The effort to recruit more Blacks and Hispanics from economically disadvantaged backgrounds inadvertently led public universities to admit more Asian students because many of them not only have good grades but are also children of poor immigrant families and would be the first generation of their families to attend American colleges. As early as 2005, universities began to argue that Asian students were "overrepresented" by pointing to enrollment data of the University of Washington: Asians represented 28.5% of the UW student body in 2004 while being less than 6% of the state population in the same year.[4]

The universities lobbied hard to bring back racial preferences in admissions because they desperately wanted to reach their racial diversity goals, even if it meant admitting more middle-class Black and Hispanic students and fewer poor and eligible Asian students. These universities conveniently omitted that, based on their proportional representation theory, white students were also underrepresented during the same period. Even though 79% of the state population was white in 2000, whites only made up 54% of the UW student body that year. Yet, none of the state's public universities advocated admitting more white students. The universities' support for I-1000 and restoring racial preferences in college admissions was criticized because it is "not about the needs of students. It is about the needs of universities. It is about universities trying to meet their racial-diversity goals," said Bruce Ramsey, a member of *The Seattle Times'* editorial board.[5]

Many Asian Americans didn't take public universities' complaints of the "overrepresentation" of Asian students seriously until the state legislature passed I-1000, and public universities gave their enthusiastic endorsement. However, several Asian American organizations, in a display of remarkable determination, mobilized and publicly opposed the I-1000 initiative out of fear that Asian American youth might be denied their fair and equal chance for college admission under I-1000's ill-defined "diversity" goals. At one of the public hearings about I-1000, dozens of Asian Americans, most of whom were members of Washington Asians for Equality, showed up at the legislative building at 5 a.m., waiting for the door to open at 8 a.m. During the hearing, more than 300 Asian Americans packed both the hearing room and the overflow hearing room behind it. The Democratic-led state legislature passed I-1000 anyway. One Democrat state senator, Bob Hasegawa, even dared those who opposed I-1000 to collect enough signatures and turn their opposition into a ballot initiative in November.[6] Since

Democrats controlled both the legislature and the governor's mansion, they felt pretty confident in ignoring Asian Americans' concerns.

Washington Asians for Equality, the Asian American Coalition for Education, and the American Coalition for Equality have stood united in their condemnation of I-1000 as "a 21st-century Chinese Exclusion Act." Their unity and determination, reminiscent of the fight against the 1882 immigration act, were truly inspiring. In a press release, Yukong Zhao, president of the Asian American Coalition for Education, strongly condemned the passage of I-1000: "For all Washingtonians, I-1000 does nothing to promote true, long-lasting diversity or to address the root cause behind failing public education in many minority communities. This politically expedient yet impractically shortsighted act only exacerbates educational inequalities across the great state of Washington!"[7] Kan Qiu, president of the American Coalition for Equality, believed that I-1000 was a divisive law that targeted Asian Americans. His organization spearheaded Referendum 88, sending I-1000 to Washington voters for a final say in that November's election. To get on the ballot, supporters of Referendum 88 had only 90 days to collect 130,000 valid signatures. They organized a signature drive and sought donations through the "Let People Vote" PAC.

Asian Americans in the state raised more than $1 million, mainly from Asian business owners and tech employees, and collected and submitted more than 213,000 signatures. Their effort put Referendum 88 on the ballot. The November election result shocked the Democrat political establishment in the state: Referendum 88 passed, meaning I-1000 was defeated, and the majority of Washington voters rejected the Democrats' attempt to restore racial preferences. The victory, according to Christopher Rufo, a fellow at the Manhattan Institute, was not just a win, but a seismic shift in the political landscape. It was "the first successful minority-run referendum in state history – and [it has] proven that the progressive mantra of 'diversity and inclusion' isn't enough to win the support of all minority voters."[8]

Asian Americans, however, knew they couldn't rest after one election victory. Linda Yang, one of the leaders of the Let People Vote group, vowed to "keep a close eye on the development [of] any executive orders or legislative bills that would circumvent people's will."[9] Yang and other Asian Americans had good reason to stay vigilant because right after I-1000 was defeated at the ballot box, the state's Democratic governor Jay Inslee sought different ways to bring back affirmative action. He released a proposed supplemental operating budget to spend a significant $5.5 million on new diversity efforts, including $1 million to create an Office of Equity to help state agencies "reach their inclusion goals." The state assembly approved Gov. Inslee's budget, indicating the Democrats and their progressive allies wouldn't easily accept defeat at the ballot box. They always try to find ways to sidestep the voters' will and patiently wait for the next opportunity to get what they wish.

Less than a year after Asian Americans in Washington State defeated Democrats' attempt to bring back affirmative action, Asian Americans in California faced a similar challenge. The state's Democratic-led legislature put Proposition 16 on that year's ballot. Prop 16 was a measure that sought to restore affirmative action in the state, meaning "universities and government offices could factor in someone's race, gender or ethnicity in making hiring, spending and admissions decisions."

Prop 16 was the progressives' attempt to reintroduce affirmative action in California by trying to overturn Proposition 209, a California state constitution amendment enacted in 1996 that mandates that the state "shall not discriminate against, or grant preferential treatment to, any individual or group based on race, sex, color, ethnicity, or national origin in the operation of public employment, public education, or public contracting."

Ward Connerly, an African American and former UC regent, played a pivotal role in the 1996 Prop 209 campaign. Connerly's personal history, with his grandfather being a slave and his father living through the Jim Crow era, gave him a unique perspective on the issue. He once wrote, "I became a full American just after my 25th birthday, when the Civil Rights Act of 1964 became law."[10] He credited his success in life to the equality principle and prohibition of discrimination based on race, color, religion, sex, or national origin. Believing affirmative action had hurt rather than helped all minorities, Connerly led the effort for Californians to approve Prop 209 in 1996.

Prop 209 made California one of eight states that ban race-based affirmative action in all public universities.[11] Since its passage, the state's public universities, including the University of California (UC) system, could no longer consider an applicant's race in college admissions. However, private colleges such as Stanford University are not governed by Prop 209. Therefore, they could consider race and ethnicity as part of their admissions process.

Contrary to the predictions of progressives in California, the passage of Prop 209 did not lead to a decline in Black, Hispanic, and Native American students' enrollment in public universities. In fact, a study by Charles L. Geshekter, a professor of African history at California State University–Chico, found that "Proposition 209 in no way hindered the progress of minorities and women in public employment. Predictions about a future deterioration of labor market positions for women and minorities proved utterly unfounded... No campus ever became remotely 'lily white' or 'resegregated.'"[12] Within a decade after the passage of Prop 209, minority students' enrollment in the UC system had steadily increased to a point where "non-white ethnic minorities constituted over 60% of all freshmen and transfers at the University of California." The trend continued in 2020, with only 21% of the UC system's 2020 freshman class being white students. The rest are minorities, including 36% Hispanics, 35% Asians, and 5% Blacks. American Indians, Pacific Islanders, and other unidentified groups comprise about 3%. This success story is a testament to the potential and resilience of minority students. Additionally, "about 44% of admitted students were low-income while 45% were the first in their families to attend a four-year university."[13]

Minority students' graduation rates had also improved since Prop 209 went into effect. Richard Sander, a University of California at Los Angeles law professor, found "a 55% increase in the number of Black and Hispanic freshmen who graduated in four years and a 51% rise in Black and Hispanic students who earned degrees in science, technology, engineering, and math." According to Geshekter, the improvement in minority students' graduation rates in the UC system is a direct benefit of Prop 209: "The elimination of ethnic preferences and the prohibition against racial double standards in admissions led to a redistribution of students among the ten-campus system," so minority students achieved better academic success when they attended a UC campus that "offered an apparently better match for their academic backgrounds and preparation."

These remarkable achievements should have indicated to progressives that disparities in outcomes are not proof of discrimination. Yet, progressives paid no heed to all empirical evidence. Rather than celebrating these minority students' achievements, the progressives insisted that Prop 209 was a failed experiment that had hurt minorities in California despite the evidence to the contrary. The progressives took advantage of the nationwide racial justice movement in the summer of 2020 to overturn the state's constitutional ban on affirmative action. They argued that some level of racial discrimination was necessary to level the playing field and fight institutional racism. As illogical as their argument may sound, more than two thirds of California's Democratic legislators voted to put Prop 16 on the November ballot, believing the initiative would easily pass in a year of racial reckoning.

The "Yes on 16'" campaign was backed by a formidable political coalition, including the state's Democratic Party and party establishment, Gov. Gavin Newsom, and national figures including then House Speaker Nancy Pelosi, Sen. Kamala Harris, and Sen. Bernie Sanders. The endorsement of progressive tech millionaires of Silicon Valley, all leftist media, higher education institutions, and other progressive organizations further bolstered the campaign.

With a substantial war chest of more than $31 million, including contributions from high-profile figures like Los Angeles Clippers owner Steve Ballmer and Patricia Quillin, wife of Netflix Inc. Chief Executive Reed Hastings, the "Yes" campaign was a force to be reckoned with.

In contrast, the "No on Prop 16" campaign was a grassroots effort. It was led by Ward Connerly, the 81-year-old Black civil rights veteran who led the passage of Prop 209 in 1996. The "No" campaign raised only a little over $1.6 million, mostly from small donations. However, the "no" camp had more voter support, especially from Asian Americans, a significant demographic in California's political landscape.

Various Asian American civil organizations, from the Asian American Legal Foundation to the Panda Kung Fu Center, formed a broad-based coalition to oppose Prop 16. According to Wenyuan Wu of the Asian-American Coalition for Education, the coalition was primarily mobilized by the fear that if Prop 16 passed "Asian-American students will be further scapegoated and penalized in college admissions."[14] Many first-generation Asian immigrants who had achieved their share of the American Dream through education attainment and hard work also believed that racial preferences in college admissions were inherently unfair, violating one of the core values that has made America great: that everyone is equal before the law. These Asian parents had been telling their children that anyone can make it in America, the land of opportunity, if they work hard. And yet, they felt betrayed when their children had to face the "Asian penalty" when pursuing higher education.

The battle between "No" and "Yes" on Prop 16 was a battle between grassroots vs. the establishment and David vs. Goliath. Still, when the "Yes on Prop 16" campaign learned it had lackluster voter support, it resorted to shameless attack ads, accusing anyone who opposed Prop 16 of being either racist or a woman hater, or calling the "No on Prop 16" campaign a white supremacist effort.[15] The name-calling was comical because the "No" camp, from leadership to volunteers, was a united front, racially and ethnically diverse.

On election day, a significant majority of Californian voters, about 57.2% (or 9.65 million), cast their ballots against Prop 16. The margin of victory was even more pronounced than that of Prop 209 in 1996, indicating a more decisive rejection of affirmative action in 2020. This victory underscores a crucial point in the most progressive state in America: the majority of voters uphold the principle of equality before the law. They believe that individuals should not be treated differently based on attributes such as race or ethnicity, characteristics over which they have no control.

Many Asian Americans regarded the defeat of Prop 16 as a "resounding victory for equality under the law." [16] Still, Asian Americans knew that the Democrats and their progressive allies were relentless and would try to restore affirmative action. Therefore, some Asian American veterans of the "No" campaign went on to create the Californians for Equal Rights Foundation (CFER), a non-profit 501(c)(3) organization. CFER was established with the mission to "safeguard and build awareness on the causes of equal rights and merit through policy monitoring, voter education, legal advocacy, rigorous research, alliance building, and media outreach." [17] This foundation plays a crucial role in advocating for equal rights and merit-based policies in California, particularly in the context of the ongoing debate about affirmative action.

California's Democratic legislators did not accept defeat gracefully, respect voters' votes, and shift their energy and resources to other pressing issues. Instead, they couldn't take "no" for an answer. It took three years for the Democrats in California to make another end run around the state constitution with a third attempt to restore affirmative action. In February 2023, Assemblyman Corey A. Jackson, D–Perris, introduced Assembly Constitution Amendment 7, or "ACA7." The bill would amend Prop 209 by authorizing the governor of California "to issue waivers to public entities that wish to use state funds for evidence-based or research-informed and culturally specific programs to increase life expectancy, improve educational outcomes, and lift specific ethnic groups and marginalized genders out of poverty." However, ACA7 was not just a sly attempt to gut Prop 209; it was a potential threat that could have made discrimination legal again in California. No wonder supporters referred to ACA7 as a "skinnier" affirmative action measure. Fellow Assemblyman Bill Essayli, R–Corona, voiced his objection to ACA7. He stated, "We need to be treating each other equally, with dignity and respect, and stop the division." Rather than debating Assemblyman Essayli on the merits of ACA7, Assemblyman Jackson resorted to name-calling, referring to Essayli, the first Muslim member of the California Assembly, as a "white supremacist."

Thankfully, Asian American activists and volunteers from the "No to Prop 16" campaigns quickly mobilized to prevent ACA7 from making it to the election-year ballot. They started the "NoACA7" campaign on social media and organized letter-writing campaigns by sending letters to Democratic leadership in the state assembly and voicing their objections to ACA7; they showed up at ACA7 hearings and gave testimony. Although ACA7 passed the state House, it was held up at the State Senate. Gail Heriot, a U.S. Commission on Civil Rights commissioner and a veteran of the "No on Prop 16" campaign, started a "No on ACA7" petition at Change.org, aiming to send a powerful message to the Senate: ACA7 is a bad idea, and senators should respect voters' wishes by not moving the bill forward. "In a state as diverse as California, it is all the more important that the government be prohibited from engaging in preferential treatment," Heriot said. The "NoACA7" campaign worked. In the early summer of 2024, Assemblyman Corey A. Jackson, the leading sponsor of ACA7, withdrew his bill, although he did vow to try it again. This victory was not just a relief for California's voters. It is also a beacon of hope for the future, signaling the possibility that California voters won't have to endure another expensive legal battle on the same issue again. But it's also a chilling reminder that voters must remain vigilant because ensuring equality under the law is a never-ending battle.

8.2 Recall San Francisco's Progressive School Board

In the fall of 2020, the San Francisco school board voted to eliminate the academic performance-based component of the admissions process to Lowell High School, one of the best high schools in the city. It is important to note that Lowell's admissions process wasn't 100% merit-based prior to 2020 due to previous lawsuits.

The case, *San Francisco NAACP v. San Francisco Unified School District*, and the 1983 Consent Decree settlement forced Lowell to adjust its merit-based admissions policy by limiting the percentage of students from a particular ethnic group that could enroll at Lowell. Lowell further watered down its merit-based admissions process in 1997 by dividing its applicants into two pools: One, which would make up 80% of the entering class, would require a minimum entrance score for all students regardless of race. The other 20% of students would come from the so-called "value-added diversity pool." These students could enter Lowell with lower entrance scores because they would gain extra points for socioeconomic factors, such as residence in public housing, eligibility for free or reduced school lunches, and other criteria, such as involvement in extracurricular activities. Students admitted from this "value-added diversity pool" are required to attend a summer school program to get them academically ready for Lowell's demanding courses. These admissions policy changes from 1983 and 1997 put an undue burden on Asian students, especially Chinese American students, who must score higher than any other ethnic group because Chinese American students represent a "disproportionate" share of students meeting the school's requirements.

In 2020, responding to a nationwide racial reckoning, the progressive San Francisco Unified School District (SFUSD) board decided to cancel Lowell's remaining academic-based admissions policy. School board president López declared grades and test scores were "biased towards Whites and Asians," even though non-white students made up 75% of Lowell's student body. Another school board member, Allison Collins, posted a series of tweets on X.com (formerly known as Twitter), claiming "'merit' is an inherently racist construct designed and centered on white supremacist framing."[18] Later, people uncovered some racially charged tweets by Collins from 2016, in which she blamed Asian Americans for using "white supremacist thinking to assimilate and 'get ahead'."[19] Collins's anti-Asian social media postings drew widespread criticism, especially from the Asian American community in San Francisco. The controversy surrounding these statements and actions should be a point of scrutiny by all those involved in shaping education policy and promoting racial equity. Yet, Collins refused to resign. She offered only a half-hearted apology, which caused further outrage in the local Asian American community.

The school board's decision to cancel Lowell's merit-based admissions came at a time when San Francisco's Asian American community's dissatisfaction with the school board was already strong. First and foremost, parents were upset about the prolonged pandemic school closure that resulted in learning loss and harm to children's mental health. By the spring of 2021, the city's public schools remained closed while 16,000 students had returned to the city's 113 private, independent, and parochial schools. Furthermore, the school board hadn't offered a clear plan of when and how it would reopen schools. Even the Democrat-led city government of San Francisco had had enough with the board. It filed a lawsuit against both the SFUSD and its board in February 2021, accusing them of "failing to come up with a reopening plan even as numerous other schools across the U.S. have reopened."[20] Yet, Board President López claimed the long delays didn't cause any learning loss because children were "just having different learning experiences than the ones we currently measure." They learned more "about their families and cultures by staying home."[21] Her tone-deaf comments angered many parents who had witnessed their kids' academic and emotional struggles at home due to the school closures. Still, the school board waited until fall 2021 to return to full-time in-person K–12 learning.

Parents were also upset that the school board had focused more on virtue signaling and progressive identity politics than educating children. The school board had done everything it could to lower educational standards and hold students back, including its attempt to gut Advanced Placement (AP) classes and dumb down math education in the K–12 system. These decisions led to a decline in academic performance, with nine public schools in San Francisco ranking in the bottom five percent of statewide schools. In 2019, the board voted to cover a mural depicting slavery and Native Americans at George Washington High School, a decision that would cost taxpayers between $600,000 and $1 million. Fortunately, the mural stayed after a San Francisco Superior Court judge overturned the school board's decision. In January 2021, the board voted to rename 44 schools, including Abraham Lincoln and George Washington High Schools, rather than developing a plan to reopen schools. Facing nationwide backlash over the renaming controversy, the school board voted to reverse its school renaming plan in April. Even Democrat Mayor London Breed expressed her disbelief, saying, "I can't understand why the school board is advancing a plan to rename all these schools when there isn't a plan to have kids back in those physical schools."[22] The editor of the "Eyes on SF Board of Education" newsletter, Laurance Lee, pointed out that many fed-up parents had pulled their kids out of the city's public schools. Consequently, the enrollment had fallen so much that the school district faced a $125 million budget deficit.

The school board's decision to eliminate merit-based admissions at Lowell High School entirely became the last straw for the city's Asian American residents. Bayard Fong, a long-time human rights activist, has two kids who graduated from Lowell. He and other Asian parents were concerned that fewer qualified Asian students, especially those from poorer immigrant families, would be admitted to Lowell without merit-based admissions. Collins's anti-Asian social media posts from 2016 only added fuel to the fire. The Asian American community's dissatisfaction with the school board finally reached a boiling point. They launched a recall campaign in January

2021, the city's first one since 1983, showing their determination to hold the school board accountable. The recall campaign aimed to recall the three longest-serving board members most responsible for the school board's bad policies: the school board's president, Gabriela López, and Commissioners Faauuga Moliga and Alison Collins, all registered Democrats.

Siva Raj, the co-founder of the recall campaign and a Democrat, said the recall campaign's initial goal was to get the school board to reopen schools. But it didn't take long for him and others to realize they were a bit naïve. He explained in an interview that he and other parents realized that "the priorities of the school board were just so disconnected... In San Francisco, it shocked us that not only were they not prioritizing the return [reopening of schools]; they were actively pushing parents away, and they were not listening to parents at all."[23] This disconnect from the community's concerns and needs was a major factor in the recall campaign.

Collins, López, and Moliga defended their records by insisting that they were elected to the school board to prioritize racial equity. In a campaign mailer to voters to protect her seat, SFUSD board member Collins identified the top three accomplishments of the board in the past few years, including "SFUSD becoming an Arts Equity District, reorganizing resources to ensure all four h [sic] and 5th-grade students received music instruction through the pandemic" and "Official reparations to the Native American / Native Alaskan communities, and for Board meetings to begin with acknowledgment that our district stands on unceded Ramaytush Ohlone land."[24] None of Collins's "accomplishments" was related to the school board's primary responsibility to ensure all kids receive a quality education, leaving the audience feeling disappointed in the board's misplaced priorities.

These three progressive board members facing recall did have their supporters. One of them was a group called "San Francisco Berniecrats," Democrat supporters of socialist Vermont Sen. Bernie Sanders' 2016 presidential campaign. Hoping to preserve the three members' seats, Berniecrats resorted to misinformation and intimidation. One of their members created a spider web meme, which demeaned the recall campaign as a deep-pocket, right-wing, anti-racist conspiracy movement. The same Berniecrat also doxed the home address of Garry Tan, a vocal supporter of the recall movement and father of two children. The Berniecrat's dirty tricks only fueled Asian Americans' determination in the recall campaign.

The recall campaign was further boosted with endorsements from some of the city's Democratic leaders, including Mayor London Breed. Matt Gonzalez, former president of the San Francisco Board of Supervisors and chief attorney in the San Francisco Public Defender's Office, also backed the recall effort. In an article for *Medium*, Gonzalez wrote, "Opponents of the recall are attempting to label all recalls as Republican-inspired. This may be a good tactical election ploy, but it isn't anywhere near the truth." Gonzalez noted that the parents who started the recall campaigns were Democrats, and most of those who signed the recall petitions were registered Democrats. In terms of funding, Gonzalez pointed out that "over 80% of the individuals contributing to the recall are San Franciscan residents, while opponents of the recall are getting over half of their contributions from outside the city."[25] Therefore, the three school board members and their supporters' claim that the recall campaign was financed by outside Republican groups was misinformation.

The recall campaign was a grassroots movement led by Asian Americans, many of whom were lifelong Democrats. Some were first-generation immigrants who had never been politically active until 2021. I had the opportunity to interview three of them. One of them was Kit Lam, an immigrant from Hong Kong and a father of two children in the SFUSD. Lam, who had worked for the school district for 12 years as a fraud investigator, was deeply affected by the closure of schools during the COVID-19 pandemic. His son, a 10th grader, became withdrawn and struggled academically and emotionally. This was a common experience among many students, and Lam was determined to "save these kids' lives."

Never interested in politics before, Lam joined the recall campaign and became the most recognized face in the local Asian American community. During the early days, the recall campaign had no money and only volunteers like him. He often rode his bike in San Francisco's Chinatown as a living campaign billboard, with "Yes to Recall" campaign signs pinned to the front of his bike and the back of his shirt. Lam went on numerous radio shows to explain the recall campaign to Asian voters. After his first radio interview, a Chinese immigrant donated $25 and signed up as a volunteer. From such humble beginnings, the recall campaign gradually built momentum. To get the recall on the ballot, recall supporters had 160 days to collect signatures from 10% of registered voters in the city, or 51,325 per board member. The COVID-19-related lockdowns made collecting signatures extra challenging. Still, with an immigrants' perseverance and work ethic, Lam and others collected more than 70,000 signature petitions for each of the three school board members to put the recall on the ballot, a significant achievement that resonated deeply within the Asian American community.

Allene Jue was another campaign volunteer and a daughter of Chinese immigrants. From when Jue was born until she was six, her family of four crammed into single-room occupancy (SRO) housing in Chinatown. SROs are one-room housing units, typically less than 100 square feet. Online photos show an SRO unit that is so small that it barely fits a bed and a small table. All occupants on the same floor shared a communal kitchen and bathroom. So, occupants on the same floor had to wait for their turn to cook a meal or take a shower. SROs are usually where low-income seniors, blue-collar workers, and new immigrants call home. As of 2022, about 15,000 Chinatown residents still live in SROs. Most of them are either low-income seniors or new immigrants.

When Jue's family of four lived in an SRO unit, Jue's dad worked as a cook, and her mom had multiple jobs, including being a hotel housekeeper. They spoke limited English and couldn't help Jue with her homework, nor could they offer her any advice on applying for college in the U.S. Jue passed a competitive entrance exam and enrolled in Lowell High School. She credited Lowell for providing her with an excellent education and plenty of support for college applications. Today, Jue is an executive at a fintech company. She learned from experience that a good education could open many doors and change an immigrant family's fortune within one generation. She believes replacing Lowell's academic-based admissions process with a lottery system would take away opportunities from qualified Asian students from low-income families like hers. Never interested in anything political in the past, Jue had been busy getting signatures, stuffing envelopes, and delivering signs for the recall campaign. She said she would pay more attention to political issues from now on.

Figure 2. Asian American volunteers for the San Francisco School Board Recall Campaign (courtesy Kit Lam)

Garry Tan, the CEO of startup incubator Y Combinator, was a well-known figure in the recall campaign. His family immigrated from Southeast Asia to Canada and the United States. Tan grew up poor. His dad "was often out of work struggling with alcoholism," and his mother "worked the night shift at the convalescent home." Tan remembered growing up, "Dinner sometimes was expired bread from the nursing home dipped in milk." Tan also wrote on

Twitter, "At age 14, I cold-called the Yellow Pages to get my first web dev job, so our family could put a down payment on a first home."[26] Like so many immigrants, Tan found his way out of poverty through education and hard work. He took AP math classes at the city's public school and studied hard. He co-founded the San Francisco–based venture capital firm Initialized Capital, with more than $700 million in assets under management.

Like many Asian residents in the city, Tan ignored politics until this recall campaign. As a parent himself, Tan shared many griev-ances that other parents had with the city's school board. In addi-tion, he was deeply concerned about the school board's attempt to gut AP classes and dumb down math education in the K–12 system. He warned his fellow Californians in a social media post: "If you don't take action now, an entire Californian generation of STEM researchers, scientists, and engineers will have never existed."[27] Tan used his wealth and influence to support the recall campaign. The school board members and their supporters tried to demonize Tan as some "right-wing" billionaire, an accusation that couldn't be further from the truth since Tan had been a lifelong Democrat. After Tan's home address was doxed by the Berniecrats, Tan told me he wouldn't be silenced by such intimidation.

Kit Lam, Allene Jue, and Garry Tan's transition from passive political observers to energetic political activists reflects both the challenge and opportunity. The challenge is that even though Asian Americans have a long history in the U.S. and a long record of civil and political engagement, the majority of Asian Americans, or about 57 percent, including more than two thirds of Asian Ameri-can adults, are first-generation immigrants.[28] Most of these new immigrants came from cultural and political environments where political activism is discouraged. However, the key to overcoming this challenge is motivation. As Kit Lam, Allene Jue, and Garry Tan demonstrated, these first-generation Asian immigrants can become politically active if they are motivated by a particular issue that resonates with them. This underscores the importance of personal motivation in driving political engagement.

February 15, 2022, was the Lantern Festival, the last day of the Chinese Lunar New Year Celebration. It also marked a new beginning for Asian Americans in San Francisco because it was an election day. San Francisco's residents finally got to vote on the ballot initiative to recall the city's three school board members. I went to San Francisco's Chinatown. On the sidewalk on Stockton Street, next to a busy bus stop, the sound of gongs and drums filled the air as a last-minute effort to drum up support for the recall campaign was in full swing, courtesy of three recall campaign volunteers: Bayard Fong, Laurance Lee, and Kit Lam. All three gentlemen are fathers, long-time San Francisco residents, and dedicated volunteers for the "Yes" to recall campaign.[29] They reminded every Asian shopper passing by to vote "Yes" for the recall. Fong, who had taken a personal day off for this, shared that he was determined to see the recall through, having found a new sense of purpose, and that he could no longer remain silent.

The recall result, a pivotal moment that unfolded close to midnight, saw an overwhelming majority of San Francisco voters choosing to oust the three school board members. This was a historic moment, marking the city's first successful recall election in living memory. Even in the most progressive city in America, the board members' performative racial-equity and social-justice policies and actions had crossed a line. An elated Kit Lam texted at 2 a.m.: "The people at San Franciso have spoken. This is democracy in action." The success of the San Francisco recall campaign drew national attention. The impact of the recall campaign on Asian Americans, especially those new immigrants' political engagement, was profound, ushering in a fresh wave of political awakening for another generation of Asian Americans and inspiring them to enthusiastically participate in the democratic process.

8.3. Recall San Francisco's Progressive DA

Following the successful recall election in February 2022, the Asian American community in San Francisco emerged as a potent

force in the city's political landscape. This momentum was demonstrated in the recall effort against the city's District Attorney, Chesa
Boudin, a few months later in June 2022.

The roots of Boudin's radical left-wing ideology can be traced
back to his parents, David Gilbert and Kathy Boudin, who were
members of the domestic terror group the Weather Underground.
Their involvement in the infamous 1981 Brink's robbery case,
which resulted in the deaths of two police officers and a guard, led
to their arrest and lengthy jail terms. Boudin, who was just 14
months old at the time, was raised by leaders of the Weather
Underground. These formative experiences significantly influenced
his worldview. Before establishing himself in San Francisco, he
spent nearly a decade in South America, where he served as a trans-
lator for late Venezuelan President Hugo Chavez, among other
roles.

When Boudin ran for the DA position in San Francisco in 2019,
he was very public about how his parents' experiences had helped
shape his view on the criminal justice system, which he called an
"inhuman system." He ran on a platform of a series of progressive
positions, including ending "mass incarceration," eliminating cash
bail, focusing on police misconduct and racial bias, refusing to
cooperate with Immigration and Customs Enforcement, or ICE, as
well as prosecuting ICE agents who violated so-called sanctuary
city laws. No wonder socialist Sen. Bernie Sanders (D–VT)
endorsed Boudin's campaign for DA of San Francisco. The 2019
race to become the DA of San Francisco was tight. Boudin won his
bid for DA in November 2019 with a narrow margin, thanks to the
city's Asian American voters, whose support was crucial in his
victory.

Boudin was part of the national wave of progressive candidates
with similar views who became DAs of some of America's largest
cities between 2019 and 2021. Then U.S. Attorney General Bill
Barr warned that these progressive DAs, including Boudin, who
"style themselves as 'social justice' reformers, who spend their time
undercutting the police, letting criminals off the hook and refusing

to enforce the law, [are] demoralizing to law enforcement and dangerous to public safety."[30] Unfortunately, Barr's warning quickly came true.

As discussed before, 2020 was a transformative year by many measures, but not always in a good way. Many people, especially young people, became reckless after enduring lockdowns and extended school closures during the COVID-19 pandemic. The tragic death of George Floyd unleashed a national racial reckoning, and one of the most-affected areas was the criminal justice system. "Defund the police" became more than a rallying cry of the racial justice movement. Many cities and states cut funding to the police force, laid off police, and redistributed law enforcement money to community programs such as housing and mental health programs. By one estimate, the "defund police" movement resulted in more than $840 million in direct cuts from U.S. police departments and at least $160 million of investments in community services in 2020.[31] For example, San Francisco officials pledged in 2020 to divest $120 million from police over two years with plans to invest in health programs and workforce training. The "defund police" movement seriously damaged the morale of the police force, leading to a significant number of early retirements and resignations. This loss of experienced officers has had a profound impact on the ability of the police to effectively serve and protect their communities.

When police retreated, criminal activities increased. During the holiday season of 2020, Democrat-run cities such as Chicago, San Francisco, and Washington, D.C., became the epicenters of "smash and grab" robberies. These robberies usually involved a large group of criminals targeting high-end stores, such as Nordstrom and Louis Vuitton, and making off with thousands of dollars' worth of luxury goods. They were a stark manifestation of the lawlessness that ensues in the absence of effective policing. The "smash and grab" robberies quickly spread from upscale stores to places like Walgreens and CVS. Since neither cops nor the stores' security guards were willing or ordered not to intervene, the stores began to lock everyday items such as shampoo and toothpaste behind plexi-glass.

The FBI crime data for 2020 show murders surged 25% – the most significant single-year increase since 1960. The Major Cities Chiefs Association reports that "63 of the 66 largest police juris-dictions saw increases in at least one category of violent crimes in 2020, which include homicide, rape, robbery, and aggravated assault."[32] The city of Milwaukee saw a 98% increase in murders as the city laid off 120 police officers in 2020. After Portland's Demo-cratic Mayor Ted Wheeler defunded the city's police department by $12 million and slashed three police units, murders increased 255%, and shootings jumped 173% in 2020. These alarming statistics underscore the direct role of the "defund the police" movement in the surge of violent crimes, calling for a reevaluation of our approach to public safety and the accountability of our leaders.

The number of violent crimes in major cities continued to rise in 2021 and victimized people of all skin colors, including Asian Americans. Additionally, since COVID-19 originated in China, many Asian Americans found themselves being increasingly target-ed for hate crimes as well, as some people expressed their frustra-tion and resentment by attacking Asians.[33] Yet, the Democrats and liberal legacy media seemed only to be interested in anti-Asian crimes if the perpetrator was white. The 2021 mass shooting in Atlanta, Georgia, that took the lives of eight people, including six Asian women, received wall-to-wall coverage. Since the perpetrator was white, Democrats and legacy media seized the Georgia case and insisted that the rising crimes against Asian Americans resulted from "white supremacy" and President Trump's rhetoric on the coronavirus. Meanwhile, the rape and murder of Ee Lee in Milwaukee, Wisconsin, that same year got little media coverage and Democrats' attention, probably because the perpetrators were Blacks, and thus, the case didn't conform to the desired political narrative.

Although the New York Police Department (NYPD) established an Asian Hate Crime task force in August 2020, the city's anti-

Asian hate crimes continued to increase. In 2021 alone, the NYPD disclosed that anti-Asian hate crimes increased by more than 300% compared to the previous year, and the majority of the perpetrators were nonwhite. For example, more than a third of the reported subway bias incidents targeted Asians. Asian victims were beaten, pushed in front of oncoming trains, spit on, and were the target of racial slurs. One of the worst cases took place on January 15, 2022; Michelle Go – an MBA graduate of NYU's prestigious Stern School of Business – was waiting for the subway at the Times Square station, and a nonwhite homeless man pushed her in front of an oncoming train. Go was killed instantly. However, the NYPD didn't classify Go as a victim of a hate crime, a decision that outraged the city's Asian community. During a candlelight vigil for Go, Asian community members demanded the town form a dedicated team, independent of the NYPD, to investigate anti-Asian hate crimes, hoping to significantly improve the investigation and prosecution of these crimes and provide the Asian American community with the justice and protection they deserve. Unfortunately, the mayor's office never responded.

San Francisco was another epicenter where crimes involving Asian victims rose sharply. The city's Asian residents blamed DA Chesa Boudin's "soft on crime" approach, which they argued often resulted in repeat offenders being set free, leading to an increase in heinous crimes.

On November 2, 2019, while Anh Lê, a 69-year-old Vietnamese American, was out for a walk in Chinatown, he was viciously attacked by the Tanners, a father-and-son duo, with a baseball bat. It was later revealed that the Tanners had targeted other Asian Americans in Chinatown on the same day. Despite the SFPD's prompt arrest of the Tanners, Chesa Boudin's DA office refused to prosecute the Tanners with hate-crime enhancements. Instead, they offered Tanner Sr. a lenient plea deal, with a misdemeanor battery charge for no jail time and only a year of probation. The DA's office didn't inform Lê about the plea deal, nor did they provide Lê an opportunity to submit a victim impact statement during the proceedings. Lê said he spent months trying to correct a Criminal Protective Order (CPO) that omitted Lê's last name and misstated his age. The DA's office ignored his requests and allegedly told him at one point that he had no right to be at hearings. Many in the community were upset by the DA's office's callous treatment of the victims.

Besides suffering physical injury, Lê said the incident had left him with post-traumatic stress disorder (PTSD), and he had to spend 52 weeks in psychiatric therapy. With the assistance of King & Spalding LLP, a member of the Alliance for Asian American Justice, Lê sued the District Attorney's Office under the Fourteenth Amendment. This amendment was invoked to accuse the office of "applying procedures that resulted in discriminatory effects on Asian Americans and creating practices that deny victims adequate due process protections."[34]

Lê was only one of many victims harmed by career criminals Boudin set free. On New Year's Eve of 2020 in downtown San Francisco, 27-year-old Hanako Abe and 60-year-old Elizabeth Platt were killed by Troy McAlister, who was trying to get away after committing a robbery when his car hit and killed both women, who were waiting to cross the street. Even though McAlister had a 25-year criminal record, DA Boudin brokered a deal and let McAlister go on parole in March 2020. San Francisco–based writer and citizen journalist Susan Reynolds found out that since being paroled, McAlister "had been arrested five times for crimes, including burglary, possession of burglary tools, vehicle theft, possession of stolen property, possession of narcotics for sale, possession of suspected methamphetamine, possession of drug paraphernalia, and, of course, parole violations." But thanks to Boudin's soft-on-crime approach, McAlister "served a combined 11 days in jail" for those five arrests.[35]

Convinced that their daughter's tragic death was entirely avoidable, Abe's parents took legal action against San Francisco and Boudin. In an interview, Abe's mother expressed her disbelief, saying, "San Francisco needs to change so that Hanako's death is not wasted... I don't understand why criminals are being protected in San Francisco. Inhumane but progressive? Is anyone responsible for Hanako's death?"[36]

In 2021, the number of crimes targeting Asians in the Bay area increased an astonishing 567% from the year before. Asian-owned businesses in Chinatown struggled with frequent robbery and vandalism. Video clips of Asian Americans, especially seniors, being pushed, kicked, and robbed when walking out of a bank, strolling down the street, or sleeping at home at night made many feel unsafe. Here are a few examples:

- San Francisco, January 28, 2021, 84-year-old Vicha Ratanapakdee, an immigrant from Thailand, was violently pushed and killed by Antoine Watson while walking outside his house.
- Oakland, February 10, 2021, in broad daylight, two young men attacked a 71-year-old Asian lady by knocking her to the ground before yanking her purse so hard the strap broke off. The woman was bruised.
- San Francisco, February 23, 2021, three people robbed and cruelly beat up a 67-year-old Asian American man in a laundromat. The suspects were arrested. They were wanted in connection with multiple auto burglaries in the area.

The family of 84-year-old Vicha Ratanapakdee was outraged after Boudin excused Ratanapakdee's murderer, Antoine Watson, for having "some sort of temper tantrum" when he committed the shocking crime. Boudin refused to retract his words or offer any public apology to Ratanapakdee's family. City residents accused Boudin of continuing to demonstrate more sympathy for the perpetrators who committed monstrous crimes than the victims of the crimes.

In addition to rising violent crime, San Francisco residents were sick and tired of widespread drug problems. However, Boudin refused to prosecute drug dealers, many of whom were illegal migrants from Honduras. Property thefts were rampant. During the Christmas shopping season, the open smash-and-grab robberies of luxury stores in downtown San Francisco shocked the nation. Small business owners said their businesses had been victims of such out-of-control robberies under Boudin's watch all too often. Yet, Boudin's office was lenient toward those who committed property crimes repeatedly.

For instance, the DA office offered a plea deal to Nathan Picco and dismissed most of the charges against him, even though he was a serial burglar convicted of 15 burglaries and theft-related felonies from 2002 to 2019. In a statement, Boudin's office explained that "the plea deal's agreed-upon sentence was that Mr. Picco receives credit for the days he spent in jail on this case, take part in a residential treatment program, and be placed on two years' probation." [37] Boudin's lenience only emboldened Picco to commit burglary against seven businesses in eight months, a clear violation of both the law and his probation agreement. But according to Boudin's office, Picco "will be issued stay-away orders, orders for restitution for all the burglaries, and be placed on electronic monitoring once he is placed in the [residential treatment] program." Only "if he fails to comply with any of the terms of his release, Picco faces up to five years and eight months in county jail."[38] In other words, the DA's office would continue to treat career criminals such as Picco with kid gloves, a practice that clearly lacked deterrence and only encouraged further criminal behavior. Property owners be damned.

Under Boudin, the percentage of shoplifting resulting in arrests dropped from 40% in 2019 to only 19% in 2021. The charging rate for theft by Boudin's office declined from 62% in 2019 to 46% in 2021; petty theft fell from 58% to 35%. San Francisco's jail population had plummeted to 766 in 2021 from 2,850 in 2019. No wonder nearly half of the retail stores in Downtown Union Square had been closed since 2019.

I took a stroll in downtown San Francisco in early 2022, and it was a jarring experience. The city's deterioration was shocking. Drug dealers operated openly, and the sidewalks were strewn with homeless tents, human waste, used needles, and all manner of refuse. The stench was overpowering, and the sight of people passed out on the streets was distressing. It was a city in decay, worse than a garbage dump. When I stopped at a Walgreens to buy a pack of gum, I was surprised to find that everyday items from toothbrushes to gum were locked behind plexiglass due to rampant robbery.

San Francisco's residents who had voted Boudin into the DA's office experienced buyer's remorse. A multiethnic coalition led by Asian Americans launched a recall campaign to get Boudin out of the DA's office. Many of the same volunteers and supporters of the school board recall campaign threw in their support to recall Boudin. Garry Tan was one of them. Tan told me he supported the recall Boudin campaign because he was concerned about "the future of San Francisco and the entire community and economy." Tan didn't believe Boudin "is doing his best to protect people and ensure those who commit violent crimes are held accountable for victimizing the poor, the disadvantaged, and the general public."

Kit Lam, another veteran from the school board recall campaign, explained in a social media post why he supported Boudin's recall by listing the rising crime, drug overdose crisis, and homeless problems.[39] The safety issue hit close to home for Lam. He told me his working-class neighbors were victims of property theft. But Boudin's office refused to prosecute the thief. They were Boudin's supporters two years ago, but they were ready to see Boudin go. Lam said, "We need to recall him [Boudin] now because the public has NO confidence in the DA office." Most other Asian voters shared Tan and Lam's concerns and were holding Boudin accountable for the city's crime surge and deterioration of its quality of life. A pre-election poll showed that 67% of Asian voters supported the recall, compared to 52% of Hispanic voters, 51% of white voters, and 34% of Black voters.

On June 7, 2022, San Francisco residents made a significant statement by ousting DA Chesa Boudin with a resounding margin. More than 60% of voters supported the recall, underscoring the depth of dissatisfaction with Boudin's soft-on-crime approach. Through both the school board recall campaign and the DA recall campaign, San Francisco's Asian voters showed that they were willing to be the vanguard to hold political leaders accountable for what they saw as destructive policies. These Asian Americans were effective at bringing change through a democratic process.

EPILOGUE

• • •

*The Year 2024 and Beyond: Shaping
America's Future*

The Asian American community has historically been a strong supporter of the Democratic Party at the polls. In the 2012 presidential election, Barack Obama achieved an impressive 73% of the Asian American vote, outperforming his support among Hispanic voters (71%) and women voters (55%). This trend continued in 2016, when 79% of Asian American and Pacific Islander (AAPI) voters rallied behind Hillary Clinton. However, in recent years, we have seen a noteworthy shift, with an increasing number of Asian Americans leaning toward the political center or right, reflecting their growing dissatisfaction with progressive policies.

One of the critical issues that has led to this shift is the Democratic Party itself, especially its leadership, which has taken a "soft on crime" approach and stood behind the "defunding the police" movement. A telling example was when, in the summer of 2020, Kamala Harris, a Democratic Senator and later vice president of the Biden administration, urged her supporters on social media to donate to the Minnesota Freedom Fund (MFF), an organization that provided bail for individuals arrested during riots post George Floyd's death. It was evident that the Democrats' "soft on crime" and "defunding the police" policies have contributed to an unsafe environment and a decline in the quality of life in cities like San Francisco and New York. The Asian community is particularly aggrieved by the lack of serious attention to crimes such as robbery and assaults against Asians, especially Asian seniors, when the perpetrators are non-whites.

The Democrats' war on merit and support for affirmative action in education has also driven away Asian voters who believe their children have been unfairly targeted and forced to sacrifice their educational opportunities and economic mobility for the sake of achieving certain racial equity goals. This issue has struck at the heart of the aspirations and concerns of many Asian American voters, who value education and economic mobility as key to their success and the success of their children. Asian immigrants who grew up in authoritarian regimes have become especially concerned that radical left-wing ideologies such as CRT are slowly turning a free society like America into the authoritarian regime they left behind.

The Democratic policies on crime and education and their underlying ideologies have prompted some Asian Americans to ask themselves crucial questions, such as "Why do we continue to support the Democratic Party? It doesn't view us as equal to other racial groups and is willing to enact laws and regulations that could harm our interests and safety, all in the name of social justice and equity." To ensure equal opportunities and the safety and well-being of our families, elders, and community, many Asian Americans have realized that we must redouble our efforts to participate in the democratic process, including showing up at the ballot box and running for political office, and never let one political party take our votes for granted.

Some Asian Americans began to move away from the Democratic Party in the 2020 presidential election. In that election, President Donald Trump made inroads with AAPI voters by winning 34% of AAPI votes. A new Pew Research report released in January 2024 shows Asian Americans have been the fastest-growing group of eligible voters in the U.S. over the past two decades, especially in the last four years since 2020; the number of eligible Asian American voters has grown by 15%. As of 2022, more than half of Asian American voters live in five states: California, New York, Texas, Hawaii, and New Jersey. What's even more striking is the record turnout of Asian Americans in every election since 2016, a clear sign of their enthusiasm and commitment to the democratic process.[1] Our vote is not just a number; it's a crucial part of the political process and is integral to shaping the future of our country.

The year 2024, an important election year, saw even greater political activism from Asian Americans than previous election cycles because more Asians recognized the necessity and urgency of engaging in the democratic process so our community will be well represented at the table to make policy decisions that affect the community the most. Asian Americans have also become confident in applying political influence after the defeat of affirmative action at the ballot box in Washington (2019) and California (2020), the successful recall campaigns in San Francisco that ousted three progressive school board members and the DA in 2022, and the Supreme Court's 2023 decision that bans affirmative action in college admissions. The 2024 election represented a pivotal moment for Asian American voters to exercise their rights and responsibilities to shape the future of our country.

Both the Democratic Party and the Republican Party recognized the growing importance of Asian American voters, as Ro Khanna (D–CA) predicted that "The Asian American vote will likely be decisive in battleground states like Nevada, Michigan, Pennsylvania and Georgia, which are decided by such a small margin."[2] Not surprisingly, both parties devoted resources to try to win over Asian American voters. Before President Biden dropped out of the 2024 presidential race, the Democratic National Committee (DNC) reportedly spent more than six figures on print and digital media ads targeting Asian American and Pacific Islander voters on behalf of President Biden's reelection campaign. Emma Vaughn, spokesperson for the Republican National Committee (RNC), said in an interview that the RNC "made a multimillion-dollar commitment to bolster our ground game in Asian Pacific American communities in key states across the country"[3] in order to take back the White House in 2024. The RNC also "opened an Asian Pacific American community center in Orange County's Little Saigon, home to a substantial Vietnamese American population," and aimed to "set up 40 of them in competitive states and districts."[4]

An AAPI 2024 voter survey showed the Democratic Party was losing support among Asian voters: "46% say they'll likely vote for Biden (down from 54% in 2020)…42% identify as Democrats (compared to 44% in 2020)."[5] Some who previously supported Democratic candidates were expected to shift their allegiance to former President Donald Trump and down-ballot Republican candidates, although former President Trump's unfavorable rate among Asian voters is still high: "62% view Trump unfavorably including 43% who view him very unfavorably…31% say they'll likely vote for Trump (compared to 30% in 2020)." Even among those who were not yet ready to switch party allegiance from the Democratic Party, there was a growing trend of breaking away from the party on specific issues such as crime and education. A prime example is the cultural and political shift in Silicon Valley.

Traditionally, Silicon Valley has been a stronghold of the Democratic Party and progressive causes. During the 2020 presidential election, employees at the top five tech companies, including Amazon, Alphabet, Facebook, and Microsoft, donated a substantial $15 million to Democratic candidates, compared to a mere $3 million to Republicans. Notably, Peter Thiel, a rare Republican voice in the Valley, openly supported Donald Trump's presidential campaigns in 2016 and 2020, a stance that likely cost him friendships and investment opportunities. The Republican Party has often accused Silicon Valley of harboring anti-conservative bias.

But in recent years, some in Silicon Valley have become fed up that their quality of life has been negatively affected by the Democrats' soft approach to drugs and street crime. Salesforce's CEO Marc Benioff threatened to pull his annual Dreamforce conference out of San Francisco due to the city's rampant homeless problem, drug addicts, and crimes that scared attendees. Another tech billionaire, Elon Musk, announced in June 2024 that he would move the headquarters of X.com (formerly known as Twitter), the social media company he owns, from San Francisco to Austin, Texas, citing the need to avoid gangs of violent drug addicts just to get in and out of the building.[6]

There's growing support for Republican candidates in Silicon Valley, as evidenced by a significant fundraising event in San Francisco in the summer of 2024. Republican presidential candidate Donald Trump received a substantial $12 million at this event, held in the heart of the Valley of the Progressive Beast. Notably, one of the co-hosts of the fundraiser was Chamath Palihapitiya, a Sri Lankan–born American venture capitalist who had previously supported Trump's Democrat opponents.

Some Asian communities declared their presidential endorsements ahead of the election. For instance, the Pakistani American Political Action Committee (PAKPAC) announced on October 17, 2024, that they endorsed Republican presidential candidate Donald Trump, stating: "after extensive meetings with the Trump & Harris campaigns, we believe the former President is the candidate who will improve the U.S. and Pakistan relations and promote true democracy in Pakistan."[7]

Garry Tan has become even more active in local politics these days. He insisted publicly he is proud to be a Democrat and has no plan to vote for Republicans. But he has emerged as a political leader who gathers other tech millionaires and billionaires to work on plans to bankroll political candidates who are less radical and who are willing to fix issues like crime, homelessness, and public education. These are issues Tan is ready to acknowledge were caused by some of the progressive policies that had gone too far to the left.

Tan and other like-minded tech entrepreneurs' political activism has already made some differences. In March 2024, San Francisco residents voted to restore some law and order to the city with two measures: Measure E expands police powers, and Measure F requires drug screenings for adults receiving welfare. In November, residents ousted Democratic Mayor London Breed, holding her accountable for doing too little to address the city's rising drug addicts and crimes. Many of the city's residents also joined other California voters in approving Proposition 36, a ballot measure that would impose stricter penalties for repeat theft and crimes involving fentanyl, by an overwhelming margin of 40 percentage points – 70.6% to 29.4%. The passage of Prop 36 was a resounding rejection of years of the progressives' "soft on crime" policy. One San Fransico voter who supported Prop 36 said in an interview: "Existing at the mercy of criminals was very disappointing, very disheartening and I guess we had to hit rock bottom before finally, people woke up and realized, it's time to take a different turn."[8]

Other tech entrepreneurs are concerned that the progressive war on merit is hurting the quality of the labor force, which in turn will constrain Silicon Valley's growth as the tech industry relies heavily on its ability to recruit talent. Alexander Wang, the 20-something founder of Scale, a Silicon Valley startup company, issued one of the most potent rebuttals against the war on merit and the whole DEI ideology on June 13, 2024. In the manifesto he published on Scale's company website, Wang wrote:

Scale is a meritocracy, and we must always remain one.
Hiring on merit will be a permanent policy at Scale.

It's a big deal whenever we invite someone to join our mission, and those decisions have never been swayed by orthodoxy or virtue signaling or whatever the current thing is. I think of our guiding principle as **MEI: merit, excellence, and intelligence.**

That means we hire only the best person for the job, we seek out and demand excellence, and we unapologetically prefer people who are very smart.

We treat everyone as an individual. We do not unfairly stereotype, tokenize, or otherwise treat anyone as a member of a demographic group rather than as an individual.

We believe that people should be judged by the content of their character — and, as colleagues, be additionally judged by their talent, skills, and work ethic.

There is a mistaken belief that meritocracy somehow conflicts with diversity. I strongly disagree. No group has a monopoly on excellence. A hiring process based on merit will naturally yield a variety of backgrounds, perspectives, and ideas. Achieving this requires casting a wide net for talent and then objectively selecting the best, without bias in any direction. We will not pick winners and losers based on someone being the "right" or "wrong" race, gender, and so on. It should be needless to say, and yet it needs saying: doing so would be racist and sexist, not to mention illegal.

Upholding meritocracy is good for business and is the right thing to do. This approach not only results in the strongest possible team, but also ensures we're treating our colleagues with fairness and respect.

In addition to supporting political candidates and challenging the war on merit, more Asian Americans were running for political offices at various levels. Laurance Lee, a father and a volunteer for the San Francisco school board recall campaign in 2022, announced on X.com that he was running for a school board seat.

Despite his initial disinterest in politics, he was deeply affected by the actions of the progressive school board members, from extended school closures during lockdowns to postponing algebra until 9th grade. His commitment to making a change was evident in his campaign post, where he promised voters, "Together we can make the changes we need! Let's ensure our schools are safe, our students are studying grade-level literacy and math, and our district is accountable."[9]

Yiatin Chu, an immigrant mother, faced a barrage of online attacks for her support of the Supreme Court's ban on affirmative action. Undeterred, she announced her candidacy for a New York State Senate seat, representing District 11 in Queens, New York, on X.com. Her campaign page presented her as a "common-sense candidate" with a diverse set of priorities that include public safety, immigration, education, and quality of life.[10]

Both Lee and Chu ran for office as either Democrat or Independent. Cao Huang, however, ran for office as a Republican. Huang came to the U.S. in 1975 as a refugee from Vietnam. He graduated from the inaugural class of Thomas Jefferson High School for Science and Technology in Alexandria, Virginia. This school was at the center of a controversy after its school board canceled merit-based admissions, aiming to reduce the number of Asian American students. Huang later joined the U.S. Navy and retired as a Navy captain.[11] He became a Republican Senate candidate after receiving former President Donald Trump's endorsement. He won more than 60% of the vote in the Virginia Senate Republican primary in June 2024.

While Lee, Chu, and Huang didn't emerge victorious in their individual races in the November 2024 general elections, the impressive voter support they received as first-time candidates was a promising sign for the future. For instance, Huang's 45.8% share of the vote in Virginia, which translates to nearly two million votes, was a significant achievement, especially when compared to Senator Tim Kaine's 54.2%, or 2.3 million votes. This strong support for these political newcomers is likely to inspire more Asian Americans to run for political offices.

Besides local and state levels, Asian American political activism has gained significant visibility at the national level, making a substantial impact on the political landscape. Robert F. Kennedy Jr. initially sought the Democratic Party's presidential nomination. However, after realizing the DNC had manipulated the party's primary process to lock in the nomination for President Joe Biden's reelection bid, RFK Jr. ended his bid as a Democrat and launched a new presidential campaign as an independent. He chose Asian American Nicole Shanahan as his running mate. Shanahan and her brother were raised by a single mother who emigrated from China. Their mother began her immigrant journey by working as a maid. Shanahan recalled in an interview that her family was so poor that she had only two T-shirts that fit her when growing up. Like a typical immigrant, Shanahan's mom never gave up on bettering herself. She later obtained an education and became an accountant in the Bay Area. Shanahan said of her mother, "Her legacy is about that immigrant, swallow the pain and do your best with what you have. That white-knuckle approach to life is tough but also effective."[12]

Shanahan's mother's resilience and determination to provide a better life for her children, despite the hardships, inspired Shanahan. Shanahan began to bus tables at a local burger restaurant. She was also a good student and eventually graduated from the Santa Clara University School of Law with a J.D. in 2014. She became a well-known patent lawyer and later married Google co-founder Sergey Brin. The couple divorced in 2023. Shanahan began to use her wealth for both philanthropy and politics. Despite having no prior political experience other than being a steadfast donor to the Democratic Party before 2024, Shanahan demonstrated her political savvy as RFK Jr.'s running mate. She was the first one from the RFK campaign to disclose in an interview in August 2024 that RFK would end his presidential bid and join hands with Republican presidential nominee former President Donald Trump. This bold move made her a significant political figure in the 2024 presidential campaign. She is someone who undoubtedly will have a lasting impact on the political landscape.

On the Republican Party side, notably, two Indian Americans, Nikki Haley, former ambassador to the United Nations, and businessman Vivek Ramaswamy, both ran for the Republican presidential nomination. After former President Donald Trump named Sen. J.D. Vance (R–OH) as his vice-presidential running mate, Vance's wife, Usha Vance, received more positive news coverage than her husband, with media outlets praising her professional background, personal story, and her potential to appeal to a diverse range of voters.

Usha Vance, the daughter of Hindu Indian immigrants, was raised in San Diego. She pursued history studies at Yale University and furthered her education at the University of Cambridge. Her professional journey led her to become an experienced litigator at the renowned Munger, Tolles & Olson law firm. However, she had to resign when her husband, J.D., accepted the nomination as the vice-presidential candidate for the Republican Party. At the Republican Party Convention in Milwaukee in July 2024, Usha Vance's debut speech about J.D. Vance was more warmly received than his. She humanized her husband by sharing how he adapted to her vegetarian diet and learned to cook spicy Indian food for her mother. She described her mixed-race family as a "testament to this great country." Her speech was not just well received but a resounding success, with many political commentators urging the Trump-Vance campaign to let Usha Vance speak more on the campaign trail. They believed that her warm and eloquent speaking style could soften some of the hard edges of J.D. Vance, and her Hindu heritage "could appeal to some South Asian voters, potentially adding value in swing states with larger South Asian communities like Arizona, Georgia, and North Carolina. The impact of her words was undeniable, resonating with the audience and potentially influencing the outcome of the campaign."[13]

On the Democratic side, following President Joe Biden's withdrawal from the re-election bid, the party nominated then Vice President Kamala Harris, whose mother was an immigrant from India. Regardless of party affiliations, many Asian Americans were excited about being well represented in both parties in the 2024 general election.

On November 5, 2024, the general election day, the exit polls confirmed a noticeable change in political allegiance among minority groups. A substantial portion of Asian and Latin Americans, along with some Black voters, broke away from the Democratic Party and supported the Republican Party instead. According to the *Washington Post*, there was a 9-point shift to the Republican Party in 2024 among Asian American voters relative to 2020. The Manhattan Institute's Neetu Arnold's own analysis of precinct-level voting data in four major urban areas found that the exit polls might be underestimating the shift. For instance, Arnold found that "majority-Asian precincts in New York City saw a rightward shift of 31 percentage points. Precincts in Dallas and Fort Bend counties in Texas both saw rightward shifts between 17 and 20 points. And precincts in Chicago saw a 23-point shift to the right."[14]

This shift had a discernible impact in some battleground states, such as Nevada. The following chart illustrates the increased support for Republican presidential candidate Donald Trump among Hispanic and Asian voters in Nevada. This shift saw Harris losing ground with these minority voters compared to their support of Biden four years ago. Trump's victory in Nevada, securing six electoral votes, marked a significant milestone as the first Republican presidential candidate to win the state since 2004.

Some Asian Americans have warned that the Republican Party should not take Asian Americans' vote for granted, as the political shift to the right may not be permanent. Asian voters are often more influenced by specific policies than by party loyalty. Pennsylvania voter Teesta Dasgupta stressed in an interview: "Dems move to the center; Asian Americans stay where they are right now but if the allegiance to gender ideology and soft on crime remains then they [Asian Americans] will move right."[15] This underscores the need for both parties to align their policies with the concerns of Asian American voters.

Nevada exit poll: Race
Polls are an approximate guide to candidate support

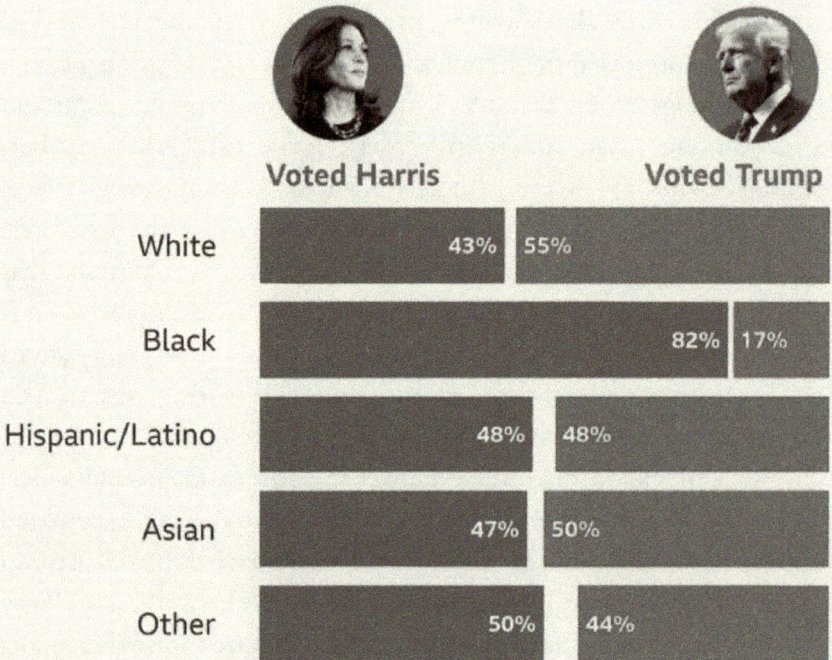

	Voted Harris	Voted Trump
White	43%	55%
Black	82%	17%
Hispanic/Latino	48%	48%
Asian	47%	50%
Other	50%	44%

Sample size: 3,473 respondents. All figures have a margin of error
Bars may not sum to 100%

Source: Edison Research/NEP via Reuters. **BBC**

Ultimately, most American voters repudiated the Democratic Party's progressive policies, leading to a landslide victory for the Republican Party on election day. The GOP gained control of both chambers of the U.S. Congress. Their presidential nominee, Donald Trump, made a remarkable comeback, winning the popular

vote and 312 electoral votes (Harris gained 226). He became the
47th president of the United States. His running mate, J.D. Vance,
assumed the role of vice president, and his wife, Usha Vance, made
history as the first Asian American second lady of the United
States. Vivek Ramaswamy, who had challenged Trump for the
Republican presidential nomination, was appointed by Trump to
lead the Department of Efficiency alongside billionaire Elon Musk.
Their goal was to reduce wasteful government spending and restore
efficiency to the federal government. Trump nominated Dr. Jay
Bhattacharya, a Stanford University physician and another Indian
American, to head the National Institutes of Health (NIH).

Shortly after taking office, President Trump signed an executive
order regarding Diversity, Equity, and Inclusion (DEI), expressing
concerns about potential "illegal discrimination or preferences." He
placed all federal employees in DEI roles on paid administrative
leave for reassessment. Trump's order also repealed former President Lyndon Johnson's Executive Order 11246, which established
affirmative action, and revoked former President Joe Biden's Executive Order 13985, which promoted "equity across the federal
government." This bold move by Trump reflects a renewed
commitment to reestablish America as a meritocratic society again.

Before the general election, Tunku Varadarajan, a *Wall Street
Journal* columnist and an Indian American himself, remarked that
Indian Americans as a group have "prospered without quotas or
affirmative action." He supported his argument with some impressive statistics about Indian Americans: "Two-thirds have college
degrees, and 40 percent have postgraduate degrees. They have the
lowest divorce rates of any ethnic group in the country and own 60
percent of all hotels. One in every 20 doctors here is Indian, as is 1
in every ten students entering medical school." [16] Varadarajan
concludes:

It is deeply unfashionable to speak these days of the American Dream. To do so marks you out, in certain circles, as

anachronistic or sentimental. But if there's one group that holds fast to its belief in the American Dream, it's Indian-Americans. Unapologetic about their drive to thrive, they are rightly scornful of those who would say that America is a place that thwarts people on the basis of race.

Varadarajan's conclusion holds true not only for Indian Americans but for the wider Asian American community. We share a deep commitment to America's founding principles, such as freedom and equality before the law. We do not seek special treatment or dwell on grievances. Our only desire is for equal opportunities to shape our destiny through our own hard work, determination, and merit. In a nation where generations of Asian Americans have contributed and sacrificed, our unwavering faith in the American Dream is a testament to our dedication. Our commitment to contribute and our determination make us an integral part of shaping the future of this great nation. I am confident that many more splendid chapters of the history of Asian American political activism are yet to be written.

APPENDIX 1

• • •

Asian Americans Compositions

Source:
https://www.pewresearch.org/short-reads/2021/04/29/key-facts-about-asian-americans

Six Asian origin groups in the U.S. had populations of at least 1 million people in 2019 ...

In thousands

Origin group	Population 2019	Population 2010	Population 2000	% growth, 2000–2019
Chinese, with Taiwanese	5,399	4,010	2,865	88%
Taiwanese	226	230	145	56%
Chinese, except Taiwanese	5,172	3,780	2,720	90%
Indian	4,606	3,183	1,900	142%
Filipino	4,211	3,417	2,365	78%
Vietnamese	2,183	1,737	1,224	78%
Korean	1,908	1,707	1,228	55%
Japanese	1,498	1,316	1,160	29%
Pakistani	554	409	204	171%
Thai	343	238	150	128%
Cambodian	339	277	206	64%
Hmong	327	260	186	75%
Laotian	254	232	198	28%
Bangladeshi	208	147	57	263%
Nepalese	198	59	9	2,005%
Burmese	189	100	17	1,031%
Indonesian	129	95	63	105%
Sri Lankan	56	45	25	127%
Malaysian	38	26	19	106%
Mongolian	27	18	6	358%
Bhutanese	24	19	<1	11,288%
Okinawan	14	11	11	33%

... accounting for 85% of the nation's Asian population

% of the U.S. Asian population that is ___, 2019

Pakistani	2%
Thai	2%
Cambodian	2%
Hmong	1%
Laotian	1%
Taiwanese	1%
Bangladeshi	1%
Nepalese	1%
Burmese	1%
Indonesian	1%
Sri Lankan	<1%
Malaysian	<1%
Mongolian	<1%
Bhutanese	<1%
Okinawan	<1%

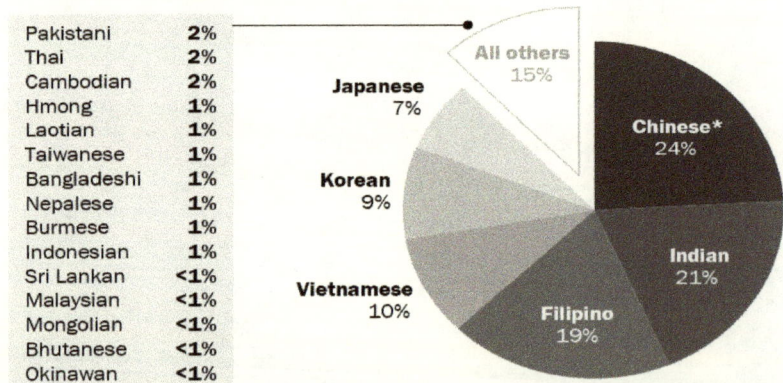

Pie chart: All others 15%, Chinese* 24%, Indian 21%, Filipino 19%, Vietnamese 10%, Korean 9%, Japanese 7%

Note: "All others" includes the category "Other Asian, not specified." Figures do not add to 100% because individuals identifying with more than one Asian group are included in all groups.
* Includes those identifying as Taiwanese; for more information, see "How many Taiwanese live in the U.S.? It's not an easy question to answer."
Source: For 2019, Pew Research Center analysis of 2019 American Community Survey 1-year estimates (Census data). For 2000 and 2010, census counts from U.S. Census Bureau, "The Asian Population: 2010" Census Brief, Table 6.

PEW RESEARCH CENTER

APPENDIX 2

* * *

Asian American Population Growth in the
United States of America

Source:
https://www.pewresearch.org/short-reads/2021/04/29/key-facts-about-asian-americans/

Asian population in U.S. nearly doubled between 2000 and 2019 and is projected to surpass 46 million by 2060

In thousands

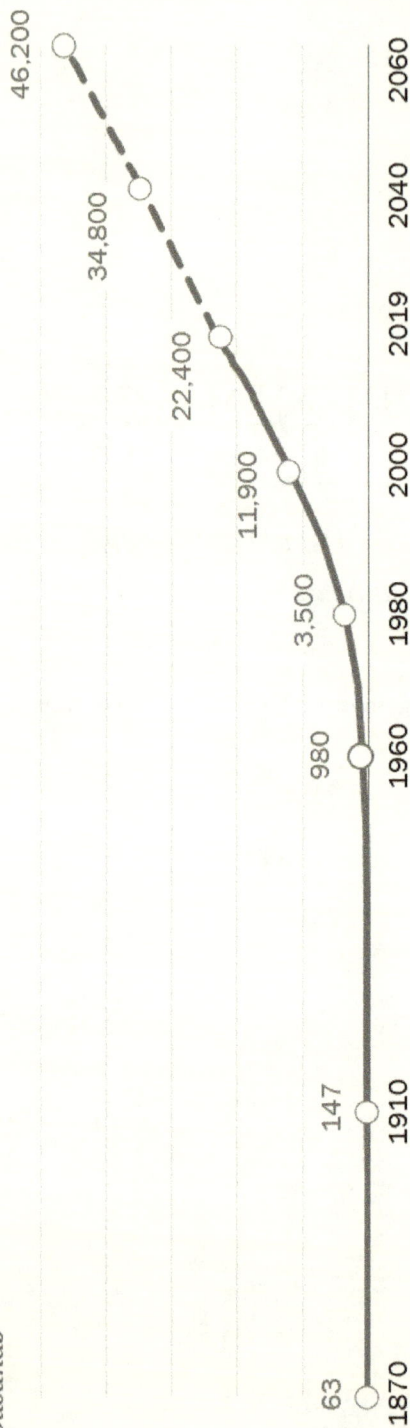

Data points: 63 (1870), 147 (1910), 980 (1960), 3,500 (1980), 11,900 (2000), 22,400 (2019), 34,800 (2040), 46,200 (2060)

X-axis: 1870, 1910, 1960, 1980, 2000, 2019, 2040, 2060

Note: In 2000 and later, Asians include the mixed-race and mixed-group populations, regardless of Hispanic origin. Prior to 2000, decennial census forms only allowed one race category to be selected. Asians include Pacific Islanders in 1980 and earlier years. Population figures for 1870-1980 are rounded to the nearest 1,000, and for 2000-2060, they are rounded to the nearest 100,000.

Source: U.S. Census Bureau 2017 population projections for 2020-2060. For 2011-2019, American Community Survey 1-year estimates (via Census Bureau data). For 2000 and 2010, census counts from Census Bureau. "The Asian Population: 2010" Census Brief, Table 6. For 1990, U.S. Census Bureau, "Asian Population: 2000" Census Brief, Table 2. For 1980 and earlier years, Campbell Gibson and Kay Jung, "Historical Census Statistics on Population Totals by Race, 1790 to 1990, and by Hispanic Origin, 1970 to 1990, for the United States, Regions, Divisions and States." U.S. Census Bureau.

PEW RESEARCH CENTER

ACKNOWLEDGEMENT

Although writing is a solo endeavor, putting a book together for publication requires teamwork. I have been fortunate to work with a fantastic team.

I want to express my gratitude to my editor, Jill Tietjen, a well-published author. Her invaluable insights and constructive feedback sharpened my focus, ensuring that my ideas in this book resonate with a broad audience.

I am equally thankful to Ms. Sara Awa, who proofread the manuscript with great attention to detail and helped me polish it by catching misspellings and grammatical errors. My collaboration with Ms. Deborah Natelson spans ten years, and her contributions have been crucial in every book I've released. Even though she has shifted away from editing, she formatted this manuscript brilliantly to ensure it's polished and ready for publication.

I want to take this opportunity to express my heartfelt appreciation for my husband, Mike Raleigh. Marriage is like a team sport, and I am incredibly fortunate to have the best teammate by my side. Mike's unwavering faith in me has been my driving force, empowering me to pursue my dreams without fear. His uncondi-tional love and steadfast support have anchored me in every deci-sion I've faced. He is the foundation of my life, and I am profoundly grateful for his presence and partnership.

The saying "teamwork makes the dream work" holds true, and I am thankful for all the individuals in my professional and personal life who have helped turn my dream of authorship into a reality.

Lastly, I owe a deep debt of gratitude to my parents, Laying and Yukun Zhou. Their tremendous sacrifices and steadfast encour-agement have been the inspiration behind my journey to the United States and my choice to embrace American identity. The profound impact they've had on my life is immeasurable, and I will always cherish their unwavering support.

CITATIONS AND
REFERENCES

Introduction

[1] Barton, N. "Redacted: An Excavation."
https://www.drnimishabarton.com/redacted?author=5bcfd41d5ce350c7a7c00c04

[2] "Key Facts About Asian Americans." (April 29, 2021). Pew Research.
https://www.pewresearch.org/short-reads/2021/04/29/key-facts-about-asian-americans/

[3] Jin, C. (May 25, 2021). "6 Charts that Dismantle the Trope of Asian Americans as a Model Minority." *NPR*. https://www.npr.org/2021/05/25/999874296/6-charts-that-dismantle-the-trope-of-asian-americans-as-a-model-minority

[4] "Key Facts About Asian Americans." Ibid.

[5] "Key Facts About Asian Americans." Ibid.

Part I. Asian Americans' First Wave of Policial Activism: From the 1850s to 1920s

Introduction

[1] "Where Are You From?"
https://www.youtube.com/watch?v=DWynJkN5HbQ

[2] See Nikole Hannah Jones' Tweets.
https://www.reddit.com/r/aznidentity/comments/iaup01/nikole_hannahjones
_is_dedicated_with_her_fixation/#lightbox

[3] Lee (October 11, 2022). "Are Asian Americans People of Color or the Next in Line to Become White?" *The Brookings*. https://www.brookings.edu/articles/are-asian-americans-people-of-color-or-the-next-in-line-to-become-white/

Chapter 1. Why Did Some Asians Choose to Migrate to America?

The Early Japanese American Experience

[1] Ogawa, D. and Kitano, C. (April 17, 2018). "Commemoration 150th Anniversary of Japanese in Hawaii: Honoring the *Gannenmono* King Kalakaua and the Issei Story."
https://discovernikkei.org/en/journal/2018/4/17/gannenmono/

[2] "Commemoration 150th Anniversary of Japanese in Hawaii." Ibid.

[3] "Commemoration 150th Anniversary of Japanese in Hawaii." Ibid.

[4] "Strikers, Scabs, and Sugar Mongers: How Immigrant Labor Struggle Shaped the Hawaii We Know Today." (August 22, 2017).
https://densho.org/catalyst/strikers-scabs-sugar-mongers-immigrant-labor-struggle-shaped-hawaii-know-today/

[5] "Strikers, Scabs, and Sugar Mongers: How Immigrant Labor Struggle Shaped the Hawaii We Know Today." Ibid.

[6] *Hole Hole Bushi: Song of the Cane Fields*. Produced by Chris Conybeare with the assistance of Franklin Odo. 30 min. KHET-TV, 1984. Part of "Rice and Roses" series on immigrant life on the plantations.

[7] "Strikers, Scabs, and Sugar Mongers: How Immigrant Labor Struggle Shaped the Hawaii We Know Today." Ibid.

[8] "Immigration and Relocation in US History: Japanese." Library of Congress.
https://www.loc.gov/classroom-materials/immigration/japanese/the-us-mainland-growth-and-resistance/

1.2 The Early Chinese American Experiences

9 "A History of Chinese Americans in California."
https://www.nps.gov/parkhistory/online_books/5views/5views3c.htm

10 "Chinese Americans in the Civil War." Battlefields.org.
https://www.battlefields.org/learn/articles/chinese-americans-civil-war

11 Jeong, M. (June 19, 2020). "Ah Toy, Pioneering Prostitute of Gold Rush California." *New York Review*.
https://www.nybooks.com/online/2020/06/19/ah-toy-pioneering-prostitute-of-gold-rush-california/ and https://en.wikipedia.org/wiki/Ah_Toy

12 "Chinese Immigrants and the Gold Rush." Ibid.

13 "The Bittersweet Memories of a Happy Dwelling." Retrieved from
https://helenraleigh.substack.com/p/the-bittersweet-memories-of-a-happy

14 "A History of Chinese Americans in California."
https://www.nps.gov/parkhistory/online_books/5views/5views3c.htm

15 Yale University website. Retrieved from http://ceas.yale.edu/yung-wing

16 Museum of Chinese in America website.
https://www.mocanyc.org/collections/stories/yung-wing/

1.3 The Chinese Rail Road Workers' Strikes

17 Workers of the Union Pacific company suffered bloody attacks by Native Americans – including members of the Sioux, Arapaho, and Cheyenne tribes. Retrieved from https://www.history.com/topics/inventions/transcontinental-railroad#section_3

18 Chang, G. (2019). "The Chinese and the Iron Road." Stanford University Press, p. 11.

19 "The Chinese and the Iron Road." Ibid, p. 10.

20 "The Chinese and the Iron Road." Ibid, p. 12.

21 "The Chinese and the Iron Road." Ibid, p. 11.

22 "The Chinese and the Iron Road." Ibid, p. 11.

23 For those who hold a deep respect for history, the documentary *Going Home*, directed and produced by Chinese American filmmaker Min Zhou, is a must-watch.[23] It chronicles the discovery of the remains of 13 Chinese workers who made a significant contribution to the construction of the Transcontinental Railroad in Carlin, Nevada. After more than two decades of archaeological excavations, research, and exhibition, the Carlin community – both private citizens and the city government – made a significant contribution. Their efforts

led to the reburial of the workers' remains in the Carlin City Cemetery on July 3rd, 2018.

[24] "The Chinese and the Iron Road." Ibid, p. 14.

[25] "American Experience: The Chinese Workers' Strike." PBS. https://www.pbs.org/wgbh/americanexperience/features/tcrr-chinese-workers-strike/

[26] The U.S. Department of Labor inducted Chinese railroad workers into its Hall of Honor in 2014.

[27] The Burlingame-Seward Treaty, 1868. https://history.state.gov/milestones/1866-1898/burlingame-seward-treaty

[28] Kennedy, L. (April 23, 2024). "Building the Transcontinental Railroad: How 20,000 Chinese Immigrants Made it Happen." History.com. https://www.history.com/news/transcontinental-railroad-chinese-immigrants

[29] "The Chinaman as Railroad Builders." *Idaho Statesman*. May 25, 1869, 3.

[30] "The Chinese and the Iron Road." Ibid, p. 288.

[31] "The Chinese Experience 1857–1892: Denis Kearney and the California Anti-Chinese Campaign." https://immigrants.harpweek.com/ChineseAmericans/2KeyIssues/DenisKearneyCalifAnti.htm

[32] The Workingman's Party changed its name soon after to the Socialist Labor Party, and it is the oldest socialist political party in the United States. It's still active today and is headquartered in Mountain View, California, about 30 miles south of San Francisco. https://www.denofgeek.com/tv/warrior-the-real-history-of-the-race-riot-that-shook-san-francisco/

[33] "A History of Chinese Americans in California." https://www.nps.gov/parkhistory/online_books/5views/5views3c.htm

[34] "Japanese Exclusion and the American Labor Movement." https://www.asianstudies.org/publications/eaa/archives/japanese-exclusion-and-the-american-labor-movement-1900-to-1924/

Chapter 2. "See You in Court!"

[1] "Chy Lung vs. Freeman (1875)," Immigrationhistory.org. https://immigrationhistory.org/item/chy-lung-v-freeman/

[2] "Before the Chinese Exclusion Act, This Anti-Immigration Law Targeted Asian Women." (April 23, 2024). https://www.history.com/news/chinese-immigration-page-act-women

[3] Page Act of 1875. The New York Historical.
https://wams.nyhistory.org/industry-and-empire/expansion-and-empire/page-act-1875/

[4] Yick Wo vs. Hopkins, 118 U.S. 356 (1886).
https://supreme.justia.com/cases/federal/us/118/356/

[5] Ross, H. "The Life and Death of a Quicksilver Mine." Los Angeles: Historical Society of Southern California, 1958, p. 75.
https://www.nps.gov/parkhistory/online_books/5views/5views3d.htm

[6] "A History of Chinese Americans in California."
https://www.nps.gov/parkhistory/online_books/5views/5views3h81.htm

[7] Ibid.

[8] Ibid.

[9] Chinese Exclusion Act of 1882.
https://www.mtholyoke.edu/acad/intrel/chinex.htm

[10] "This paper certified that Wong Kim Ark was able to follow through with his plan to leave the United States and return. Three men signed this letter attesting to his identity. Included with the attestation is a signature of the witness, who is the notary Robert M. Edwards, and a photograph of Wong Kim Ark."
https://catalog.archives.gov/id/2641490?objectPage=2

[11] "History of CACA." http://cacanational.org/htmlPages/history.html

[12] "Gentlemen's Agreement." (October 29, 2009).
https://www.history.com/topics/immigration/gentlemens-agreement

[13] "Ozawa v. United States (1922)." U.S. Supreme Court Justia.
https://supreme.justia.com/cases/federal/us/260/178/

[14] "Ozawa v. United States." Retrieved from
http://encyclopedia.densho.org/Ozawa_v._United_States

[15] "Ozawa v. United States (1922)." Ibid.

[16] "United States v. Bhagat Singh Thind (1923)." U.S. Supreme Court Justia.
https://supreme.justia.com/cases/federal/us/261/204/

[17] According to CACA's website, "In 1977, another milestone in membership was achieved when women were admitted as members for the first time. Since then, a number of women have been elected to hold office in local lodges, including the office of president. By the national convention in Houston in 1993, the numbers of male and female presidents of regional lodges were almost equal. In 1997, at the convention in Phoenix, Nancy Ann Gee was elected as the first woman to hold the office of National Grand President." CACA History.
http://cacanational.org/htmlPages/history.html

Part II. Asian Americans' Second Wave of Political Activism: From WWII to the 1990s

Chapter 3. "Are You Loyal to America?" – How the Internment Reshaped the Japanese American Experience

[1] Tiezzi, S. (Aug 15, 2015). "When the U.S. and China Were Allies." *The Diplomat.* https://thediplomat.com/2015/08/when-the-us-and-china-were-allies/

[2] "Repeal of the Chinese Exclusion Act, 1943." Office of the Historian, The Department of State of the United States of America. https://history.state.gov/milestones/1937-1945/chinese-exclusion-act-repeal

[3] The repeal of Chinese exclusion paved the way for measures in 1946 to admit Filipino and Asian-Indian immigrants. https://history.state.gov/milestones/1937-1945/chinese-exclusion-act-repeal

[4] "Immigration and Relocation in US History: Japanese." Library of Congress. https://www.loc.gov/classroom-materials/immigration/japanese/.

[5] Kumamoto, B. 1979. "The Search for Spies: American Counterintelligence and the Japanese-American Community 1931–1943." *Amerasia Journal* 6:45–75. https://www.du.edu/behindbarbedwire/history.html

[6] Ibid.

[7] Ibid.

[8] The Munson report about Japanese Americans' loyalty was first uncovered in 1946.

[9] "Pearl Harbor Attack." https://www.britannica.com/event/Pearl-Harbor-attack/The-attack

[10] Kumamoto, B. Ibid.

[11] Multiple sources confirmed that the U.S. government had plenty of warnings before the Pearl Harbor attack: "Roosevelt and a small circle of advisors had been following Japanese policy through radio intercepts. Incriminating coded messages had been translated by American cryptographers, and were delivered to the Secretary of State prior to the attack. Though American intelligence did not know the precise location of the attack, they knew of Japan's plan for military retaliation in the event negotiations broke down." "Pearl Harbor: Japanese vs. American Civilian Perspectives." https://library.tamucc.edu/exhibits/s/hist4350/page/pearl-harbor-japanese-vs-american-perspective. Maechling, C. "Pearl Harbor: The First Energy War." *History Today*, vol. 50, no. 12, December (2000). P. 41. And "Adm. Husband E. Kimmel and Lieut. Gen. Walter C. Short, who shared command at Pearl Harbor, were warned of the possibility of war, specifically on October 16 and again on

November 24 and 27. The notice of November 27, to Kimmel, began, "This dispatch is to be considered a war warning," went on to say that "negotiations have ceased," and directed the admiral to "execute an appropriate defensive deployment." Kimmel also was ordered to "undertake such reconnaissance and other measures as you deem necessary." The communication of the same day to Short declared that "hostile action is possible at any moment" and, like its naval counterpart, urged "measures of reconnaissance." "Pearl Harbor Attack." https://www.britannica.com/event/Pearl-Harbor-attack/The-attack

[12] Wakida, P. (September 23, 2021). "American Experience: How a Public Media Campaign Led to Japanese Incarceration during WWII." PBS. https://www.pbs.org/wgbh/americanexperience/features/citizen-hearst-japanese-incarceration/

[13] Ibid.

[14] "Decision to Evacuate." https://www.du.edu/behindbarbedwire/decision_to_evacuate.html

[15] "Sold, Damaged, Stolen, Gone: Japanese Americans' Property Loss During WWII." April 4, 2017. https://densho.org/catalyst/sold-damaged-stolen-gone-japanese-american-property-loss-wwii/

[16] History.org website. http://www.history.com/topics/world-war-ii/japanese-american-relocation

[17] "Ralph Carr." Denver Public Library Special Collections and Archives. https://history.denverlibrary.org/colorado-biographies/ralph-carr-1887-1950

[18] "Gordon Hirabayashi." Densho Encyclopedia. https://encyclopedia.densho.org/Gordon_Hirabayashi/

[19] "Letter from Min Yasui to General John L. DeWitt. Minoru Yasui Project. https://56a00056-2dab-4ddb-af19-6a2f0bab8ec0.filesusr.com/ugd/6c3aec_eea0f448a8244eb48a9dfe5538f247c5.pdf

[20] "Facts and Case Summary: Korematsu v United States." United States Courts. https://www.uscourts.gov/educational-resources/educational-activities/facts-and-case-summary-korematsu-v-us

[21] Ibid.

[22] http://www.ucs.louisiana.edu/~ras2777/pres/korematsu.html

[23] "A Quiet Civil Rights Hero: Mitsuye Endo's Landmark Supreme Court Case." February 1, 2024. California Historical Society. https://californiahistoricalsociety.org/blog/a-quiet-civil-rights-hero-mitsuye-endos-landmark-supreme-court-case/

[24] Ibid.

[25] "Loyalty Questionnaire." Densho Encyclopedia.
https://encyclopedia.densho.org/Loyalty_questionnaire/

[26] Ibid.

[27] "Heart Mountain." Densho Encyclopedia.
https://encyclopedia.densho.org/Heart_Mountain/#Resistance

[28] Interview of Norman Mineta and Alan Simpson by the Academy of Achievement.
https://www.crono911.org/Fonti/226_Mineta_Academy_of_Achievement0306 2006.pdf.

[29] "Yasui v United States." Densho Encyclopedia.
https://encyclopedia.densho.org/Yasui_v._United_States/

[30] Brown, D. (2021). "Face the Mountain: A True Story of Japanese American Heroes in World War II." Random House, New York, p. 790.

[31] "Face the Mountain." Ibid.

[32] "Face the Mountain." Ibid.

[33] "Minoru Yasui." Densho Encyclopedia.
https://encyclopedia.densho.org/Minoru_Yasui

[34] "Japanese Evacuation Claims." Densho Encyclopedia.
http://encyclopedia.densho.org/Japanese_American_Evacuation_Claims_Act/

[35]
https://www.fordlibrarymuseum.gov/sites/default/files/pdf_documents/library /document/0159/1670001.pdf

[36] "Redress Movement." Ibid.

[37] "Facts and Case Summary: Korematsu v United States." Ibid.

[38] "Coram Nobis Cases." Densho Encyclopedia.
https://encyclopedia.densho.org/Coram_nobis_cases

[39] The bill President Reagan signed is H.R. 442, or "An Act to implement recommendations of the Commission on Wartime Relocation and Internment of Civilians." It provides for a restitution payment to each of the 60,000 surviving Japanese Americans of the 120,000 who were relocated or detained.

[40] Reagan, R. (Aug 10, 1988). "Remarks on Signing the Bill Providing Restitution for the Wartime Internment of Japanese-American Civilians."
http://faculty.history.wisc.edu/archdeacon/404tja/redress.html

[41] Siek, S. (January 6, 2012). "Remembering Gordon Hirabayashi, Japanese American Civil Rights Hero." CNN.

https://www.cnn.com/2012/01/06/us/remembering-gordon-hirabayashi-japanese-american-civil-rights-hero/index.html

[42] Minoru Yasui Community Volunteer Award.
https://www.sparkthechangecolorado.org/mycva.html

Chapter 4. "Our Blood Is the Same" – How the Murder of Vincent Chin Reunited the Pan-Asian Civil Rights Movement

[1] The War Bride Act and the G.I. Fiancées Act of 1945 permitted Chinese American veterans to bring their wives into the United States.

[2] "Killing of Vincent Chin." *Wikipedia.*
https://en.wikipedia.org/wiki/Killing_of_Vincent_Chin and "About Vincent."
Vincent Chin Institute. https://www.vincentchin.org/about-vincent

[3] "Oil Shock of 1978 to 1979." Federal Reserve History.
https://www.federalreservehistory.org/essays/oil-shock-of-1978-79

[4] "Understanding the 1979 Energy Crisis." *Investopedia.*
https://www.investopedia.com/terms/1/1979-energy-crisis.asp

[5] "About Vincent." Vincent Chin Institute. https://www.vincentchin.org/about-vincent

[6] "Facts vs. Fiction." Vincent Chin Institute. https://www.vincentchin.org/facts-vs-fiction

[7] Moore, M. (August 30, 1987). "The Man Who Killed Vincent Chin."
https://rumble.media/the-man-who-killed-vincent-chin-by-michael-moore/

[8] Ibid.

[9] Judge Kaufman was held by Japanese military as a prisoner of war during WWII, but he denied that his wartime experience influenced his ruling in Vincent Chin's murder case.
https://en.wikipedia.org/wiki/Killing_of_Vincent_Chin

[10] "Killing of Vincent Chin." *Wikipedia.* Ibid.

[11] Burke, Meghan A. (2008). "Chin, Vincent (1955-1982)." In Schaefer, Richard T. (ed.). *Encyclopedia of Race, Ethnicity, and Society.* SAGE Publications. pp. 276–278.

[12] In 1982, about 20,000 Chinese immigrant women took to New York City's Chinatown streets to demand benefits, fair wages, and better working conditions. Their determination and resilience were evident in the fact that it was the largest protest in Chinatown's history. The strike workers got what they asked as employers backed down within a few days.
https://en.wikipedia.org/wiki/1982_garment_workers%27_strike

¹³ "The Man Who Killed Vincent Chin." Ibid.

¹⁴ Renee Tajima-Peña, who co-directed the film *Who Killed Vincent Chin?*, said in an interview: "We knew who killed Vincent Chin, but the real question was why? Was it because of his race? For me it was a Rashomon-like enigma, trying to untangle the conflicting perspectives of the people who lived through the case. It also revealed the fractures in America itself, and ultimately, how people bridged those divides to fight for justice." https://www.pbs.org/pov/pressroom/who-killed-vincent-chin-encore/

¹⁵ "Man convicted of Vincent Chin's death seeks liens removed, still owes millions." (December 11, 2015). *NBC News*. https://www.nbcnews.com/news/asian-america/man-convicted-vincent-chins-death-seeks-lien-removed-still-owes-n478766

¹⁶ "Estate of Vincent Chin Seeks Millions from His Killer." (June 27, 2017). *The Detroit News*. https://www.detroitnews.com/story/news/local/oakland-county/2017/06/24/vincent-chin-th-anniversary/103167672/

¹⁷ Phe, N. and Yap, E. (May 20, 2022). "40 Years After Vincent Chin." https://www.natlawreview.com/article/40-years-after-vincent-chin

Chapter 5. "We Were Targeted and Isolated" – How the 1992 LA Riots Changed Korean Americans Forever

¹ "The Los Angeles Riots." History.com. https://www.history.com/topics/1990s/the-los-angeles-riots

² "How Rooftop Koreans Took Back Los Angeles." Popo Medic (June 2, 2022). https://www.youtube.com/watch?v=xWMj-mFUDGA

³ "History of Korean Immigration to America, from 1903 to Present." https://sites.bu.edu/koreandiaspora/issues/history-of-korean-immigration-to-america-from-1903-to-present/#_ftn1

⁴ Constante, A. (April 25, 2017). "25 Years After LA Riots, Koreatown Finds Strength in 'Saigu' Legacy." *NBC News*. https://www.nbcnews.com/news/asian-america/25-years-after-la-riots-koreatown-finds-strength-saigu-legacy-n749081

⁵ "Latasha Harlins' Death and Why Korean-Americans Were Targets In The '92 Riots." (April 2017). https://laist.com/shows/take-two/latasha-harlins-death-and-why-korean-americans-were-targets-in-the-92-riots

⁶ Holguin, R. and Lee, J. (June 18, 1991). "Boycott of Store Where Man Was Killed Is Urged: Racial tensions: The African-American was slain while allegedly trying to rob the market owned by a Korean-American." *LA Times*. https://www.latimes.com/archives/la-xpm-1991-06-18-me-837-story.html

⁷ "Boycott of Store Where Man Was Killed Is Urged." Ibid.

⁸ "25 Years After LA Riots, Koreatown Finds Strength in 'Saigu' Legacy." Ibid.

[9] "How Rooftop Koreans Took Back Los Angeles." Ibid.

[10] Fuchs, C. (April 25, 2017). "Communities Work to Build Understanding 25 Years after LA Riots." *NBC News*. https://www.nbcnews.com/news/asian-america/communities-work-build-understanding-25-years-after-la-riots-n748591

[11] Luhar. M. (November 9, 2015). "'April's Way' Captures Stories of Korean-American Merchants During LA Riots." *NBC News*. https://www.nbcnews.com/news/asian-america/aprils-way-captures-stories-korean-american-merchants-during-l-riots-n456016

[12] Kang, H. (April 29, 2022). "Korean American–Black Conflict During LA Riots Was Overemphasized by Media." https://www.nbcnews.com/news/asian-america/korean-american-black-conflict-l-riots-was-overemphasized-media-expert-rcna26547

Part III. The Third Wave of Asian American Political Activism: From 2010s to Present

Introduction

[1] "Key Facts About Asian Americans." Pew Research. https://www.pewresearch.org/short-reads/2021/04/29/key-facts-about-asian-americans/

Chapter 6. How "The Asian Penalty" Motivated a New Generation of Political Activists and a Supreme Court Case

[1] Mansky, J. (June 22, 2016). "The History Behind the Supreme Court's Affirmative Action Decision." *The Smithsonian Magazine*. https://www.smithsonianmag.com/history/learn-origins-term-affirmative-action-180959531/

[2] Bloom, A. (1987). "The Closing of the American Mind." Simon & Schuster, New York, NY. P. 93.

[3] Bloom, A. (1987). Ibid. p. 94.

[4] "Regents of the University of California v Bakke." https://constitutioncenter.org/the-constitution/supreme-court-case-library/university-of-california-v-bakke

[5] "Graze v Bollinger." Cornell Law School. https://www.law.cornell.edu/supct/html/02-516.ZC.html

[6] "Grutter v Bollinger." Cornell Law School. https://www.law.cornell.edu/supct/html/02-241.ZS.html

[7] Anderson, S. (December 1, 2023). "How Sandra Day O'Connor Brought Compromise to the Supreme Court." *Smithsonian Magazine*.

https://www.smithsonianmag.com/history/sandra-day-oconnor-compromise-supreme-court-smithsonian-180983353/

[8] The final sentence in Justice O'Connor's opinion in *Grutter* read, "We expect that 25 years from now, the use of racial preferences will no longer be necessary to further the interest approved today."
https://supreme.justia.com/cases/federal/us/539/306/

[9] "Fisher v University of Texas at Austin." U.S. Supreme Court Justia.
https://supreme.justia.com/cases/federal/us/579/14-981/

[10] See Dr. Thomas Sowell's *C-Span* TV interview about his book, *Preferential Policies: An International Perspective.*
https://www.youtube.com/watch?v=VVvnTByzTmA

[11] "Indians in the U.S. Factsheet." Pew Research.
https://www.pewresearch.org/social-trends/fact-sheet/asian-americans-indians-in-the-u-s/

[12] "Indians in the U.S. Factsheet." Ibid.

[13] Unz, Ron. (November 28, 2012). "The Myth of American Meritocracy." *The American Conservative.* https://www.unz.com/runz/the-myth-of-american-meritocracy/

[14] Sun, Shuyun. (January 30, 2011). "*Battle Hymn of the Tiger Mother* by Amy Chua – Review." https://www.theguardian.com/books/2011/jan/30/battle-hymn-tiger-mother-review

[15] "Admission Preferences for Minority Students, Athletes, and Legacies at Elite Universities." (2004). Princeton Survey Research Center.
https://psrc.princeton.edu/publications/admission-preferences-minority-students-athletes-and-legacies-elite-universities

[16] English, B. (June 1, 2015). "To Get into Elite Colleges, Some Advised to 'Appear Less Asian'." *Boston Globe.*
https://www.bostonglobe.com/lifestyle/2015/06/01/college-counselors-advise-some-asian-students-appear-less-asian/Ew7g4JiQMiqYNQlIwqEIuO/story.html

[17] Chapter V. "Abbott Lawrence Lowell and Discrimination in Admissions and Housing." Harvard and the Legacy of Slavery.
https://legacyofslavery.harvard.edu/report/abbott-lawrence-lowell-and-discrimination-in-admissions-and-housing

[18] "Stanford apologizes for admissions limits on Jewish students in the 1950s and pledges action on steps to enhance Jewish life on campus." (October 12, 2022). *Stanford Report.* https://news.stanford.edu/stories/2022/10/task-force-report-jewish-admissions-and-jewish-life

[19] "The Myth of American Meritocracy." Ibid.

[20] Mounk, Yascha. (November 25, 2014). "Is Harvard Unfair for Asian Americans?" *The New York Times.* https://www.nytimes.com/2014/11/25/opinion/is-harvard-unfair-to-asian-americans.html

[21] Schlott, R. (June 29, 2023). "Why I helped strike down Harvard affirmative action in the Supreme Court." *The New York Post.* https://nypost.com/2023/06/29/why-i-helped-strike-down-affirmative-action-in-the-supreme-court/

[22] Schlott, R. (June 15, 2023). "Asian and Black Students Reveal Why They Oppose Affirmative Action." *The New York Post.* https://nypost.com/2023/06/15/asian-black-students-on-why-they-oppose-affirmative-action/

[23] Lepore, S. (June 9, 2023). "The Asian American teen who could end affirmative action." *The Daily Mail.* https://www.dailymail.co.uk/news/article-12175915/The-Asian-American-teen-end-affirmative-action-Supreme-Court-case.html

[24] "Students for Fair Admissions v Harvard." Civil Rights Litigation Clearinghouse. https://clearinghouse.net/case/14188/

[25] "Students for Fair Admissions v Harvard." Ibid.

[26] "Students for Fair Admissions v Harvard." Justia. https://docs.justia.com/cases/federal/district-courts/massachusetts/madce/1:2014cv14176/165519/672

[27] "Students for Fair Admissions v Harvard." Ibid.

[28] Eustachewich, L. (October 17, 2018). "Harvard Gatekeeper Reveals SAT Cutoff Scores Based on Race." *The New York Post.* https://nypost.com/2018/10/17/harvards-gatekeeper-reveals-sat-cutoff-scores-based-on-race/

[29] "Asian and Black Students Reveal Why They Oppose Affirmative Action." Ibid.

[30] Kendall, B., and Korn, M. (January 24, 2022). "Supreme Court to Review Race-Conscious Admissions Policies at Harvard, UNC." *The Wall Street Journal.* https://www.wsj.com/articles/supreme-court-to-consider-challenges-to-race-conscious-admissions-policies-at-harvard-unc-11643035684?mod=article_inline

[31] "Justice Department Sues Yale University Over Admission Practice." (October 8, 2020). *The Wall Street Journal.* https://www.wsj.com/articles/justice-department-sues-yale-university-over-admissions-practices-11602194974

32
https://www.supremecourt.gov/oral_arguments/argument_transcripts/2022/21-707_bb7j.pdf

33 Ibid.

34 Ibid.

35 Draeger, J. (August 17, 2022). "Less than Two Percent of Harvard Faculty is Conservative: Survey." *The College Fix*. https://www.thecollegefix.com/less-than-two-percent-of-harvard-faculty-is-conservative-survey/

36
https://www.supremecourt.gov/oral_arguments/argument_transcripts/2022/21-707_bb7j.pdf

37 Ibid.

38 There are other studies which show that racial and gender quotas do not improve an organization's performance. https://thefederalist.com/2018/03/13/evidence-from-norway-shows-gender-quotas-dont-work-for-women/

39 https://www.law.cornell.edu/supct/html/02-241.ZO.html

40 "More Americans Disapprove than Approve of Colleges Considering Race, Ethnicity in Admissions Decisions." (June 8, 2023). Pew Research Center. https://www.pewresearch.org/politics/2023/06/08/more-americans-disapprove-than-approve-of-colleges-considering-race-ethnicity-in-admissions-decisions/

41 Pew Research Center. Ibid.

42
https://s.wsj.net/public/resources/documents/2023SCOTUSAFFIRMATIVE.pdf

43 "Harvard Rated Asian-Americans Lower on Personality Traits, Suit Says." (June 15, 2018). *The New York Times*. https://www.nytimes.com/2018/06/15/us/harvard-asian-enrollment-applicants.html

44 https://studentsforfairadmissions.org/wp-content/uploads/2023/06/SFFA-Scotus-Opinion-Issued-Press-Release-June-2023.pdf

45 "Why I helped strike down Harvard affirmative action in the Supreme Court." Ibid.

46 https://x.com/jemelehill/status/1675203147504005121

47 https://www.nbcnews.com/news/asian-america/asian-americans-say-affirmative-action-ruling-used-pawns-rcna91861 and

https://www.npr.org/2023/07/02/1183981097/affirmative-action-asian-
americans-poc, and https://www.thenation.com/article/society/asian-american-
conservatives-white-supremacy/

[48] https://lieu.house.gov/media-center/press-releases/rep-lieu-statement-
supreme-court-decision-affirmative-action

[49] Ford, R. (July 10, 2023). "The Supreme Court's Segregationists." *The Chronicle
of Higher Education.* https://www.chronicle.com/article/the-supreme-courts-
segregationists?utm_source=Iterable&utm_medium=email&utm_campaign=ca
mpaign_7225671_nl_Afternoon-
Update_date_20230710&cid=pm&source=ams&sourceid=

[50] Hess, F. and Fournier, G. (June 24, 2024). "Don't Trust Colleges on Race-
based Admission." The James Martin Center for Academic Renewal.
https://www.jamesgmartin.center/2024/06/dont-trust-colleges-on-race-based-
admission/

[51] After facing backlash, within days, Columbia Law School removed the video
statement requirement. https://freebeacon.com/campus/columbia-law-school-
said-it-would-require-applicants-to-submit-video-statements-in-the-wake-of-
affirmative-action-ban-then-it-backtracked/

[52] "Don't Trust Colleges on Race-based Admission." Ibid.

[53] Perez, K. (August 3, 2023). "Legacy Admissions Are Being Rolled Back." *The
USA Today.*
https://www.usatoday.com/story/news/education/2023/08/03/legacy-college-
admissions/70511866007/

[54] Ibid.

[55] Hunter, B. (March 6, 2024). "A Mother's Fight to End Discrimination and
Protect Merit-based Public Education." https://pacificlegal.org/a-mothers-fight-
to-end-discrimination-and-protect-merit-based-public-education/

[56] Ibid.

Chapter 7. Asian Americans Fought Back Against the War on Merit

7.1 The Acronyms

[1] Green, J., and Hand, J. "McKinsey's Diversity Matters/Delivers/Wins
Revisited." *ECON JOURNAL WATCH* 21(1) March 2024: 5–34.
https://econjwatch.org/File+download/1296/GreenHandMar2024.pdf?mimety
pe=pdf

[2] Bannister, C. (April 4, 2024). "No Science doesn't Show Diversity Lead to
Higher Profits." The Media Research Center.

https://www.mrctv.org/blog/craig-bannister/no-science-doesnt-show-diversity-leads-higher-profits-study-reveals

[3] Brownlee, D. (September 15, 2019). "The Dangers of Mistaking Diversity for Inclusion in the Workplace." *Forbes.*
https://www.forbes.com/sites/danabrownlee/2019/09/15/the-dangers-of-mistaking-diversity-for-inclusion-in-the-workplace/

[4] Weiss, B. (November 7, 2023). "End DEI." *Tablet Magazine.*
https://www.tabletmag.com/sections/news/articles/end-dei-bari-weiss-jews

[5] "Key facts about Asian Americans, a diverse and growing population." (April 29, 2021). The Pew Research Center. https://www.pewresearch.org/short-reads/2021/04/29/key-facts-about-asian-americans/

[6] "At Forum on NYC High School Admissions, Frustration Rules." (April 12, 2019). *NBC News.* https://www.nbcnews.com/news/asian-america/forum-nyc-s-high-school-admissions-frustration-rules-n993966

[7] "How it Feels to be an Asian Student in an Elite Public School." Ibid.

[8] "How it Feels to be an Asian Student in an Elite Public School." Ibid.

[9] Salamy, E. (March 1, 2021). "BLM Raised $90m Last Year, But Where is the Money Going?" *ABC News.* https://wjla.com/news/nation-world/blm-raised-90m-last-year-but-where-is-the-money-going

[10] Rufo, C. (March 30, 2021). "Critical Race Theory: What It Is and How to Fight It." https://imprimis.hillsdale.edu/critical-race-theory-fight/

[11] "CACAGNY Denounces Critical Race Theory as Hateful Fraud." (February, 2021). Chinese American Citizens Alliance of Greater New York (CACAGNY). https://nebula.wsimg.com/9499c73d959b9f49be9689476a990776?AccessKeyId=45A6F09DA41DB93D9538&disposition=0&alloworigin=1

[12] Michael Gilday, the chief of naval operations, admitted in testimony at the U.S. House Armed Services Committee in 2021 that he asked sailors to read books like Ibram X. Kendi's *How to Be an Antiracist* in response to conversations with sailors after the murder of George Floyd.
https://taskandpurpose.com/news/us-navy-reading-list-how-to-be-an-antiracist/

[13] Kendi, I. "Pass an Anti-Racist Constitutional Amendment."
https://www.politico.com/interactives/2019/how-to-fix-politics-in-america/inequality/pass-an-anti-racist-constitutional-amendment/

[14] Duffy-Alfonso, D. (February 2, 2021). "Whistle Blower: Coca-Cola Uses Antiracist Training that Tells Employees to be Less White." The Federalist.com. https://thefederalist.com/2021/02/20/whistleblower-coca-cola-uses-antiracist-training-that-tells-employees-try-to-be-less-white/

7.2 "Meritocracy is Racist"

[15] "Asian and Black Students Reveal Why They Oppose Affirmative Action."
Ibid.

[16] Rufo, C. (Jan 12, 2021). "Woke Elementary."
https://christopherrufo.com/p/woke-elementary

[17] "End DEI." Ibid.

[18] "California Judge Rules Law to Include Women on Boards of Directors
Unconstitutional." (May 16, 2022). *NBC News.*
https://www.nbcnews.com/business/business-news/california-judge-rules-law-
include-women-boards-directors-unconstituti-rcna29071

[19] "Ten Years on From Norway's Quota for Women on Corporate Boards."
(February 17, 2018). *The Economist.*
https://www.economist.com/business/2018/02/17/ten-years-on-from-
norways-quota-for-women-on-corporate-boards

[20] Chen, T., and Weber, L. (July 21, 2023). "The Rise and Fall of Chief Diversity
Officer." *The Wall Street Journal.* https://www.wsj.com/articles/chief-diversity-
officer-cdo-business-corporations-e110a82f

[21]
https://x.com/realchrisrufo/status/1816163390483751265?utm_source=substa
ck&utm_medium=email

[22] https://x.com/ByronYork/status/1283372233730203651

[23] Arness, C. "Capitalism is the Real Target." *The Commentary* (July–August 2024).
https://www.commentary.org/articles/clifford-asness/pro-hamas-protests-
capitalism/

[24] The *USA Today* article "Critical Race Theory Defined" provides definitions of
these DEI- and CRT-related words.
https://www.usatoday.com/story/news/education/2021/07/22/critical-race-
theory-defined/8045511002/

[25] Eustachewich, L. (February 23, 2021). "Coca-Cola Diversity Training Urged
Workers to be Less White." *The New York Post.*
https://nypost.com/2021/02/23/coca-cola-diversity-training-urged-workers-to-
be-less-white/

[26] Greene, Jay, and Paul, James. (July 27, 2021). "Diversity University: DEI Bloat
in the Academy." The Heritage Foundation.
https://www.heritage.org/education/report/diversity-university-dei-bloat-the-
academy

[27] Sailer, John. "Diversity Statement, then Dossier." National Association of Scholars.
https://www.nas.org/storage/app/media/Reports/Cluster%20Hiring/Cluster_Hiring_Report_Diversity_Statement_Then_Dossier_V.pdf

[28] Landrum, Eric. (April 12, 2024). "Most Colleges Demand DEI Requirement in Order to Graduate." American Greatness.
https://amgreatness.com/2024/04/12/report-most-colleges-demand-dei-requirements-in-order-to-graduate/

[29] Wong, Alicia. (February, 6, 2023). "Why are Colleges Offering Up More DEI Degrees?" *USA Today*.
https://www.usatoday.com/story/news/education/2023/02/06/dei-diversity-equity-inclusion-programs-growing/11155271002/

[30] Bronk, Emily. (April 22, 2024). "Test Optional Colleges." The Student Research Group. https://studentresearchgroup.com/test-optional-colleges/

[31] Kuncel, N. R., and Hezlett, S. A. (2007). "Standardized tests predict graduate students' success." *Science, 315*(5815), 1080–1081.
https://doi.org/10.1126/science.1136618 and Park, G., Lubinski, D., Benbow, C. (2007). "Contrasting Intellectual Patterns Predict Creativity in the Arts and Sciences: Tracking Intellectually Precocious Youth Over 25 Years."
https://journals.sagepub.com/doi/abs/10.1111/j.1467-9280.2007.02007.x

[32] Reese, R. (June 29, 2023). "Harvard Hints At How It Will Keep Considering Race In Admissions Despite SCOTUS Ruling." *The Daily Caller*.
https://dailycaller.com/2023/06/29/harvard-circumvent-supreme-courts-affirmative-action/

[33] Jorgensen, J. (August 23, 2019). "A Look at How NY Charters Performed on State Tests Compared to Public Schools." https://ny1.com/nyc/all-boroughs/news/2019/08/23/2019-new-york-test-scores-charter-school-students-compared-to-public-school-students

[34] https://twitter.com/rweingarten/status/1412482850729963521

[35] https://twitter.com/thomaschattwill/status/1412792885892812804

[36] https://twitter.com/thomaschattwill/status/1412793225140703234

[37] Williams, A. (August 20, 2020). "'White Privilege' is the Biggest White Lie of All." *The Hill*. https://thehill.com/opinion/civil-rights/511323-white-privilege-is-the-biggest-white-lie-of-all/

[38] Murphy, Sara C., Klieger, David M., Borneman, Matthew J., and Kuncel, Nathan R. (Spring 2009).

"The Predictive Power of Personal Statements in Admissions: A Meta-Analysis and Cautionary Tale." *Proquest* Vol. 84, Iss. 4: 83–86, 88.

https://www.proquest.com/openview/cde6b6b6519abfab73e2175d5b9917a4/1?pq-origsite=gscholar&cbl=1059

[39] Alvero, A.J., Giebel, S., Gebre-Medhin, B., Antonio, A.L., Stevens, M.L., & Domingue, B.W. (2021). "Essay Content is Strongly Related to Household Income and SAT Scores: Evidence from 60,000 Undergraduate Applications." (CEPA Working Paper No.21-03). Retrieved from Stanford Center for Education Policy Analysis: http://cepa.stanford.edu/wp21-03.

[40] Although the vote took place in 2020, the school district started to phase out the G & T program in 2024 and expected to complete the process by the 2027–2028 school year. https://www.msn.com/en-us/news/us/seattle-public-schools-shuts-down-gifted-and-talented-program-for-being-oversaturated-with-white-and-asian-students/ar-BB1l0pB5

[41] "Debate emerges over racism and white supremacy in Oregon math instruction." (February 26, 2021). *KATU.com*. https://katu.com/news/local/debate-emerges-over-racism-and-white-supremacy-in-math-instruction

[42] Betz, B. (October 18, 2020). "San Diego School Districts Overhauls Grading System to Combat Racism." *Fox News*. https://www.foxnews.com/us/san-diego-school-districts-grading-system-racism

[43] Cromer, A. (October 22, 2020). "No Test for Three Boston Exam Schools for Incoming Fall Class." Boston.com. https://www.boston.com/news/schools/2020/10/22/no-test-boston-exam-schools-fall-class/

[44] Pacific Legal Foundation. CACAGNY v Mayor Adams. https://pacificlegal.org/case/christa-mcauliffe-pto-v-de-blasio/

[45] Nomani, A., and Margulies, N. (December 17, 2020). "The Nation's No. 1 High School Poised to Pick Students Based On Race, Not Achievement." The Federalist.com. https://thefederalist.com/2020/12/17/nations-no-1-high-school-poised-to-pick-students-based-on-race-not-achievement/

[46] https://www.youtube.com/watch?v=w5RcAhRyB6g

[47] Raleigh, H. (March 2, 2022). "Court Ruling Deals a Decisive Blow to Race-Based Admission Policy at Top High School." https://thefederalist.com/2022/03/02/court-ruling-deals-decisive-blow-to-race-based-admission-policy-at-top-high-school/

[48] "Court Ruling Deals a Decisive Blow to Race-Based Admission Policy at Top High School." Ibid.

[49] Woosley, A. (March 1, 2022). "Court Ruling on Thomas Jefferson High School Admission Changes Draws Mixed Reactions." *FFX Now*. https://www.ffxnow.com/2022/03/01/court-ruling-on-thomas-jefferson-high-school-admissions-changes-draws-mixed-reactions/

[50] Graff, N. (February 25, 2019). "Most Americans Say Colleges Should not Consider Race or Ethnicity in Admissions." The Pew Research. https://www.pewresearch.org/fact-tank/2019/02/25/most-americans-say-colleges-should-not-consider-race-or-ethnicity-in-admissions/

[51] "CACAGNY Congratulates TJ and PLF." (February 25, 2022). https://nebula.wsimg.com/3df32f87c3a22cdaa030853aabef4aa6?AccessKeyId=45A6F09DA41DB93D9538&disposition=0&alloworigin=1

[52] "FCPS Wins Appeal of Lawsuit Challenging TJ Admissions." (May 23, 2023). *FFXNow*. https://www.ffxnow.com/2023/05/23/breaking-fcps-wins-appeal-of-lawsuit-challenging-tj-admissions/

[53] Howe, A. (February 20, 2024). "Justices Decline to Intervene in Another Dispute over Race and Admissions." *SCOTUSblog*. https://www.scotusblog.com/2024/02/justices-decline-to-intervene-in-another-dispute-over-race-and-school-admissions/

[54] Constantinto, A. (August 23, 2023). "Thomas Jefferson High School Drops to 5th in Latest US News Ranking." *US News*. https://www.insidenova.com/headlines/thomas-jefferson-high-school-drops-to-5th-in-latest-us-news-ranking/article_b4ce2886-4692-11ee-a98b-4b0dbcb840c2.html

[55] Lundquist-Arora, S. (March 5, 2024). "Thomas Jefferson Principal Celebrates Remedial Math Achievements." *The Washington Examiner*. https://www.washingtonexaminer.com/restoring-america/2901327/thomas-jefferson-principal-celebrates-remedial-math-achievements/

[56] Asness, C. "Capitalism is the Real Target." *Commentary Magazine*. July–August 2024. https://www.commentary.org/articles/clifford-asness/pro-hamas-protests-capitalism/

7.3 The DEI and CRT Bubble Popped

[57] Vincent, I. (November 11, 2021). "How Hawk Newsome Went from High School Dropout to BLM Leader." *The New York Post*. https://nypost.com/2021/11/11/how-hawk-newsome-went-from-high-school-dropout-to-blm-leader/

[58] "California Threatens to Hold BLM Leaders Personally Liable for Missing Financial Records." *The Daily Mail*. https://www.dailymail.co.uk/news/article-10466461/California-threatens-hold-BLMs-leaders-personally-liable-missing-financial-records.html

[59] Park, C. (September 22, 2023). "Fed-up Staff Seethe over Boston U's Antiracist Center." *Fox News*. https://www.foxnews.com/media/fed-up-staff-seethe-boston-us-antiracist-center-colossal-waste-millions-dollars

[60] Fara, Z. (September 21, 2023). "Ibram Kendi's Antiracist Center Was a Multi-Million Dollar Grift All Along." *The Washington Examiner.* https://www.washingtonexaminer.com/opinion/2434020/ibram-kendis-antiracist-center-was-a-multi-million-dollar-grift-all-along/

[61] Rufo, C. (July 22, 2021). "Ibram X. Kendi Is the False Prophet of a Dangerous and Lucrative Faith." *The New York Post.* https://nypost.com/2021/07/22/ibram-x-kendi-is-the-false-prophet-of-a-dangerous-and-lucrative-faith/

[62] Sibarium, A. (August 27, 2024). "Robin DiAngelo Plagiarized Minority Scholar, Complaint Alleges." *The Washington Free Beacon.* https://freebeacon.com/campus/robin-diangelo-plagiarized-minority-scholars-complaint-alleges/

[63] Wren, K. (March 28, 2022). "Q&A: Stuart Schmill on MIT's decision to reinstate the SAT/ACT requirement." *MIT News.* https://news.mit.edu/2022/stuart-schmill-sat-act-requirement-0328."

[64] Leonhardt, D. (January, 7, 2024). "The Misguided War on the SAT." *The New York Times.* https://www.nytimes.com/2024/01/07/briefing/the-misguided-war-on-the-sat.html

[65] Clark, J. (January 9, 2024). "SAT Defended." *The New York Post.* https://nypost.com/2024/01/09/news/sat-defended-from-misguided-attacks-as-test-increasingly-becomes-optional-for-students/

[66] "The Misguided War on the SAT." Ibid.

[67] "The Rise and Fall of Chief Diversity Officer." Ibid.

[68] Chen, T., and Smith, R. (July 3, 2023). "No One is Happy About Diversity Efforts at Work." *The Wall Street Journal.* https://www.wsj.com/articles/diversity-workplace-affirmative-action-dei-3646683b?mod=article_inline

[69] "Diversity, Equity, and Inclusion in the Workplace." (May 17, 2023). *The Pew Research.* https://www.pewresearch.org/social-trends/2023/05/17/diversity-equity-and-inclusion-in-the-workplace/

[70] "Jewish TikTok Staff Reveal Rampant Antisemitism, Israel Hate in Workplace." *The Times of Israel.* https://www.timesofisrael.com/report-jewish-tiktok-staff-reveal-rampant-antisemitism-israel-hate-in-workplace/ and "TikTok Users Still See Widespread Antisemitism on App." *Fox News.* https://www.foxbusiness.com/lifestyle/tiktok-widespread-antisemitism-app

[71] Chang, D. (April 23, 2024). "Columbia's hyper-privileged protestors are being fed by buffet spread." *The Daily Mail.com.* https://www.dailymail.co.uk/news/article-13340891/columbia-palestine-protestors-buffet-spread-food.html

[72] https://x.com/sfmcguire79/status/1713664285212061774

[73] Egan, B. (October 17, 2023). "Wexner Foundation Cuts Ties with Harvard over 'Tiptoeing' on Hamas."
https://www.cnn.com/2023/10/16/business/wexner-harvard-hamas-israel-antisemitism/index.html

[74] Sibarium, A. (January 1, 2024). "Harvard President Claudine Gay Hit with Six New Charges of Plagiarism." *Freebeacon*.
https://freebeacon.com/campus/harvard-president-claudine-gay-hit-with-six-new-charges-of-plagiarism/

[75] In August 2024, Columbia University's president, Minouche Shafik, resigned. During her short tenure of merely 13 months, the New York campus of Columbia experienced some of the most disruptive pro-Palestine protests. Columbia moved its classes online for the end of the academic term and canceled the university's main graduation ceremony. She is the fifth Ivy League president to step down over the past year.

[76] Kabbany, J. (May 9, 2024). "After Increasing Demands for her Resignation, Embattled President of Cornell Announces Retirement." TheCollegeFix.com.
https://www.thecollegefix.com/after-increasing-demands-for-her-resignation-embattled-president-of-cornell-announces-retirement/

[77] Weiss, B. (November 7, 2023). "End DEI." *Tablet.com*.
https://www.tabletmag.com/sections/news/articles/end-dei-bari-weiss-jews

[78] Please note that this new admissions data by race does not add up to 100% because some students identify as more than one race or ethnicity.
https://www.bbc.com/news/articles/c8rxvd2z6ldo

[79] Looker, A. (August 22, 2024). "Top University Says Diversity Slumps After Affirmative Action Ban." *BBC*.
https://www.bbc.com/news/articles/c8rxvd2z6ldo

[80] "Harvard Reports Drop in Black Enrollment after Supreme Court Affirmative Action Ruling." *CBS*. https://www.cbsnews.com/boston/news/harvard-admissions-black-supreme-court-affirmative-action/

[81] "Top University Says Diversity Slumps After Affirmative Action Ban." Ibid.

[82] Confessore, N. (October 16, 2024). "The University of Michigan Doubled Down on DEI. What Went Wrong?" *The New York Times*.
https://www.nytimes.com/2024/10/16/magazine/dei-university-michigan.html

[83] Ibid.

[84] Ibid.

[85] The WSJ Editorial Board. (August 29, 2024). "Businesses Back Away from DEI." *The Wall Street Journal.* https://www.wsj.com/opinion/brown-forman-dei-rollback-lowes-robby-starbuck-business-hiring-politics-833e6a3d

Chapter 8. Winning at the Ballot Box

8.1 We Are Not Going Back

[1] "Washington Initiative 200, Affirmative Action Measure (1998)." https://ballotpedia.org/Washington_Initiative_200,_Affirmative_Action_Measure_(1998)

[2] Robertson, S. (October 25, 2019). "Voters to Decide if Affirmative Action Returns to Washington." https://www.king5.com/article/news/politics/washington-r-88-i-1000-affirmative-action/281-22f6a03a-b964-46cb-b211-aec422a416ba

[3] https://www.youtube.com/watch?v=hudVi6wcwzI

[4] Ramsey, Bruce. (February 23, 2005). "Diversity, Preferences and Race/Class Debate." *The Seattle Times.* https://www.seattletimes.com/opinion/diversity-preferences-and-the-race-class-debate/

[5] "Diversity, Preferences and Race/Class Debate." Ibid.

[6] https://www.facebook.com/kan.qiu.1/videos/2610641222292926

[7] "AACE Denounces the Passage of Initiative 1000 by the Washington State Legislature." (May 2, 2019). https://asianamericanforeducation.org/en/pr_20190502/

[8] Rufo, Christopher. (October 8, 2019). "Asian Americans in WA State Break Away with Progressive Consensus." *City Journal.* https://www.city-journal.org/article/asian-americans-for-equal-opportunity

[9] O'Sullivan, J. (December 29, 2019). "With the Loss of Referendum 88, Affirmative Action Advocates Wonder What's Next." *The Seattle Times.* https://www.seattletimes.com/seattle-news/politics/with-the-loss-of-referendum-88-affirmative-action-advocates-wonder-whats-next/

[10] Connerly, W. (June 24, 2020). "America Isn't a Racist Country." *The Wall Street Journal.* https://www.wsj.com/articles/america-isnt-a-racist-country-11595628914

[11] Eight states ban race-based affirmative action at all public universities. California, Washington, Michigan, Nebraska, Arizona, and Oklahoma passed bans through voter referenda. In Florida, Governor Jeb Bush issued an executive order creating the ban. And in New Hampshire, the legislature passed a bill banning the consideration of race. https://tcf.org/content/commentary/what-can-we-learn-from-states-that-ban-affirmative-action/

[12] Geshekter, C. (September 25, 2008). "The Effects of Proposition 209 on California: Higher Education, Public Employment, and Contracting." National Association of Scholars. https://www.nas.org/blogs/article/the_effects_of_proposition_209_on_california_higher_education_public_employ

[13] Watanabe, T. (July 16, 2020). "For the first time, Latinos are the largest group of Californians admitted to UC." *The Los Angeles Times.* https://www.latimes.com/california/story/2020-07-16/latinos-uc-berkeley-diverse-class-history

[14] McGurn, W. (June 1, 2020). "Ward Connerly Rides Again." *The Wall Street Journal.* https://www.wsj.com/articles/ward-connerly-rides-again-11591032423

[15] "Truth be told: A Look at Affirmative Action and Yes on Prop 16 ads." https://www.10news.com/news/election-2020/truth-be-told-a-look-at-affirmative-action-and-yes-on-prop-16-ads

[16] Mai-Duc, C. (November 4, 2020). "Measure to Restore Affirmative Action in California Fails." *The Wall Street Journal.* https://www.wsj.com/articles/measure-to-restore-affirmative-action-in-california-fails-11604517345

[17] https://www.cferfoundation.org/about

8.2 The Recall of Progressive School Board Members

[18] https://x.com/AliMCollins/status/1315789903842566146

[19] https://x.com/AliMCollins/status/805475649133551616

[20] Calton, J. (February 3, 2021). "San Francisco City Attorney Sues School District Over Reopening Plan." *The Wall Street Journal.* https://www.wsj.com/articles/san-francisco-city-attorney-sues-school-district-over-reopening-plan-11612376184?mod=article_inline

[21] "San Francisco City Attorney Sues School District Over Reopening Plan." Ibid.

[22] Chan, S., and Jackson, A. (January 27, 2021). "San Francisco School Board Votes to Rename 44 Schools." *CNN.* https://www.cnn.com/2021/01/27/us/san-francisco-school-name-changes-trnd/index.html

[23] Young, D. (February 2, 2022). "Breaking down the SF School Board Recall Election." *SF Bay View.* https://sfbayview.com/2022/02/breaking-down-the-sf-school-board-recall-election/

[24] "Breaking down the SF School Board Recall Election." Ibid.

[25] Gonzalez, M. (January 31, 2022). "Why I Support the San Francisco School Board Recall." *Medium*. https://mtt-gonzalez33.medium.com/why-i-support-the-san-francisco-school-board-recall-e95c74ab2e5b

[26] https://mobile.twitter.com/garrytan/status/1488590809230315520

[27] https://twitter.com/garrytan/status/1467221526520872960

[28] "Key Facts about Asian Americans." Ibid.

[29] Please check out my interview with some of the recall volunteers at: https://helenraleigh.substack.com/p/fire-in-my-belly.

[30] Smith, A. (December 16, 2019). "Chesa Boudin is San Francisco's New District Attorney." *NBC News*. https://www.nbcnews.com/politics/elections/parents-guilty-murder-raised-radicals-chesa-boudin-san-francisco-s-n1101071

[31] Levin, S. (March 7, 2021). "These U.S. Cities Defunded Police." *The Guardian*. https://www.theguardian.com/us-news/2021/mar/07/us-cities-defund-police-transferring-money-community

[32] Tucker, E. (April 3, 2021). "The US Saw Significant Crime Rise Across Major Cities in 2020. And It's Not Letting up." *CNN*. https://www.cnn.com/2021/04/03/us/us-crime-rate-rise-2020/index.html

[33] "The Return of Yellow Peril." https://stopaapihate.org/2020/10/21/the-return-of-yellow-peril-2020-candidates/

[34] Samson, C. (January 25, 2022). "Elderly Man with PTSD from SF Chinatown Baseball Bat Attack Sues DA Chesa Boudin for Mishandling His Case." https://nextshark.com/anh-le-suffering-files-federal-suit-against-sf-district-attorney

[35] Reynolds, S. (December 17, 2021). "Hanako Loved San Francisco." https://susanreynolds.substack.com/p/hanako-loved-san-francisco?s=r

[36] Reynolds, S. (September 09, 2021). "73 Felonies and 34 Misdemeanors." https://susanreynolds.substack.com/p/73-felonies-and-34-misdemeanors-in?s=r

[37] https://abc7news.com/sf-crime-burglary-plea-deal-chesa-boudin/11833000/

[38] Sierra, S. (May 9, 2022). "Serial Burglar Convicted of Targeting SF Businesses Gets 'Lenient Plea Deal,' Court Documents Show." *ABC News*. https://abc7news.com/sf-crime-burglary-plea-deal-chesa-boudin/11833000/

[39] https://twitter.com/ManKitLam4/status/1519391291641008128

Epilogue. The Year 2024 and Beyond: Shaping America's Future

[1] "AAPI Data Releases 2024 Asian American Voter Survey Amid Unprecedented Election Year." (July 10, 2024). https://aapidata.com/press-releases/2024-asian-american-voter-survey-release

[2] Kapur, S. (August 23, 2023). "As the 2024 Election Revs up, Asian Americans Rise as a Powerful Voting Bloc." *NBC News.* https://www.nbcnews.com/politics/2024-election/2024-election-revs-asian-americans-rise-powerful-voting-bloc-rcna99875

[3] Ibid.

[4] Ibid.

[5] "AAPI Data Releases." Ibid.

[6] https://x.com/elonmusk/status/1813295846710206811

[7] https://x.com/PAKPAC/status/1847092107065925972

[8] Lim, D. (November 6, 2024). "How the Passing of Prop 36 Will Impact California." *ABC News.* https://abc7news.com/post/prop-36-retail-theft-drug-crimes-what-to-know-california-props/15519446/

[9] https://x.com/eyessfboe/status/1800262578373034238

[10] https://www.yiatinforny.com/

[11] From Huang Cao's campaign website: https://www.hungforva.com/

[12] Schaefer, P. (March 26, 2024). "55 Things You Need to Know about Nicole Shanahan." *Político.* https://www.politico.com/news/magazine/2024/03/26/nicole-shanahan-rfk-jr-2024-bio-00149015

[13] Bharath, D. (September 2, 2024). "Is Usha Vance's Hindu identity an asset or a liability to the Trump-Vance Campaign?" *AP News.* https://apnews.com/article/usha-vance-hindu-faith-2024-election-509313f4b9fc33f92e7846a31ea2025a

[14] Arnold, N. (November 19, 2024). "Here's Why Asian Americans Shifted Right." *Real Clear Politics.* https://www.realclearpolitics.com/articles/2024/11/19/heres_why_asian_americans_shifted_right_151965.html

[15] Ibid.

[16] Varadarajan, T. (July 16, 2024). "J.D. Vance and the Indian American Dream." https://www.wsj.com/articles/j-d-vance-and-the-indian-american-dream-2024-election-usha-81ddedd0#cxrecs_s

www.ingramcontent.com/pod-product-compliance
Lightning Source LLC
Chambersburg PA
CBHW031120020426
42333CB00012B/156